Pearl's once beautiful face was now just a few bones with skin stretched across them. Only fifteen years old and she looked like an old lady. She wore a rag of a dress and was covered with mud and filth. She was suffering terribly. For a brief moment, her eyes focused on mine. She struggled to speak.

"Every . . . thing . . . gonna be . . ." Her lips turned upward in the tiniest smile and she reached toward me with her tiny, deformed hand. "Y'all be . . . a big boy . . . now, chile—"

From somewhere in my mind I heard laughter and saw again her black eyes dance happily in the sunlight, and we were tumbling in the grass as she tickled my nose, then my chin and neck. Her smile fixed itself on my face, and it was once again summer somewhere— somewhere, my Pearl and I were frolicking, laughing, and she telling me with her sweet kisses and squeezes there was hope, there was hope.

HELP ME Remember...
HELP ME Forget

ROBERT SADLER
With
MARIE CHAPIAN

BETHANY HOUSE PUBLISHERS
MINNEAPOLIS, MINNESOTA 55438
A Division of Bethany Fellowship, Inc.

Formerly published under the title, *The Emancipation of
Robert Sadler*, 1979

ISBN 0-87123-203-0

Printed in the United States of America

The story of Robert Sadler is true. A few names and certain incidents have been altered slightly to protect the privacy of individuals involved, but the authors have striven to maintain authenticity and accuracy in documenting this book.

ACKNOWLEDGMENTS

We wish to thank the many people who gave selflessly of themselves during the researching of this book and whose lives touch these pages. A special thanks to Jeanette Patterson, John and Lillian Sadler, Buck Moore, Connie and Alice Lee, Eugene and Josephine Mattison, and Ronald and Marilyn Rolph. For their faithfulness, support and continuing prayers: Myra Gebhard, Gladys Dunbar, Dorothy Jordan, Frank and Kathie Kripaitis, Jacqueline Sadler, and Peter, Christa and Liza Chapian.

Thanks to our editors and publishers for their sustaining concern and love, with a specific grateful note to Kent Garborg.

To the countless people who have waited to see Robert Sadler's story in print, and to the many who have helped and encouraged us, we give our deepest thanks.

Robert Sadler
Marie Chapian

ABOUT THE AUTHOR

MARIE CHAPIAN, well-known author of Christian books, has written, among others, the best selling *Free To Be Thin*, the Overeaters Victorious life-changing plan for losing weight forever, and *In the Morning of My Life*, story of singer Tom Netherton. Marie co-authored *Telling Yourself the Truth*, the book that explains the Misbelief Therapy method of controlling our thoughts and filling our minds with the truth. She has also written the true, heart-gripping story of a Yugoslav family during the war, *Of Whom the World Was Not Worthy*. Marie is a professional psychotherapist and served on the staff at the Center for Christian Psychological Services in St. Paul, Minnesota, from 1973-1979 before moving to southern California. She travels widely as Bible teacher and popular conference speaker. She is the mother of two daughters.

PREFACE

It was a cold, snowy day in New Brighton, Minnesota, the first time I met Robert Sadler. I was in a laundromat hurling clothes into a dryer. My two little daughters were climbing into laundry carts and asking for lunch. Glancing up, I saw an impressive looking man about sixty years old, skin the color of rich walnut, tufts of white hair at his ears. He was smiling.

Walking directly toward me, he stopped and asked softly, "Excuse me, are you a writer?" His face was kind and his voice little above a whisper.

My mouth dropped open in surprise. I finally managed, "Uh, well, yes. I am a writer."

"Well," he smiled, "I have a story for you."

"A story?" I tossed a wet towel in the dryer.

"That's right. Would you be interested?"

What next? First I lose a quarter in the soap machine; now this strange man wants to tell me his story.

"I've had a very interesting life—"

"Well, actually, I'm a poet. I write—" Out of the corner of my eye I saw my four-year-old drinking out of the returned soda bottles by the soft drink machine. "Liza! You'll get sick doing that!"

"Marie," the soft voice said, "I'm Robert Sadler."

"Robert Sadler!" I gasped. He had my full attention.

"I've been praying for pretty near forty years for somebody to write my story," he laughed, taking me by the shoulders. "Then the Lord told me you were the one. Oh, thank you, Jesus! Thank you, Lord!" And I was laughing and thanking Him, too—I had wanted to write this story for a long time.

My husband, who knew Robert Sadler personally, was waiting for us at the car and drove us home. Peter had told Robert of my desire to write his story. He had been delighted because he knew the story should be told.

It was another five months of preparation before my husband packed our two little daughters and me onto a train to Bucyrus (Bew-si´-rus), Ohio, to the Sadler home. Work on the book began in the spring of 1973.

We traveled with our friend Bob through the South, the Midwest, and up into Canada. We stayed in Anderson, South Carolina, and spent several days at his mission there, visiting and interviewing other former slaves in that town. We saw the plantations where Bob had been a slave—the now run-down Beal* Plantation and the Billings* Plantation where we talked to Miss Billie* who still lives there.

We drove with Bob through small towns handing out free clothing and food. He would often stop the car to help someone in need. (He kept paint brushes, tools and work clothes for this purpose in the back of the station wagon along with the food and clothing.) We heard him preach in churches and homes in the mountains of the Virginias, the Carolinas, and in Indiana, Ohio, Michigan, Illinois, and Ontario, Canada.

Researching and gathering boxes of Sadler memorabilia, I found letters from people of all ages and in every walk of life who loved him. And I knew why. Loving, gentle, humble and unselfish, his was a personality of magnitude. He had been through hells that those of this generation in America can hardly imagine, and he had overcome. Overcome! He looked down on no man. Every person—young, old, rich, poor, sick, well, happy, sad—he found intensely important.

I marveled at Bob's capacity to love people. He was never too tired or too busy to help someone or to make somebody feel special.

People from everywhere, from all stations in society, visit the Sadler home in Bucyrus. One man helplessly crippled with cerebral palsy visited regularly. Bob would hold his plate and feed him, wiping his mouth for him, and carry on full, happy conversations with him when no one else in the room could understand a word of the garbled noises made by the handicapped man.

Living and working with Robert Sadler has been a high point in our lives. I consider it one of the greatest honors to know him and to have written his story.

Marie Chapian
St. Paul, Minnesota

---

* These names have been changed.

CONTENTS

PART I

Slavery

1

A streak of sunlight shone on Ella's face and on her dusty, corn-rowed hair as she laughed and wriggled in Mama's lap. She was two years old that day. Mama had saved up and bought some fresh fruit from the white folks' fruit stand about a mile down the road, a pear and a peach for everybody. We had eaten the fruit happily and eagerly for breakfast with the whole family. There were eleven of us children, though all were not living at home then, and I was the tenth.

We laughed as Mama tickled Ella's toes and kissed us both. Her white teeth shone as she laughed and sang to us. She was the warmth and brightness of our lives.

Our birthday fun together soon ended when Father's large figure appeared in the doorway. He was over six feet tall and his eyes always had a little bit of rage in them. Whenever he appeared, we children had a way of disappearing. We were never sure what kind of mood he'd be in. This day he was in a bad mood and Ella and I scurried outside. We could hear him in the cabin cursing and yelling at Mama. We knew there'd be no more singing that night and Ella's birthday would not be mentioned again.

Our small, three-room shanty was on a large plantation south of Anderson, South Carolina, about a quarter of a mile off the road. Our cabin was built of pine board and leaned slightly to one side. Its wooden window frames had no screens or glass and inside there were no ceiling or floor coverings. During the day we could see the chickens running underneath the house and at night we could see the stars through the boards of the roof. We had a barn of unpainted wood for our mule and buggy, a chicken coop, and a pigpen for the pig, when we had one.

Mama cooked over the fireplace at one end of the kitchen. There was a long wooden table with two benches on either side in the center of the room. The straight-backed chair Father sat in was in one corner, Mama's rocking chair by the fireplace, and along the wall was the cupboard with wooden doors that swung open. An old wooden box and the butter churn made up the rest of our furniture. Pots and pans hung from nails on the wall. Even with two windows in the room, it was never very bright. The sun seemed to shine in for a few feet and then stop.

"I'm hungry!" my father snapped. We could hear Mama's quick movements getting his supper on a plate. There was hot corn bread baking in the ashes near the fire and fatback frying in the skillet. She rarely answered Father back, even if he was in a good mood.

Ella and I were sitting close together burying our toes in the dirt alongside the house when we heard a loud smack from inside. Then there was a tumbling, and we held our breath. Father had hit Mama and knocked her down. We crawled under the house to be outside his reach when he came out of the house. As I sat in the darkness underneath the house, I fought tears of fright and anger. Even though I was just a small child, I wanted to jump up and defend Mama.

It was not long before Father had finished eating and was fixing to leave again.

We could hear Mama pleading with him, "Please stay home, honey. Don't go out again tonight. . . ." His curses rang through the air, and soon he stomped out of the cabin and was walking up the road. That night in our bed on the floor we could hear Mama's soft crying coming from the room next to ours where she slept. By morning Father still wasn't home.

The days and nights continued like that—Father ranting and Mama crying. On the rare nights he stayed home, he'd be drunk.

Two of my brothers had moved into town to find jobs, my sisters Ada and Janey were hired out, my brothers Leroy and Johnny were dayworkers on the plantation where we lived, and Pearl and Margie helped Mama work the land we rented and with the work at home. With everybody working, that left Ella and me to ourselves most of the time.

We usually played together in the dirt outside our cabin, or we'd play near wherever Mama was working. In the autumn when most of the family was picking cotton for the white farmer in his fields, Ella and I played at the edge of the field Mama was in. It was a happy sight to see Mama coming for us at noontime. We'd go home and she'd cook the noon meal and then return to the field until quitting time. Sometimes we'd eat lunch in the field, and always, no matter where it was, Mama bowed her head and thanked the Lord for the food. One day as we sat at the edge of a small grove of trees eating our lunch, Mama looked at me soberly and said, "Robert, some day you learn to read, hyar? Then you set down and read to me from the Bible."

"Yes, Mama," I said.

It was nearly hopeless for me to learn to read. Not many of the blacks in our area ever got a chance to go to school. But the way Mama was looking at me, I knew it was important and might happen some day.

There were other workers' children playing with us while we waited in the fields for our mamas. Many of the families who sharecropped worked their own land as well as the white man's they rented from. That was one of the reasons we couldn't go to school.

In the mornings everyone in our cabin was up before daybreak. The older children got up and fed the mule. Mama fed the pig and the chickens. Then on certain days there'd be the washing done outside in the big pots in the yard. Everybody would come in for breakfast by sunup, and then they'd be leaving for the field, where they worked all day.

My sisters Pearl and Margie especially wanted to go to school. They begged and begged Mama to find a way to let them to go school. One day after they had done their morning work, Mama announced she had made arrangements for them to go to the little Negro school about two and a half miles away. My sisters were so excited they danced and jumped around the cabin until I thought we might fall through the cracks in the floor. There was much singing and laughter in the cabin that morning as they got ready.

Both sisters had one dress, and after they finished their work, they'd stick their heads in the rain barrel outside and then rush inside and put on the one dress they each owned. I watched them hurry out of the house and begin the two-and-a-half-mile walk down the road to school. Mama would holler after them, "Be sure'n be home about 10:30 so's to knock down cotton stalk!"

In a few hours they'd be home, and the first thing they would do would be to wash their dresses in the basin and hang them over the chair to dry before the fire until they'd take the smoothing iron the next morning and iron them for wearing. They came home with stories of danger and adventure nearly every day.

"The big white school bus driv by, an' they aholler an' spit on us, Mama."

One morning they came home crying so terribly I thought maybe the white children had beat on them. It was worse than that. They had been walking up the dusty road the two and a half miles to school when the white farmer we rented from approached Father.

"Whar those children of yors goin', Jim?"

"They's goin' to school, jes like yors."

"Oh no they ain't, Jim. *My* children is goin' to school, yor children is goin' to the field!"

From the fierce look on his face, Father knew that he'd better send his children to the man's field. Though they worked for nothing, he knew if they didn't some mighty bad things could happen to him.

"Git out the field, chillren," he said.

The crying lasted about a week. They never went back to school again because soon they were doing Mama's work too. Her health was failing and she didn't have much energy. Some days she could hardly get out of bed. But she tried to work in the field nearly every day.

Ella and I played in the clearing during the day with the other children, waiting for our mamas to come for us. My older sisters were working with Mama in the field. At last we saw her coming for us. Her forehead and fine high cheek bones shone with sweat. Her small but strong body stooped low and her walk was slow. As she drew near to us a broad smile spread across her face. We ran to her arms and kissed her wet face. Mama's health was getting worse. I began to feel protective of her, and I worked hard at cleaning the house, sweeping, and feeding the animals.

One night Leroy and Johnny moved out of the cabin to join the other brothers and get jobs. Mama said good-bye to them tearfully. As she embraced each one individually, she looked as though she wanted to tell them something— something special, something that would make sense of everything and give it all a purpose and meaning. But instead she kissed them each quickly and said, "The Lord watch over you."

When they were gone, and the house was still, Mama sang to us. It was as though she was praying. She was part Indian and usually wore her long black hair in braids tied around her head. This night her hair hung loose and fuzzy around her shoulders, and I thought she looked like an angel. The other children must have thought so too, for we all sat real quiet, watching and listening as Mama sang to us. We joined in, too, and sang until it was time to go to bed.

As tender and loving as Mama was, Father's disposition was growing worse and worse. He came home that night, drunk as usual. I heard him call for Mama. I crawled out of bed and watched from the shadows. He was teetering on his feet and in an ugly mood. Mama got out of bed and came into the kitchen where he stood. Without a word he raised his arm and struck her a blow across the head, and she was sent sprawling to the floor.

I ran across the room with a scream and grabbed a stick. I leaped at my father and beat his legs with all my might. "Stop it! Stop it! Stop it!" I screamed at him. "Don't you hit Mama!"

Before I knew it, he had me dangling from his hand in the air. Then with a howl he hurled me the length of the cabin into the wall, knocking me unconscious.

Mama fussed over me for a couple of days, and I ached and hurt everywhere. She was afraid something had been broken in my head.

Mama's health continued to grow worse. By cotton-picking time the following year she was unable to rise up out of the bed. She cried often for her children. I would hear her in the bed as I brought in the wood in the morning.

"O Lor', have mercy. Have mercy. Take care of my chillrens, Lor'."

"Where you goin', Mama?" I would ask her.

"Son, you gonna have to be mighty strong, hyar? Yor Mama's goin' home soon."

"Goin' home? But you *are* home, Mama."

"No, son. Mama means home in heaven. With the Lord—that's real home."

"You leavin' us, Mama?"

"I believe so, son."

She had that look in her eye again—that look as though she had something very important to say. Something that would explain everything. Like why Father was so cruel, and why things were the way they were—things like that.

"Lor', have mercy," she said instead.

I was sweeping out the cabin one afternoon and it began

to rain. We dreaded rain because it poured in on everything. The cabin was like a sieve. Mama lay on her bed with the rain dripping down on her pillow by her head. I stood near her bed watching her. She lay so still in the darkness of the afternoon, I was afraid she might have been serious about leaving us and going to her real home. The cabin had been so gloomy since she took sick that there was little joy anywhere. Even Ella, who was always happy and laughing, became grave and sullen. There was no singing anymore without Mama to sing with us, and one day followed the other like a string of cold stones.

It rained for three days. Father took Janey, Pearl, and Margie to the field with him, and Ella and I stayed in the cabin alone until they came home at night. Ella got a fever and had to stay in bed, so I was alone during the day.

At the end of the third day of the rain, I heard Mama calling for Father from her bed. "Jim ... Jim ... " Her voice was weak. I ran to her. " ... Yor father, honey. Git yor father."

"Yes, mam," I said, and ran out of the cabin to get my father. When I found him I shouted almost hysterically, "Mama! Mama! It's Mama! She wants you! She's real sick, Father! She's callin' for you!" He didn't even look up as he worked. Finally he muttered something under his breath.

By the time Father arrived at Mama's bedside that evening, she had slipped into unconsciousness. She never spoke or opened her eyes again. In another day she was dead.

The days which followed were a daze. The funeral was held in a little church on the hill about a mile away. I saw her laying in the box they had built, and I wanted to scream, "Mama, get up. Get up! Mama, why you layin' there like that?"

The only one of the family who wasn't there was Ella. She was still sick. A friend of Mama's sat with her during the funeral. The little church was crowded with Mama's friends and some of our relatives. My older brothers were there, brothers I had hardly even seen. I stared at them, wondering what life off the farm could be like. Did they know how to read and write? There were many things I wanted to ask them, but as it was I didn't get a chance to speak with them at all because they left right after the funeral. I don't think they were even aware that I was their little brother. There were lemonade and sugar cookies at our cabin after the funeral.

"Yoll eat aplenty, Robert," my sister Margie told me. "It'll be a long time before we see cookies agin!" I took two cookies and some lemonade and went into the bedroom where Ella lay sick.

"Ella, how long you gonna lay up in that bed?"

"I dunno."

"Well, Mama's daid now."

"I know it. What are you fixin' in yor mind to do now?"

I looked at her face and was startled to see how thin it had become. She was small for her age to begin with, but now she looked so tiny and so helpless. I felt panic rise within me.

"Ella!" I shouted.

"What you shoutin' on, Robert?"

"Are you gonna die, Ella? Are you gonna die?"

Ella's condition didn't get any better. A doctor came and left some tonic in a bottle for her to take, but she didn't get well. Soon she couldn't eat anything, and it was only one month after my mother died that she was dead, too.

All I had in the whole world was gone—Mama, the light of our life, and now my only friend, Ella.

Father worked extra jobs as a basket maker and a blacksmith, but every cent he made he spent on liquor, and there were days when there was not a crumb of food in the house. One day Margie and I were coming back from the mill with the sack of cornmeal in the back of the buggy, and we saw an old apple core on the side of the road. I held the reins and Margie made a dive for the apple core, and we ate it right there. The rest of the way home we looked hungrily for more apple cores.

Margie and Pearl were good to me. They played with me, talked to me, put me to sleep in the bed with them, and tried to show me love. Margie brought singing back into the cabin, and at night we would sing around the fire; or else, all tucked into our bed, we'd sing to the moon peeking through the boards of the roof.

Father was home less and less. Whenever we did see him he would be drunk. Then one day he came home and announced that he was getting married, so late that spring Father, Pearl, Margie, and I left our little cabin and moved to the north side of Anderson to live in our new mama's home. It was a little nicer than our cabin, but it, too, was unpainted and had no ceiling, floor coverings, window glass, or screens, and the yard was grey dirt. Standing beside the porch were two boys, younger than us, about four and five years old. The thing that interested me the most was that both children were fat. If they were fat, then maybe we would get some good food to eat.

"Them's Rosie's chillren," Father told us. "Yor new brothers."

Our life in Rosie's shanty with her two children was a nightmare. Rosie hated us. She pulled Margie's hair, screamed at Pearl, and would hit us at any time. While she ate at the table with her own children, we had to eat our food on the floor.

The hopes of getting good food or enough to eat were quickly squelched. We got only what they didn't want. Some days we would get just one bowl of grits. We were hungrier at our stepmother's house than we had been before.

One night when Rosie was making chicken and corn bread, Margie and Pearl ran into the kitchen, tossed some pieces of chicken into their aprons, and ran out again. We ate the chicken behind the shed in back. Rosie told Father that night that we were thieves and that he ought to get rid of us. We were outside, but we could hear her screaming at Father about us.

"Lazy, thas what! Don't do no work! Now they's stealin' food as well. Since you brought them three no-accounts into mah house, it's been jes trouble."

We were certain that Father wouldn't listen to her lies. He knew we were good workers and would know that we took the food because she wasn't feeding us.

But when he called us in to him, we knew he had sided with Rosie. One by one he whupped us with the buggy trace for stealing.

It got worse. Father was not taking care of the farm the way he should and was staying out all night drinking. When he'd come home, he'd be so drunk that he would sleep all day. He started keeping company with another woman, and Rosie took her fury out on us children. She would beat us for no reason whatsoever.

"They don't mind me nohow, Jim, hear? They don't mind me nohow! They're good-for-nothin' no-accounts, each one of 'em!"

As he listened to Rosie's lying accusations, Father began to form a plan in his mind. It was early spring, plowing time. One terrible day he came into the room where my sisters and I slept together and woke us up, ordering us to get into the wagon outside. We quickly scrambled out of bed into the cool morning air and climbed into the wagon, never dreaming what was in store for us. In fact, we thought it was a special treat to be receiving any attention from Father. Maybe we were going to town to pick up seed; maybe we were going to the blacksmith's where Father worked. We were so glad to be getting away from Rosie and her two boys that we didn't really care where we were going.

Little was said during our ride down the Abbeville Road, through Anderson and on south. The morning air was cool and damp, and my sisters and I huddled together in the corner of the wagon, bouncing against the rough boards as we rolled across the deep ruts and holes in the road. Wherever Father was going, he was mighty intent on it. His face was grim and his eyes blazing.

Soon we passed the cabin where all of us had been born. I held my breath as I looked at the old deserted shanty. Margie and Pearl looked as though they might cry, but they held their chins stiff. The door of the shanty was open, and inside it was dark and empty. How I longed to jump from the wagon, run down the path, and into Mama's arms. If only Ella's little round face would appear from around the side of the sloping porch, and I could run to her and squeal and laugh again and then sit at Mama's knee and hear her sing to us. As we passed over the top of the hill, I began to cry. Pearl pinched my arm in case Father would turn and give me a lick for crying.

We bumped along the road without a word for more than an hour. Finally Pearl said to Father, "Where we goin'?" He sat almost motionless on the small seat at the front of the wagon. He did not so much as whisk a hair at her question. His silence meant don't ask any questions.

We grew hungry as the morning wore on, and a little sore from the bumpy ride. Still, we said nothing as we watched the South Carolina countryside slowly pass by us. Finally, we left the main road and turned into a long driveway. On top of a hill was a large, beautiful house, the biggest I had ever seen. I wondered why Father was turning in here. It was not the home of anybody we knew, and obviously it belonged to a white man. We saw several shanties near the back of the property like our cabin north of Anderson.

Father halted the mule, got out of the wagon and started for the back door.

"Why is we stoppin' here? Who lives in that big house?" I asked. Margie and Pearl didn't answer, for those same questions were in their minds.

The dogs in the yard barked as Father made his way to the back door. He took off his large brimmed hat and held it in his hand. He looked tall and shabby standing there on the step; his black hair and the dark skin of his face shone in the early morning sun. Soon the door was opened by a white man as tall as Father. They talked for a while and then Father turned and pointed to us. He turned several times, pointing to us, and then he and the white man went inside the house. When they came out, Father ordered us to get out of the wagon. Margie and Pearl jumped down first and then helped me down. We stood in our bare feet on the cold ground staring at the white man, Mr. Tom Billings, a cotton farmer.

"Y'say the boy is only five years old?" the man asked.

"Yessuh. Five years old, suh," my father answered.

"Hmmm . . . I don't like 'em so young."

"Take 'em all or take none," my father said.

The man narrowed his eyes, then said, "OK, I'll take 'em."

"Git over there by the house and stand still!" he ordered us roughly. We did as we were told and when we turned around, Father was in the wagon and turning it back the way we had come. I called out to him, but he didn't turn his head. Then Pearl called, "Father, wait! Don't leave us!" and she ran after the wagon. It was no use. Father didn't even look at her. His fierce gaze was on the road ahead of him, and he didn't pay any mind to our cries and pleas.

The wagon disappeared down the driveway and onto the main road. Pearl and Margie and I stood trembling against the side of the house, our feet digging into the cold earth. It was spring of 1916 and my sisters and I had just been sold as slaves.

2

Margie and Pearl held onto my hands so tightly it hurt. When I looked up at them, they were both crying. The white man stood in front of us, looking at us with cold, hard eyes. Then, without a word, he disappeared into the kitchen. In a moment a large black woman hurried out of the door and bustled over to where we were cowering against the side of the house. She reached for our hands and said in a soft voice, "You chillrens come along." Hesitantly, we followed her. The sun was shining hot overhead, and I could hear the sound of birds twittering in the trees.

"My name is Sarah, what's yours?" the soft-spoken woman asked. We told her our names, and I began to shiver and tremble. Margie picked me up in her arms and held me.

"You'll help me with the washing," Sarah told my sisters. "And you, Robert, can you sweep with a broom?" I nodded dumbly.

Sarah gave me a broom and explained that the porch had to be swept and kept clean every day. Then she took my sisters with her inside the house. Margie squeezed my hand.

"We'll be back, hyar?" I watched them leave me, and then standing alone on the large wooden porch, I began to cry. I was afraid I'd get a whupping for not doing what I was told, but I was too scared to move. When I turned around, a blond-haired young lady dressed in a pink and white dress that went down to her toes was standing in the doorway. I stared at her, frightened, and she stared back at me, amused.

"Who are you?" she asked.

I tried to answer, but no words came out.

"Well, I hope you can work better'n you can talk," she said with a little giggle as she brushed past me and out the door.

I watched her through my tears and saw her climb into a buggy drawn by a fine brown horse that a black man was driving. Where was my father? Why did he leave us here?

After what seemed like hours, Margie and Pearl came through the porch following Sarah. They carried large bundles of laundry in their arms. I cried out in relief when I saw them, but when Margie saw that I hadn't swept yet, she snapped, "Get busy, hyar? Sweep this porch!" They followed Sarah out into the backyard, and I could see them as they pounded the clothes with the paddle on the three-legged battling bench.

Margie's sharp words had their effect on me, and I hurriedly swept the porch so I could join them in the yard. It took most of the morning and early afternoon to finish the washing. The dirt had to be paddled out of the clothes and then they were boiled in soapy water in the big black iron pots. I stirred the clothes with a big stick. Then they had to be renched three times and finally hung to dry.

Later I saw the blond-haired young lady return, and I stared at her with wonder. I had never seen a sight like her before. Sarah saw me and pulled me around facing the other direction.

"What you starin' at, boy?"

"Nothun, mam."

"Keep it that-a-way, hyar?"

"Yezmam."

The day continued and so did my crying. That night, huddled between my sisters on the floor of Sarah's cabin, we all cried ourselves to sleep.

The days wore on. I cried a lot and kept waiting for Father to come for us. It was cotton planting time, and almost all of the slaves were working in the fields. Margie and Pearl were taking care of the slaves' children as well as helping Sarah in the big house. I was given jobs such as sweeping, carrying trash, feeding chickens, chasing cows, and kitchen work.

I discovered who the lady in the pink and white dress was. She was Miss Billie, Tom Billings' fifteen-year-old daughter. She took a liking to my sister Pearl, who was thirteen. She had Pearl comb her hair and tend to her personal needs. If it weren't for her, Margie and Pearl would have been sent to the fields to work, and I'd have been all alone in the big house.

One day Pearl was heating irons on the stove to iron Miss Billie's dresses, and I was standing nearby watching her.

"How old is Robert?" Miss Billie asked Pearl.

"He was five June last, mam."

Miss Billie's eyes grew wide. "He is young to be separated from his mama, isn't he?"

"His mama be dead, mam."

"But he has a daddy—?"

"Yes, mam."

Miss Billie stared at me and I shrank back. White people were frightening to look at.

"Do you like it here, boy?" she asked me.

I didn't know what to answer. If I said no, I might get a whupping. I stared back at her, speechless. Then I began to cry.

"Oh, he must miss his mama!" Miss Billie exclaimed.

Pearl didn't say a word.

Miss Billie reached her hand out to me and said, "Come here, honey." She took my hand and walked me into a long, narrow pantry where she opened a big jar and gave me a cookie.

"Thank you, mam," I mumbled. I had never tasted anything so delicious.

As the weeks passed, Miss Billie grew more and more distressed at my being bought as a slave and often would complain to her father. "It ain't right!" she would argue. Finally she threatened to run away if he would not take me back to my home. He only told her to hush up and mind herself.

The Billings family had few guests; but one day early in the summer, some of their friends from Hartwell, Georgia, came to visit. The house slaves had been busy preparing for their arrival—scrubbing, polishing, waxing, and washing. The grounds were cleaned, mowed and trimmed flawlessly. When their horses pulled the buggy up in the driveway, slaves stood waiting to help them and tend to their horses. As I watched them enter the house in a flurry of chatter and excitement, I didn't realize that they would bring another tragedy into my life.

Margie, who was just fourteen, had been a hard worker around the plantation. She was strong and they worked her like a mule. She worked from sunup until late at night. She was working in the big house while the visitors from Hartwell were staying there. Mrs. Billings, a large, stern-faced woman, boasted about her slaves to the visitors. She called for Margie and showed them what a fine buy they had made when they purchased her.

"Can't read or write," she boasted. "That's how to keep 'em."

"And who is the little niggerboy?" the plump, red-faced friend asked.

"Tell her your name, boy," Mrs. Billings ordered.

" . . . Wobber."

Mrs. Billings sat upright, enraged.

"Robert *what*, boy?"

"Wobber Sadder," I mumbled.

Mrs. Billings was furious. I had humiliated her in front of the guest she was trying to impress.

"You say *mam* when you talk to me, boy!" she shouted.

Suddenly she grabbed me by the ear and yanked me across the floor. She hit me in the face several times. "I ought to have you whupped, boy!" she shouted. "Now how do you talk to me?"

"Mam, mam," I stammered.

"Now git out, both of you," she ordered.

"Yes, Missus Billings, mam," Margie answered.

After we had left the room, Mrs. Billings sold Margie to her lady friend. The next morning after our breakfast of molasses drizzled over corn bread in Miss Sarah's shanty, Margie was called to the big house. Pearl and I went with her. We played a little game as we walked in the early morning light up the damp path. Walk two steps, hop one step, jump two steps, hop one step. When we got to the clearing, we saw the buggy hitched up and the visitors climbing into it. Then Mr. Billings called Margie.

"Git in," he ordered, and he pointed to the back of the buggy. Margie cried out in alarm. "Lor', have mercy!"

"Git in, I said!"

We followed Margie to the edge of the buggy. Her eyes were wide with fright. She reached down to hug me.

"Take care of Pearl, Robert darlin'; she ain't as strong as you." Her voice was all broken up.

Pearl and I began to cry. "No! No!" Pearl screamed. "Don't take my sister! Don't take her!"

I felt a hard blow across my head and shoulders, and I fell tumbling to the ground. I looked up in time to see Mr. Billings' boot kick Pearl in the back as she too rolled to the ground. Blood trickled down my neck.

The buggy began moving, and soon it was being drawn down the driveway. Margie's face was torn with pain. "Please, Robert . . ." I heard her call, "Please be a good boy. . . ." When she saw our sister lying on the ground, she cried, "Pearl! Pearl!" The lady in the front of the buggy turned and ordered, "Shut up, girl! Shut up, hyar?"

"Git back to the kitchen, girl," Mr. Billings snarled at Pearl. "And you, boy, git over here and sweep up this yard!"

In the weeks that followed I received many blows for crying. Master Billings often beat me with a peach tree switch. It stung terrible. I could hardly do the tasks I was given. Something else happened to me which added to my misery. I had trouble pronouncing words and speaking right, but up until now I was hardly aware of it. Nobody had ever made anything of it and so it didn't bother me. Now, however, I completely lost my speech. I could not form any words at all, and when I did try to talk, it came out all garbled and nobody could understand me. I became the "backward nigger brat," and it made Mr. Billings furious just to look at me.

Billie Billings continued to beg her father for my release. It seemed to cause her particular distress to see a five-year-old boy cowering in corners and crying all the time, even though I was a slave boy and hardly worth her attention.

Pearl was working in the kitchen all the time now, where she remained all during the summer months. She worked from sunup until late at night, and I was able to be with her most of the time. I was glad she wasn't sent to the fields. Nearly every night I'd fall asleep waiting for her. She'd carry my sleeping body home to Miss Sarah's shanty and then she'd go back to work.

Pearl was a frail girl in the first place, and now she seemed to be becoming more thin and more worn looking. One morning when she was cleaning the kitchen after the white people's breakfast, Miss Billie came in, looked at her and said, "Pearl, you set down a spell; you look plumb tuckered!"

"Thank you, Miss Billie, mam," Pearl answered, "but ah's fine, jes fine."

Master Billings happened to overhear Miss Billie's words, and he burst into the kitchen in a rage and screamed at Pearl, "You get busy, nigger, you hear? Don't you pay no mind to settin'!" He ordered Miss Billie to her room, and we could hear their voices in hot argument as Pearl trembled and worked and I helped her in the kitchen. We were scared, because when Miss Billie fought with her father about us it made him so angry he would often whup us in revenge.

I hated him so much I was afraid my heart might stop

beating. I wanted desperately to tell Pearl, but I couldn't form the words in my mouth. It was as though I had a clump of weeds growing on my tongue and there was no room for words to get out. *Hate. Hate. I hate! I hate! I hate!* If only I could say it.

Pearl rarely sang to me or held me anymore. It seemed I was more often in her way than anything else. "Robert, bring this inside," "Robert, sweep the porch," or "Robert, wash this"—never "Robert, honey, come here and let me love you," like she used to.

One hot afternoon when she was preparing the food for the white folks' dinner, she told me to bring a bowl of fresh fruit to the dining room table. I picked it up and it was heavy. "Don't drop it, hyar?" She snapped at me. The minute she said the words, my hands slipped and the bowl of fruit fell to the floor. Glass shattered and the fruit rolled in all directions. Pearl flew at me in anger and hit me hard upside the head. I was so stunned and hurt, I wailed helplessly. Then I ran out of the kitchen and across the yard and hid behind the smoke house. I heard Miss Sarah calling me. "Robert, Robert! Where are you, boy?" I held my breath. Miss Sarah was talking to somebody else. "Poor chile is dumb, can't talk. They done beat the sense out of him."

Pearl didn't get back to the shanty until almost dawn. I had been waiting all night for her. She lay down on the floor beside me with her back to me and without a word faced the wall. Her body shook badly and I reached out for her. "Peh, Peh—" I called, pulling her arm. She did not turn around to me, and I could hear her softly crying until she finally fell asleep.

I could not understand Pearl's coldness toward me. It hurt and confused me. A few days later Miss Sarah took me to her knee and said, "Honey, don't you fret yourself over Sister, hear? She be wanting you to grow up now so's you can learn how to take care of yourself. She be afraid you gonna stay a baby, an' if she be sent away, what'd happen to you?"

Pearl's rejection of me just made me cling to her all the more. I held her skirts while she worked; I cried and whined beside her all day long. Miss Billie would often find us together in this way. Pearl would be trying to do her work, and I would be clinging to her skirts and whimpering. If Pearl would wash Miss Billie's hair or help her with her bath, I'd be nearby, sniffling and crying.

Then one morning early in September, after we had been Tom Billings' slaves for about five months, Pearl and I were summoned to get into the buggy which was hitched up in the driveway. This time Pearl swooped me up in her arms and held on to me for dear life.

"I won't let them take you away from me, chile, I won't!" she cried. "They have to kill me fust!" She held me with all her strength. Her thin young face was fierce.

Master Billings strode out of the house and climbed into the driver's seat. "Git in!" he ordered. "Both of ye!" We did as he commanded, and Pearl never let her grip loosen on me. It was as though she were hanging on to life itself.

We bumped along the driveway, then turned on Abbeville Road toward Anderson. I looked back at the Tom Billings Plantation and saw my last glimpse of Miss Sarah as she came running to the driveway to watch us leave.

Pearl held me tight, and kept her gaze fixed on the back of Master Billings' head. Hatred filled her eyes like I had never seen before. As we bumped along the dirt road, I wondered where we were going. The hope that things could get better had long ago left me.

The hours went by and we found ourselves pulling up in front of Father and Stepmother's shanty north of Anderson. I could hardly believe my eyes. Even Pearl seemed a little excited. Her eyes were big and her mouth parted, but her grip on me tightened.

"Git out," Master Billings ordered. We climbed out of the buggy over the wheel caked with dried mud, and ran toward the house. Father came to the door and looked with stunned surprise at his two children returning home. He grabbed us by the arms and took us back to the buggy. Before he could ask why we were being returned, Master Billings shouted, "Keep 'em, hear?"

It was then we learned that Miss Billie had threatened to commit suicide unless he returned us to our home. Master Billings, although furious about it, returned us to our father.

Hungry and exhausted, our bodies aching from the long bumpy ride on the floor of the buggy, we entered the familiar cabin. Rosie actually seemed glad to see us. She held out her arms to us and hugged us. When we told her how Margie had been sold and taken off to Georgia she cried real tears. We ate ravenously of corn bread, molasses, greens, and salt pork. Then Rosie put us to bed on the straw pallet on the floor.

I heard her say in a trembling voice to Father, "They look half dead, Jim, half dead shor 'nuff."

3

Our happiness at being free and home again did not last. Rosie did not let us rest for a minute. She was glad to have Pearl back so she had someone to do her work for her, and Pearl set to work immediately cleaning, cooking, washing, and tending the garden. I was so happy to be home that I did my chores eagerly and without complaining. Father seldom spoke to us. Then, not even a week after we had been home, Rosie started telling him lies about us again.

"They's stealin' food!"

"They be underfoot!"

"Them chillrens is lazy, no-good, that's the God hepp me truth!"

"They's just plain devilment!"

Pearl and I were hurt and angry that Rosie would lie about us that way, especially when we worked so hard for her.

Mealtime was once again cornmeal mush thrown to us like we were animals, while Rosie and her boys ate at the table. Pearl and I would take our bowls and sit on the steps outside and eat. Pearl would talk about Mama, Ella, and Margie. She comforted me, telling me we would see Margie again, and we would talk about our other brothers and sisters who were now gone and far away. Then she would talk about heaven where Mama and Ella were. Tears would roll down my face as Pearl would tell me stories about how Mama was singing to Ella and how happy they were.

"They is no slaves in heaven, chile," she would explain, "and they is always plenty to eat."

When she saw my questioning face, she answered as though she knew what I wanted to ask.

"Oh, Robert, it be in the *Bible*, that's what I heard!"

The Bible. The Bible. I remembered Mama telling me in the field that day long ago that I must learn how to read so I could read to her from the Bible. Pearl couldn't read or write, and I had never even seen a book. I had no idea what the Bible was, but I nodded to Pearl that I understood what she meant.

Father stayed away most of the nights and when he came home, he was always drunk and he fought with Rosie.

We were home about two weeks when Father called me to run an errand.

"Take this here sack and buy some cornmeal from Zeke, boy."

Zeke Miller's cabin was about a mile away across the creek and over the field.

I took a small cloth bag and headed through the garden down a footpath in the direction of the creek. Pearl was gathering sticks in the wooded area behind our shanty. When I went past her, she jumped at me playfully, whirling me around to tickle me. We tumbled together, laughing and getting dirty in the red dust of the earth. Lying together under the blue sky all out of breath, I looked at her face and kissed her dusty cheek and said my first words in almost six months. "Pearl, yoll shure be pretty."

Pearl sat upright in the dirt.

"You talked! You talked! Jesus, mah Robert done talked!" A joy filled her face that I had not seen since before Mama died.

I was so happy as I ran down to the creek's edge, I felt like flying. I could talk! I didn't dare try it again for fear of sounding like mush, but I couldn't forget the look on Pearl's face. I had made her happy, genuinely happy, and I believed in my heart that everything was going to be all right after all.

The creek was lonely and still. The water moved lazily along in the heat of the mid-morning, the sun dancing off its surface making patterns and shiny shapes. After a few minutes of wading, I climbed the far bank and headed through the field toward Zeke's shanty. When I arrived I knocked on the wooden door frame. Zeke's wife called, "Yoll come in!" I entered the room and held out the little sack and grunted. I was afraid to try to talk, afraid it wouldn't work.

"What you want, boy?" Mrs. Zeke asked pleasantly.

I took a breath and said, "Uh—uh—uh c-c-c-orn meal, mam." She smiled at me and I was delighted with myself. I had spoken again! I had formed good words! The sensation that my mouth was filled with sand was still there, but I had spoken, I had really spoken! I grinned broadly.

I danced all the way through the field to the creek.

"C-c-c-orn meal, mam! Corn m-meal, mam!" I sang.

I stopped and looked for frogs along the creek banks, but I could find none. Finally, in the early afternoon I arrived back at our shanty. Only Rosie was at home. I looked around for Pearl. I searched the cabin, the yard, and then I saw that the buggy and the mule were gone. Fear clutched me. I ran screaming inside to Rosie. My mouth wouldn't form any recognizable sounds. "Peh! Peh! Ahhhhh! Ahhhhhh!" Rosie didn't even look at me. Her face was cold and smug.

Panicked, I ran as fast as I could up to the main road and looked in both directions. No sign of the wagon. "Pehhhhhh!!"

Father did not return that night and neither did Pearl. I slept beside the door shivering and crying all night. When I awoke in the early grey morning it was raining. When I heard the sound of the mule, I ran outside. The smell of whiskey was strong, and Father was alone in the wagon. "Peh! Peh!" I wailed. Father ignored me and slid down from the wagon into the mud. He walked right past me. I grabbed his trouser leg wailing unintelligible sounds. He shook me off with a drunken snort and went inside the cabin. I didn't dare go inside. My thin shirt was soon soaked through to my skin, and I shook with cold. I knew that Father had sold Pearl again, and the life and hope drained out of me like the rain as it dripped down my face and fell to the wet mud at my feet.

My loneliness in the next days was as strong as my hunger. I was so hungry most of the time that I ate grass and once even tried eating dirt. Mostly, I lived on the peanuts my father was growing. He didn't know that I was eating them, half-grown and all.

One day in early October Father called me.

"Git into the wagon, boy!"

My heart began to beat faster, but I knew it would be useless to ask him where we were going. The road was dry and dusty and we bumped along, not speaking. This time I rode on the seat next to him in the front of the wagon. I felt a slight tinge of excitement, but fear had become so much a part of me that I sat trembling on the edge of the seat.

We entered Anderson and turned west on the main road. After about a half hour we came to a crossroad and turned south. The farms were large and I looked in wonder at the immense cotton fields. There were many Negroes working in the fields and around the big barns. I tried not to think about where we might be headed and why.

Soon another farm came into view on the west side of the road. It made the Billings Plantation look small by comparison. We pulled into the curved driveway, and I was awed by the majesty of the house. The sloping yard was beautifully kept and groomed. Flowers grew in artistic groupings and huge oak trees lined the driveway. This was the Sam Beal Plantation.

Father whoa'ed the mule and sat silent, waiting. In a few minutes I heard a door slam and footsteps come running around the side of the house. Pearl! She stood barefoot, wearing the same dress she wore when I had last seen her. She wore a muslin apron over it. She was very angry.

"You wicked man! You bringin' this chile to this evil place? You is jes plain evil and wicked!"

Father ignored her. He jerked his head, indicating for me to get out of the wagon. I did so quietly and stood beside it. But Pearl continued.

"How can you sell my mama's baby like this! He a dumb chile!" Father curled his lip. "Shut yo' mouth, Sister."

At that moment a short, stocky man with a red, swarthy face came toward us. He wore overalls and dirty flannel shirt and thick, heavy boots. Father talked to him in a low voice. The man looked at me and then continued talking with Father. The white man gave him some money. Then my father drove the buggy out of the driveway without a glance backward toward his children. I was sold as a slave once again.

4

I was so happy to see Pearl that I didn't care about anything else. Mr. Beal hurled some orders at Pearl to take me to the slave quarter, and with a "Yessuh, Massuh Beal, suh," she took my hand and began running around a wooden walk alongside the house, past a kitchen door, then across the yard past a smoke house, chicken coop, barn, and down a dirt path to the rows of shacks the slaves lived in.

"Peh—Peh," I pleaded. I had so many questions to ask her. Where were we? Would we stay together now? Was it really a wicked place? Would Father come back for us?

Pearl knew exactly what was in my confused mind. She sat me down in some dirt next to one of the shacks. "This be the Sam Beal Plantation," she told me. "Father done sold us again. This be home now."

I nodded.

"We be together and you don't be down in the mouth."

Again I nodded.

"It be evil here, but you do what be told you, an' yoll be jes fine. Come on, let me love you now. You got any love for me, chile?"

With that I leaped into her lap hugging and wrestling, and we tumbled in the dirt together laughing just like always. Being sold as a slave boy didn't bother me because Pearl and I were together again. I forgot Rosie and Father's cruelty. I forgot Father's drunkenness. I forgot the loneliness and the despair—Pearl was here.

Later, Pearl stood me up and looked at me; then under her breath she said, "Pappy never done shoulda carried yoll here. Yoll jes a dumb old baby chile."

Pearl was staying in one of the shanties with a married couple named Buck and Corrie Moore. They were both field hands and they worked in the fields from sunup to sundown every day. Buck and Corrie had shown Pearl kindness in sharing their cabin and food with her, and now I was added to the family. They took to me right away and I felt at home with them. We had corn bread, molasses, greens, and corn tea for supper that night, and I ate like I hadn't ate in a age.

Corrie said quietly, "He plumb starvationed."

Pearl explained to me what life at the Big House was like. She told me that Mr. Beal was a hard and tough boss-man and that we should stay away from him when he was drinking. He was especially evil then and enjoyed torturing his slaves.

Mrs. Beal, Pearl told me, was a kind enough lady, as far as white ladies come, but she didn't trust her nohow.

There were six children in the Beal family: John was eight years old and very mean; Thomas, six years old, just sort of mean; Juanita was five years old; Virginia, four; Ethel, three; and lastly, the baby Anna, who was a year and a half.

There were about five house slaves. There was Big Mac, who was the hired hands' cook; then there was Mary Webb, who was the family cook. Harriet was the housekeeper and she had two helpers, a girl named Daisy and my sister Pearl.

I was overjoyed when I was told that I would be working in the Big House, too. That meant I could be with Pearl all day.

Pearl and I slept together on the floor of Buck and Corrie's shanty on a pile of dirty rags, and there was no blanket to pull over us. We were better off than we had been at the Billings Plantation, though.

In the Big House it was Big Mac who gave me my duties. I liked him right off. He was a tall, lean man with very dark skin. He had a scar that ran from his forehead to his chin, just missing his eye and spreading out like a row of tulips on this cheek. He had a large booming voice and hands the size of two big kettles.

"Every morning before daybreak, yoll git some sticks and light this hyar fire in the cookstoves," he ordered. Then he took me from fireplace to fireplace in the bedrooms, showing me how to light them as well. I was also to keep the woodboxes filled.

I was amazed as we passed from room to room in the Big House. Even though the Beals were not rich white folk, I thought the house was dazzlingly beautiful. I saw carpets for the first time in my life, stuffed chairs with anti-macassars draped over their arms and backs; I saw carved hutches and rows of china dishes sitting inside them. I saw polished tables and ornate kerosene lamps. I saw curtains and bedspreads. There were pictures hanging on wall-papered walls, and in some of the rooms, wonder of wonders, I saw toys. I had never dreamed of playing with a toy because I had never seen a real one.

Big Mac caught me staring at a large stuffed bear. He laughed and said, "It ain't real, boy." I grunted, trying to ask him what it was for.

Big Mac said, "Dem's de white chillen's, and they's soon as cut off yor black fingers 'n let you tech it."

It was also my job to sweep the back porch, the wooden walk, and the yard. If I didn't keep these clean, Big Mac warned, I would get whupped good until I learned how to do it right.

I wanted to say, "Yes sir, Mister Mac, sir," but it came out like, "yassahmassamasuh." It *almost* sounded like talking. Big Mac didn't even seem to notice. In fact, Big Mac never once made mention of my speech problem in all the years I was a slave on the Beal Plantation. And he never once referred to me as "dumb." I think he must have been a very great man.

I had very little contact with the white folk, and although the white children were strangely interesting to me, I didn't have to have anything to do with them. That is, not right away.

When I finished my chores at the Big House, I would run back to the slave quarter and play with the other children whose parents were out in the fields. I was delighted to have some friends to play with. I learned new games and new sports, ones that my little sister Ella and I never knew about. There was a game called baseball, and we played with a stick and a stone. I loved it, although I couldn't hit the stone with the stick at all, nor could I run and catch the stone very well when somebody else hit it. The enemy in all of our games was always the white man. The white man was hated with fierce intensity in the quarter, and the children especially expressed their hatred in their games and sports. They had one game they played called "Kill Missah Thrasher," where they beat rocks on a pile of dirt until it was flattened. I learned that Thrasher was the name of the chief overseer, the most hated and dreaded white man on the Beal Plantation. He was known to have whupped slaves until they fainted just because they stood up and broke the bent-over posture they were forced to keep while picking cotton.

Every night after supper I'd go to the Big House to be with Pearl, and I'd stay there until she was through work. Sometimes she would be working until 10:00 at night, and she would have to be back at 4:00 in the morning. I just liked being near her so I waited in the big kitchen for her or on the steps outside, being careful to stay sway from the white folk. Then we'd walk to our shanty together and maybe we'd sing or maybe not say anything. It didn't matter. It would seem like we'd just get to sleep when Pearl would nudge me to wake up, and I'd run to the Big House to light the fires while it was still dark out and everyone was still asleep.

The slaves' children ate their noon meal from a large pot of boiled cornmeal that was brought down to the quarter by either Pearl or Daisy or one of the bigger slave boys. This was dumped into a large wooden trough and set on the ground. All of the children came running with pieces of shingle or cardboard or a tin can to scoop out what they could get. If you ate fast and got there first, you'd get the most. If you were like me, you got there last and never ate fast enough. Nobody was ever filled up though—no slave child ever had enough to eat.

I usually ate breakfasts at the Big House. After I started the fires, Big Mac would give me a hunk of corn bread and some hot coffee. I'd crouch down by the cookstove and gulp it down. I was up long before the sound of the horn was heard in the quarter waking the slaves. One morning before the overseers came to eat, Big Mac gave me an apple and said, "Beat it, now, hyar?" I ran out of the kitchen and stood breathless in the dark by the side of the smoke house. I was almost six years old and had never before eaten a whole apple. I ate the whole thing—core, seeds and all.

Mary Webb, the family cook, was a surly little woman with flashing black eyes and a thin pointed nose that shot out from her face like a bullet. Her mother was a slave and her father was a white man. She was one of the many transferred slaves that came from another plantation. Often a slave's family was torn up like Mary's, leaving husband and children behind, and they would never know where their family was taken off to.

Mary Webb was filled with nastiness—demonized, I think she was. She had a high-pitched, railing voice you could hear for two miles. "Git that skillet yonder!" she'd shriek at me, and if I didn't jump with all my might to do as she said, she'd scream so loud my ears would ring. Or she'd throw something.

One day while I was helping Pearl finish scrubbing the large griddle, Miss Mary screamed at me to take out the garbage. I didn't move fast enough to please her, and a terrible rage came over her. I froze as I saw her spring for a large carving knife. She lunged at me just as Big Mac hollered, "Move, boy!" I jumped, grabbed the can of garbage, and flew out of the door. The knife whizzed through the air and missed my head by a hair.

Another time when my response to Miss Mary's command was not to her liking, she hit her target. She threw a heavy cast-iron biscuit pan at me and got me right on the forehead. I was knocked unconscious.

"Robert, honey," I heard Pearl call. She was stroking my cheek and holding a tin cup of yellow flower tea.

"Robert, honey, you know what?"

"Uh?"

"Yoll be six years old now. You is a big boy!"

"Ahz?"

"You done become six June 27 las'. Don't you forgit that date now, hyar? Some people jes don't know 'zakly when they was born. But you do, hyar? You is six years old June 27 las'."

I didn't feel any different being six than I had felt when I thought I was five, except for the large bump on my head, but Pearl seemed to think it was important I be six.

Pearl was growing prettier all the time. She had high cheek bones like Mama, soft full lips and small, even teeth. Her eyes were large and deep set, and she always looked as though she was studying in her thoughts. She was almost fifteen. Her good looks bothered Buck and Corrie. They said a black slave girl is better off ugly.

I had some bad headaches after the blow Mary Webb gave me. Big Mac would get irritated if I talked about it, so I learned early not to complain of physical pain. Slaves just don't complain about pain.

Sundays were my favorite day. The white folks usually went out on an outing after church, so Pearl could leave the Big House and we could go for walks together, or go visiting some of the other slaves.

One autumn Sunday about 5:00 in the evening, Miss Harriet, the Beals' housekeeper, came down to the quarter looking for Pearl.

"Come on," she called, "Massuh callin' yoll."

Pearl's eyes widened in fright. "What he want wi' me?"

"Mary Webb, she be drunk and can't cook nothing nohow. He want you to come cook up a meal for him and his friends."

Reluctantly, Pearl followed Miss Harriet up the path to the Big House. Buck's face was solemn as he watched her go. I ran after her to go along, but Miss Harriet shooed me off.

Pearl did not come back that night. In the morning before sunup I ran up the cold dirt path to the Big House to light the fires as usual. I picked up a load of wood from the woodpile first and carried it to the house. There was a small light flickering in the kitchen window. I entered the room and saw Big Mac hovering over something on the floor. It was Pearl.

He saw me coming and put his hand up. "Go 'way, son. Ain't nothin' fuh yoll to see."

"Peh! Peh!" I screamed. Big Mac couldn't keep me from her, and being afraid I'd wake the entire house, he didn't hold me back. Pearl was lying on the floor so badly beaten I could barely recognize her.

"The massuh an' his friends . . ." Big Mac sobbed.

They had beaten and burned her with the poking iron. She was bloody from head to toe.

Something happened to me when I saw her lying there. A cold, icy, finger-like vise grabbed my body, and with every ounce of strength I had, I hated the white man. Big Mac picked the thin, broken form of my sister up in his big arms and carried her outside, down the path, and to the quarter to Buck and Corrie's. In his strong arms she looked no bigger than a child like myself.

Corrie fixed up some ointments to lay on Pearl's body and face. Some places she put leaves, other places lard, other places some grease gotten from the wagon wheels. Pearl was conscious and screaming in agony. Big Mac had to leave right away to cook the breakfast for the overseers. Some women field workers came and prayed over Pearl; some cried, but most of them just looked at her with hard, cold faces. They knew what had happened, and there wasn't a court in the world that cared.

As the days wore on, Pearl began to get better. Soon

she was out of bed and able to use her hands. Her hands had been burned the worst. They had put them right into the fire. The rest of her body had open sores which festered for many months.

Pearl didn't go back to work in the Big House after that. She was sent to work in the fields. I was heartsick over it. She went to the fields before sunup and didn't get back till sundown. The only time I could see her would be at noon when they let the slaves eat dinner, and at night. She was sullen and quiet now. And she was always exhausted.

Field work was hard on Pearl. She wasn't strong to begin with, and being outside in the cold, barefooted and wearing only a thin cotton dress, she developed a cough that wouldn't stop. The wounds on her body were still healing, and it pained her terrible each time she coughed.

Corrie gave her everything she could think of. She made special root teas, she made a syrup with molasses and some bitter leaves, she put hot poultices on her chest, but the cough wouldn't leave.

Then, to my complete horror, early in the winter I was moved out of Buck and Corrie's shanty and into the Big House. I was not allowed off the grounds, which meant I couldn't go to the quarter. They put me in the same room with the white sons, John and Thomas, who were eight and six, and the baby Anna, who was almost two. My new chore was to mind baby Anna.

I sat crying on the woodbox in the kitchen the first morning I was ordered to live up at the Big House. Big Mac saw me, and he came striding over to me and slapped me hard across the cheek.

"There'll be no more of that, hyar?" I was stunned. I knew nothing else to do but cry. I couldn't fight back, I couldn't even talk. I could only hate and cry.

It was almost noontime of the first day at the Big House when I got what you might call my official welcome. It came in the form of the dreaded overseer, Thrasher.

I had heard many terrible things about him from the other slaves, but I had never seen him. When the overseers came for their meals, I had made it my business to be out of sight. This day, however, I was caught off guard. Besides, the Big House was now my home, and I was not allowed to go to the slave quarter anymore. I could go only as far as the woodpile, by orders of the master.

It was while I was coming from the woodpile with wood

and sticks in my arms for the cookstoves in the kitchen that I met up with Thrasher. I was trying to hurry with my errand because I didn't want another biscuit pan in the head from Mary Webb.

Around the corner of the yard came Thrasher riding on his powerful brown and white horse, and he straightened in the saddle when he saw me. I stopped, bowed slightly, and tried to say "Good day, suh."

Thrasher's voice boomed at me, "Niggerboy!"

I whirled in my tracks as he removed the long black whip he carried on the horn of his saddle. He raised his arm high in the air and the whip came cracking down on my neck and shoulders. The blow brought me to my knees with wood and sticks falling to the ground.

"You black niggerboy, you call me *Mr. Thrasher, suh*, hyar?"

Mary Webb came to the kitchen door when she heard the sound of the whip. Thrasher turned his rage on her.

"You better learn this hyar black nigger slave boy how to talk right or he goin' to be a dead niggerboy, hyar?"

"Yessuh, Missah Thrasher, suh," she said in a high mocking voice.

When I tried to get up, I wobbled on my feet and fell backwards in the dirt. Mary Webb watched me go down, wiped her nose on the back of her hand, and went back into the kitchen to finish her work.

The pain burned like a hot fire on my neck and shoulder. I finally struggled to my feet and dragged myself to the kitchen door of the Big House. Mary Webb was standing at the cookstove. Her eyes flashed when she saw me. Then in a high, shrill voice, she called, "Roberrrrrt! Where's that wood I tole you to git?"

5

It was the winter of 1917. I was six years old and so was Thomas Beal. We discovered one another the very day that Thrasher had given me the lash in the yard.

I was standing by the doorway of the room I was to sleep in with the white children. The pain in my neck and shoulders was awful bad, and I was feeling nauseous. I wanted to lie down but I was afraid to in that room where the white children were.

Thomas saw me standing in the door and he said, "What's yor name, boy?"

"Robert," I answered. (It came out like "Wobber.") I wasn't sure if I was supposed to call him sir or not.

"My name is Thomas. Are you seven yet?"

I couldn't answer that. I didn't know if seven came before or after six.

"I'm gonna be seven and have a birthday," Thomas told me proudly.

He showed me the bed he slept in and the bed his brother, John, slept in. Anna's crib was right near the little cot that had been set up for me. In addition to the little cot, there was a tiny dresser for me. I had nothing to put in it, of course. I stared at the room. There was a real ceiling, and the walls had blue flowered wallpaper on them. The bare wood floor was polished, and there were little rugs here and there. There were pale blue curtains on the long, low windows, and the sun was shining in the room, making it seem warm and cheerful.

"Yoll ought to clean yourself up," Thomas told me. "Yoll got blood all over you. Ugh."

Big Mac washed me up outside in the yard by the side of the house. "You do your own cleanin' up after this, boy," he told me. He washed me by pouring icy cold water from a bucket over my body and scrubbing me with a bar of hard soap. He used dried leaves as a scrub brush, but he was very gentle around the cut of the lash on my neck and shoulder.

"Got you deep, boy," he said with a tone of disgust.

After the icy bath, which left me chattering, came the worst part. It was the putting on of the new flax shirt. The coarseness of the fabric was like a million tiny pins sticking into my skin.

"In a few days this hyar shirt'll be smooth as a rose petal," Big Mac assured me.

I stumbled inside after him, feeling feverish and cold. He fixed me a cup of sassafras tea and told me to drink it down. He even tied a clean rag around my wounds.

In spite of the pain I felt from the lash wound and the pricks of the shirt, I lay down that night in my new bed with a feeling of excitement. It was the first time I had ever slept in a real bed, and I was sleeping in it all alone. I had a blanket that was clean all for myself, too. I did not stir until the next morning when Big Mac tugged at my foot.

"Fires need lightin', boy," he said softly.

I stared dumbly around me in the darkness. For a moment I had forgotten where I was. The pain in my neck and shoulder reminded me, and my body felt raw and sore from the scratching of the new shirt. I struggled out of bed into the cold air and hurried to the woodpile for sticks and wood to start the fires.

By 4:00 a.m. I had all of the fires lit, including the ones in the cookstoves. I was still in the kitchen when the dreaded crew of overseers filed into their special dining hall for breakfast. There were eleven of them, including Thrasher. They were mean men with dirty mouths. They looked like giants, and it seemed to me they hated everything, even each other. They all lived on the Beal Plantation in dwellings within a few minutes of the Big House. Some had families and some didn't. Most of them were heavy drinkers just like Mr. Beal, who was an alcoholic.

Thrasher caught sight of me and hollered across the room, "Nigger, you got some manners yit?"

I stood to my feet, "YessuhMassuhThrashuhsuh," I mumbled. Thrasher snorted. "What's your name, nigger-boy?"

"Wobber, suh, MassahThrashuhsuh."

Thrasher laughed and the others laughed with him. "He's a *dumb* nigger slave boy too, ain't he? You want another lash, nigger?"

"NosuhMassuhThrashuhsuh."

Big Mac passed by with a bowl of hot biscuits and Thrasher's attention was then drawn to the food. I hurried for the broom and the scrub brushes to begin my chores. First the porch, then the steps, and then the yard . . .

6

"We got a new black puppy. Want to see him?" John Beal walked through the front hallway with a stringy-haired friend his age.

"Nah. I knows what a nigger looks like. Ain't no different from any othern. They all the same."

Big Mac told me that the white folks liked to have "little black puppies" around. Some folks had two or three of them like me sleeping in their bedrooms with them. It was our job to run around after the white masters, cleaning up their chamber pots and doing other dirty work they didn't want to do.

One day as I was finishing my work, Miss Harriet was taking the sheets off the children's beds to put into the laundry pile. She was a large, stern-faced woman, and this day her mouth was drawn tight and her eyes had a distant look.

"I done raised these chillrens," she said aloud. Although I was the only one in the room, I had the feeling she wasn't talking to me.

"I done nursed them all at my breast. Each one o' them. I done washed their bodies and tuk care of 'em when they was sick. I done fed 'em they meals and I done put 'em in the bed at night...." Her voice trailed off and I saw tears streaming down her face.

Later that morning Big Mac told me her own baby had died the night before in the quarter. Her other children had neglected to feed him right and he starved to death.

The slave women bore children by their own men as well as by the white bosses who used them whenever they wanted to. These women worked either in the field from 4:30 in the morning till after dark, or like Harriet, worked at the Big House all day and night. When they finally were home for the few hours before they'd have to return to work, they'd be too exhausted to care for and feed their own families rightly. So the job was left up to the children themselves. The older children had the responsibility of taking care of the babies and little ones. Sometimes an old slave granny was put to work minding the children in the quarter when she got too old to go to the field.

I learned that Harriet had seven children of her own, and while the master's babies were sucking at her breast, her own children were neglected and going hungry down in the slave quarter.

Harriet had a husband once but he had been sold to a plantation owner in Alabama. "After he gone," Big Mac said, "Harriet never smile no more."

These were things my child's mind could not understand, but even if I couldn't understand, I felt bad about Harriet's baby dying because I remembered how bad I felt when Mama and my little sister, Ella, died. Dying was not good. It meant they weren't anymore. Just like my mama. She was there all the time, and then one day she wasn't there. She was no more. It makes you sad and it makes you lonesome.

Saturday night was supposed to be payday for the slaves. Since the Big House was now my prison, I could see what went on from there. The slaves would line up at the smoke house, or the plantation store, and the man there would give them their provisions—usually flour, sugar, some salt pork, beans, cornmeal, and some tobacco. Then they'd tell them how much they owed, and it was always more than what the pay was. So the slave didn't get paid. Sometimes when they'd come for their pay the man would say, "Master Beal is out of town. Won't be back till Monday. He'll pay yoll then." Of course Master Beal never did pay them on Monday, or any day for that matter. It was very rare when he would throw a dollar or two at the slave.

With winter coming, shoes were needed and so was warmer clothing. Not everybody got shoes, and not everybody got another layer of clothing. Many slaves died in the winter months, and many were crippled up by the cold. I hoped I would get some shoes or maybe some trousers. I began to ask Harriet about it. She was indifferent, and I realized it was hopeless to continue to ask.

I missed Pearl. I longed to see her, and soon I became desperate to see her. Knowing that my punishment would be a whupping if I were caught, I began planning to sneak down to the quarter. I got my first chance one evening when the children were in bed sleeping. Master Beal was away, and Miss Harriet was upstairs with Mistress Beal. The house was still. I crawled out of bed quietly, and barely breathing, moved through the kitchen, the porch, and then out the door and down the steps. I was careful to keep in the shadows of the yard. When I passed the woodpile and the stable, I came to the dirt path to the quarter and broke into a run.

When I reached Buck and Corrie's shanty, they were surprised and then excited to see me. Pearl held me in her arms and squeezed me so tight she took the breath out of me. We laughed and cried and hugged, and everybody talked at once.

"They gonna whup you for this, chile," Pearl warned.

Pearl was coughing bad and she looked worn out and so thin. The wounds on her body still weren't completely healed. I asked her if they had given her any shoes, and she shook her head no.

The wind blew through the boards of the little shack, and I knew there would be no way for her to be warm. There was the little pile of rags she slept on and that was all.

We huddled before the fire in the hearth, and when it began to go out I put more sticks on it and then kissed Pearl goodnight. I promised myself the next time I came I would come bringing something for them.

The moon was full and the sky covered with stars when I left the quarter. I ran up the hard, cold dirt of the path in the moonlight, rounded the yard, the stable, and the wood-pile.

The Big House looked like a bulging many-sided monster in the moonlight. The kitchen side jutted out like a long flat finger; the sun porch on the east side sat dark, cold, and square beneath the looming two-story arm behind it. Windows peered at me like enemy eyes.

My successful brief escape gave me new courage. My thought night and day now was when I could make another break for the quarter and what I could bring with me for my sister.

I began following Miss Harriet around as she cleaned the house. I would hold baby Anna and follow along behind Miss Harriet, learning where everything was. At first she didn't like it, but then she allowed me to tag along with her. When I saw the huge linen closet on the second floor filled with towels, sheets, pillows, and blankets, I made plans to steal a blanket for Pearl. Miss Harriet must have seen the expression on my face as I gazed into the closet. She lifted my chin with her big hand and looked me in the eye.

"We is cold and shiverin' an' they has got blankets enough to fill a room, Robert. But lissen up, chile, to what I'm sayin'. Massah don't have no mercy nohow on no thiefs. Don't you start figurin' a way to carry any o' these fine blankets to the quarter, hyar? Massah'll cut off yor lil black fingers!"

That week I was being rusted to give baby Anna her lunch occasionally. There was fresh fruit, sandwiches, cookies, and other wonderful things. I fed her under the watchful eye of Mary Webb, and if I so much as licked a crumb from the table top, she would scream and call for Mistress Beal and tell her I was eating the baby's food.

One afternoon I had peeled an orange for Anna, and I stuck one of the peels into my mouth. Mary Webb saw me from across the kitchen and let out a high, shrill scream. She rushed over to the table where I sat with the baby, grabbed me by my ear, and marched me into the sitting room where Mistress was sewing.

"This nigger done et Miz Anna's orange, Missis, I see'd him!"

Mistress put her sewing down, and with a stony glare at me, said in a low voice, "I'll speak to my husband about it. Now get out both of you." I tried to protest but it was no use. Mary Webb hit me hard with the palm of her hand and then yanking my ear, she pulled me back to the kitchen. I cried, knowing I would get the lash when the master came home.

Master Beal came home in time for dinner. After he had eaten, he came looking for me. "Robert," he called, "come hyar!"

He took me by the hand and in his other hand he held the dreaded leather strap. He led me out of the side door and took me around to the side of the house where Mac had given me my bath. Then he said, "Take off your shirt and lie down." The grass was wet and cold, and the sky was already dark in the early evening. I could hear a cricket chirping happily near my cheek as the first lash of the leather bit into my back. I don't know how many times it came down cutting into me, but when it was all over, he said, "You steal from me agin, boy, and I'll show your black hide what a whuppin' really tastes like, hyar?"

"... yesssuhmassah ... suh."

And he walked away.

7

The days grew colder, and the activity around the plantation decreased for the winter months. Some of the overseers left until spring, and the field slaves were used to fell trees, dig river banks, build, mend barns, and do the many other jobs necessary to keep the large plantation running. Although it was not a wealthy plantation and Sam Beal was not a rich man, there was enough work for the slaves to be kept busy from sunup to sundown.

Baby Anna was put in Miss Harriet's charge again since my experience with the orange peel. As I did my chores around the Big House, I made plans to pay a visit to the quarter to see Pearl again.

I got my chance the day I received my first pair of trousers and shoes. John had worn and outgrown them, and Harriet said Mistress Beal wanted me to have them because she couldn't stand looking at me so shabby and barefoot all the time. The shoes were too small and the trousers too big, but I felt like the richest boy in the world.

Then Mistress gave me a shirt to wear, too—a cotton one that buttoned like the ones white children wore. It was smooth on my skin, and I stroked it continually. I had never worn anything but coarse flax shirts and this soft piece of clothing was a wonder to me.

That night after the evening meal, I waited until the kitchen was cleared out, and then I sneaked into the pantry and took a jar of strawberry preserves and another jar of peach slices. Then I fled from the house as though the devil himself were chasing me. I reached Buck and Corrie's shack panting and gasping for breath.

"Chile!" Corrie exclaimed. "Is they after you?"

We opened the peaches right then and passed them around, eating them with our fingers. Pearl's hands were scarred and disfigured from her bitter experience with Master Beal.

There was a fourth person in the shanty that night, one I had never met. His name was George Murphy, and he was new on the plantation. Master Beal had hired him to do some special carpentry.

He was a handsome young man as black as the night. "Ain't no white blood in me," he boasted. I liked him right off because of his easygoing manner, his self-assurance, and his lack of fear of the white man. Pearl was completely taken by him. I had never seen her so radiant.

I sat with Pearl's arms around me on the floor near the fire listening to George tell us stories about his dangerous exciting escapades. He had done all sorts of jobs, from working on the railroad to building barns. He peppered his stories with traveling news. He is the first person I can ever remember telling us that slavery was against the law. "It ain't legal for a man to own another man," he insisted. "They's a law!"

George could read a little and tell numbers. That way, he said proudly, nobody could cheat George Murphy of what was rightfully his.

The moments passed swiftly, and then I gave Pearl a kiss and said good-bye. I promised I would be back soon. George Murphy put his hand out and shook mine. I felt very important and manly, especially since I was wearing such fine clothes.

The clothes didn't go unnoticed, by the way. But the reaction wasn't quite what I had expected. Pearl looked at me oddly, and Buck and Corrie stared with no expression at all. "You look fine, boy," Buck said finally in a dry voice. That's all that was said about it.

I got back to the Big House safely again that night and tiptoed to my bed. I slept in my new clothes and shoes, not knowing enough to take them off.

The stolen items went unnoticed, and I was thankful and encouraged by it. Next time maybe I could bring more. Pearl was still coughing bad. I would remember to ask Big Mac about coughing and what would cure it.

A few evenings later while the white folks were having their supper in the dining room and Big Mac and I were eating grits and gravy in the kitchen, we heard a tremendous ruckus in the yard. Big Mac went to the window to see what it was.

"Wal, Thrasher got hisself another one," he said. Mac opened the backdoor. Thrasher had a black man hooked under his arm. He had been slapped around plenty.

"Fetch the bossman!" he commanded.

Minutes later, Master strode out of the dining room, angry at being interrupted during his meal.

"This hyar nigger lef his job before quittin' time, Boss,"

I heard Thrasher shout. "He's a uppity one, that's for certain. Thinks he can do jes as he pleases."

"I was done with my work!" I heard a voice insist. I recognized the voice. Quickly, I went to the window and cupped my hand to see outside. A wave of horror filled me. It was George Murphy.

Master Beal shouted back, "We'll see how uppity he can be! We'll jes bring him down to meet some of my friends and have a little talkin' over. Hold him till I get ready."

I saw Thrasher drag George Murphy to the horse barn. Master Beal stormed out of the backdoor. He had been drinking. They threw the tied-up figure on a horse and galloped out of the driveway.

"What'll they do to him, Mac?" I asked, terrified.

"They's gonna tear him apart," Mac answered. "And if they don't kill him, he'll wish they had."

"Oh, no!"

"That's the way they do, son; them Ku Klux, that's the way they do."

I couldn't sleep that night thinking about George Murphy and what they were doing to him. When at last I heard horses and voices in the yard, I ran to the window. It was hard to see, but I made out the drunk swagger of Master Beal crossing the yard. He used the side entrance and went right upstairs. When it became quiet, I crept down to the kitchen, across the cold porch, down the steps, around the yard, and instead of using the path, I ran through the brush to the quarter. When I arrived, I heard voices coming from Buck and Corrie's shanty. Someone was crying. Several of the slaves were up and around the door. I pushed through them. What I saw on the floor was worse than anything I had expected.

He was lacerated practically beyond recognition. He had been beaten so badly there was hardly any skin on him, and his flesh looked like hamburger. His face was torn up and his head crushed. He was twisted up funny.

Pearl was crying and putting some grease on his head and back. He was barely conscious.

Corrie was on her knees at his feet with a pail with water in it. Some other people were praying.

"I'll be on the job tomorrow," I heard George swear through cut and swollen lips.

"Never you mind," Pearl whispered.

I don't think anybody saw me come or leave the shanty that night. I shall never forget what I saw.

George Murphy became the talk of everybody in the quarter in the days that followed. News came to us through the house slaves who lived in the quarter, like Mary Webb, Daisy, and Harriet. The next day after his beating, he actually did get up on his feet and put in a day's work. He became a symbol to the slaves of the strength of the black man.

After several weeks, he became well enough to run away. He made it, too, in spite of the hounds and searches, and nobody ever heard from him again. He remained our hero. Wherever he was, we knew he wasn't owned by any man.

The white children taught me games, and we played almost as any normal children played—normal, that is, except I was not allowed to win or be first in anything, and if they wanted to fight, I was not allowed to hit back. If I had something in my hand, they could grab it if they wanted to, and I was not to protest.

Yet the children were kind to me. At mealtimes they often sneaked food from the table to give to me. They would sneak sandwiches and cake and sometimes a slice of ham or other meat. I gobbled the food hungrily, and they would laugh with delight to see me go at it.

One cold afternoon we were playing in the music room when Mistress Beal came in. "Mama," Juanita asked suddenly, "how come Robert's skin is dark and ours is white?"

Mistress answered coolly, "Because Robert and his people were created to be the white man's slave. They are dark because they sinned against God and God punished them."

I listened in alarm.

"Because they sinned, they have to pay for it. And that is why they are meant to serve the white man."

"Are there any niggers in heaven, Mama?"

"If there are, dear, they're serving the white people."

I lowered my head in shame. Juanita seemed embarrassed too. She was learning that a slave was not considered a real person.

"Robert don't have a soul, honey," Mistress said without blinking an eye. "Negroes don't have souls. They are just like animals that way."

"Don't Harriet have a soul neither?" asked Juanita.

"No dear, she is a Negro too, and Negroes don't have souls."

Juanita looked as though she would cry. Mistress

laughed softly. "Now, honey," she cooed, "instead of putting on a sad face, you ought to thank the good Lord for giving you some niggers to take care of you."

". . . Yes, Mama."

We left the music room quietly, and Juanita went upstairs to her room without a word. I went outside to the woodpile. Pearl must have told me wrong. Mama and Ella weren't happy and free in heaven, after all. They were black slaves serving the white angels. Whatever our sin was to deserve such an awful fate, it must have been real bad.

8

The winter days were long and I was worried about Pearl. On a grey, windy afternoon when there was a lot of activity around the Big House, I planned another escape to the quarter. Visitors were expected at the Big House that evening. I was put to work cleaning the halls and the bathrooms. All day long tension filled the air. Mistress Beal was shouting orders, the house slaves were running around trying to obey them, the children were underfoot and misbehaving, and Mary Webb was throwing things in the kitchen. In my effort to avoid everybody, I got in everybody's way. Not only did I receive the heel of Mistress Beal's foot, but of Mary Webb's and Harriet's as well.

"Robert, get outa here!"

"Roberrrt! You brought in wet logs for the fire! Git out there an' bring in dry logs!"

"Robert, git over hyar!"

"Robert, fetch some water!"

"Roberrrt, scrub these pots!"

"Robert, you ain't nothin' but somethin' dumb!"

I was made to scrub the wooden planks of the front porch and steps and the wooden walkway leading to the circular drive. My hands in the icy water were numb, but I hardly noticed it because I was so excited about seeing Pearl again. I planned to make my getaway to the quarter when everyone was asleep that night.

Every once in a while I thought about Margie, and I wondered if they were treating her bad where they had taken her off to. I wondered if she was a house slave like me or a field slave like Pearl. I longed to see her.

When the chores were done, the house slaves were allowed to eat supper in the kitchen—fatback fried crisp, corn bread, and molasses. I asked Big Mac some questions that he seemed to understand the meaning of.

"Where Hartwell, Georgie?"

"A long ways off, boy."

"How long?"

"Too long for you to think about. If it was jes yonder

down the road, it would be too far for you to think about."

I looked at him sadly. "Margie in Hartwell, Georgie."

Big Mac finished his food and said somberly, "Let me tell you about a woman who used to live on this here plantation, boy."

I listened closely.

"She quite a woman. Her name Lois. A good worker. She work the fields like a man. And she bring three little babies into this world, too. When she done bore her third baby, the boss, he call her and he say, 'You leavin' this place tonight. You done been sold to a new boss.' It done tore out her heart and she scream and cry and beg the boss. 'Don't send me from my chillrens! Please don't send me from my chillrens!' But the boss, he don't pay her no mind nohow and he pack her up in the wagon. When she scream and grab his leg beggin' him to let her stay with her chillrens, he give her a kick in the face, and she fall in the ground crying and prayin' to almighty God to help her and help her chillrens. They throwed her in the back of the wagon and off they goes down the road. They tuk her more'n a hundred miles away, way across the state to a great big farm where they put her to workin' the field cuttin' cotton stalk. She done ran away one night she was so grievin' for those chillrens. She jes had to get to her chillrens. She done run night and day through the woods, the marshes, across the rivers, in wilderness and towns; that woman done run to git back here to her chillrens and her man. She knew that no man slave can take care of the chillrens. They didn't catch her nohow. She got as far as the road up here jes a mile away. She was half-dead from running and being hongry. She got up here jes about a mile—" His voice broke.

Mac's strong, wide shoulders crumpled and shook, and he sobbed and gulped.

"Oh Lord," he cried, "she got all the way to the plantation! Jessa few minutes from her babies who was cryin' for their mammy—"

I sat still, my heart beating loudly.

"They done catched her and throwed her in the jail until the new owner come and fetched her. She never saw her chillrens agin."

Tears burned in my eyes. The agony of being torn from those you love was common to us. Big Mac pulled his shoulders back and said quietly, "Boy, that woman was my wife."

The visitors arrived and I helped carry their traveling cases to the guest rooms. Three young children eyed me with contempt as they moved around the rooms. There was food prepared for them, and the two families sat down to eat in the dining room. From the kitchen we could hear their laughter and loud talking. Master was not yet home, but we expected him soon.

At last the white folks went upstairs to their rooms. When the children were in bed, I set to work cleaning up after them and helping in the kitchen.

Mary Webb, Harriet, and Daisy were cleaning and preparing for the next day's meals, and when nobody was looking, I sneaked out the door of the sun porch and ran through the yard, careful to dodge any light spots. As I made my flight, I had forgotten that Master Beal had not returned home yet.

I got as far as the woodpile when I heard heavy footsteps in the dark. I froze in my tracks and listened. Soon the hulking form of Master Beal approached. It was too late to duck. He had already seen me.

"Whozzat?" he demanded.

"W—W—Wobber, Massuh Beal, suh," I answered in a voice barely audible. He was drunk and could hardly balance himself. "Whatchou doin' outchere, niggerboy?" he asked with a growl.

I quickly answered, "Fetchin' wood, Massuh Beal, suh, I be fetchin' wood."

He growled again and staggered toward the house. "Git movin' then," he said over his shoulder.

With trembling hands, I filled my arms with pieces of wood and hurried back to the Big House. That was my last attempt to get to the quarter that winter. It was many weeks before I got another opportunity.

The next days brought merrymaking and fun for the Beal family and their visitors. They had activities planned for each day, and the house was filled with the sounds of their voices and the smells of liquor and tobacco.

It was at this time I got my introduction to a torturous form of entertainment which gave them much pleasure.

After breakfast one cold morning, I was bringing in water from the well on the porch to be put on the cookstove to heat. "Robert," Daisy said from the door, "Massuh callin' you." I hurried as fast I could and practically ran to the parlor where he was sitting with his friends. He had already been drinking. I could tell by the way he sat and the crooked look on his face.

The fire was going in the fireplace, and the room was cozy and warm. "Put some coal on the fire, boy," ordered Master Beal. "Yessuh, Massuh Beal, suh," I responded properly.

I bent to pick up the coals as I was told when suddenly I felt a searing pain in my back, and the smell of burned flesh stung my nose. I whirled around, shocked and yelping. Master Beal stood behind me with a red-hot poking iron from the fire. He was laughing and so were his friends. "Let's see how high you can jump, slave boy," he cawed, jabbing the poking iron into my belly. The burning pain caused me to fall backwards onto the floor. He continued, laughing hilariously.

"Oh, that ain't high enough, niggerboy. Let's see you do a little jig!" He thrust the glowing end of the poking iron into my face, and I rolled over and scrambled to my feet, crying and squealing in terror.

"I said a jig, niggerboy. A jig!" Again the poking iron came at me and I hopped out of its way. Again and again he pushed the fiery end of the poking iron at me. I leaped and hopped and turned and twisted each time to escape its sizzling my flesh. Sometimes I made it, but sometimes I didn't. When the iron bit into me, tearing the skin off, I screamed and yelled, much to the master's delight. Their laughter and excitement over this sport built to a frenzy as I wept and begged, "No Massuh, no, please Massuh—" jumping around the room to miss the deadly sear of the iron.

At last, when they tired of their fun, Master Beal shouted, "Stand still, niggerboy." I did, shaking and crying miserably. Then with one final jab to my body, he said calmly, "You didn't put any coal on the fire, boy!"

Those burns took many weeks to heal. Master Beal loved to show off on his slave boy and for eight winters when guests came I was often called to "put the coals on. . . ."

There was no such thing as doctor care for the slaves on the plantation. The animals had better medical treatment. Many slaves died during the winters from exposure and hunger. Disease and filth were common among the shacks in the quarter. Death was a victory.

One miserable day after another passed by, and I didn't know any better but to believe I was what they said I was —a dumb niggerboy with no soul. I was the little puppy dog who did the dirty work for the white folks, and that's all my people were meant for. And the white folks expected us to be grateful for the honor of serving them. They had some kind of idea that we should be *happy* as slaves, and if we weren't slaving and dying, we were supposed to be singing and dancing and being just plain dumb and happy-like. I didn't feel that way, but I acted that way. I had to.

9

The spring of 1918 came, and the plantation buzzed with activity. The overseers returned to their jobs, the slaves were put to the fields, and the cultivating was begun. Everybody was nervous and tense, and tempers flared continually.

Then came the rains. It rained night and day. It was cold, too, and the mud was deep in the yard. I made my runs to the woodpile to catch a glimpse of Pearl when the slaves filed by on their way to the field each morning.

I'd see her bent, downcast, moving toward the field. I'd jump with joy. She'd lift up her head and smile at me for a flashing moment. My heart would sing at the sweet sight of her. Then I'd watch her disappear over the hill and down to the deep muds of the field.

Each day I'd run to the woodpile at the same time, and each day I'd see Pearl moving behind Buck and Corrie toward the field. Some days the rain would be falling so hard that I could barely see her face, but I knew it was Pearl and that's all that mattered.

One morning when the rains had passed, I stood at the woodpile waiting to catch sight of Pearl, but when the slaves filed by, I didn't see her. I didn't see Corrie either.

I knew it was a very serious matter for a slave not to show up for work. They could get whupped practically to death for that.

I dropped the sticks in my hands. "Buck!" I called, "Where's Pearl?" Buck looked down and said in a low voice, "She be ailin', son." He moved away before I could ask more.

I hurried to light the fires and fill the woodboxes, and then I told Big Mac, "I'm goin' to Pearl!" not caring whether I got whupped or not. I ran out of the house as fast as I could to the quarter.

I arrived at Buck and Corrie's shanty out of breath and scared to go inside. I took a breath at last and rushed through the door. Pearl was lying on Buck and Corrie's cot making awful rasping, gurgling sounds.

Corrie saw me and tried to turn me away. "No, son. Sister's ailin'. You ought'n see her jes now."

I screamed and threw myself at the bed. I could form no words with my mouth. It was as though I had never spoken. She was little more than a skeleton as she lay there gurgling and glassy-eyed.

"The rains," Corrie cried. "The rains done did her in. They sent her to the fields with her ailin'. We begged for a doctor—we *begged* for a doctor—" She buried her face in the folds of her skirt and sobbed.

Pearl lay half-conscious in the darkness of the shanty. It was damp and cold in the room, and she had no covering on her. Her feet were caked with dried mud. She had still not gotten any shoes. I could see the scars on her body from the beating she had last summer. There were shiny grey pits and holes on her arms, legs, and neck.

Her once beautiful face was now just a few bones with skin stretched across them. Only fifteen years old and she looked like an old lady. She wore a rag of a dress and was covered with mud and filth. She was suffering terribly. For a brief moment, her eyes focused on mine. She struggled to speak.

"Every . . . thing . . . gonna be . . ." Her lips turned upward in the tiniest smile and she reached toward me with her tiny, deformed hand. "Yoll be . . . a big boy . . . now, chile—"

From somewhere in my mind I heard laughter and saw again her black eyes dance happily in the sunlight, and we were tumbling in the grass as she tickled my nose, then my chin and neck. Her smile fixed itself on my face, and it was once again summer somewhere—somewhere, my Pearl and I frolicking, laughing, and she telling me with her sweet kisses and squeezes there was hope, there was hope.

The hours of the morning passed by, and I stayed by Sister, never taking my eyes from her face. I gasped with each painful breath she took. And then they stopped.

Her eyes were wide open with a look of desperate agony when it happened, and her mouth hung stupidly downward. There she lay—everything pure, beautiful, and alive that I had known. Pearl's tortured body lay still now. I kissed her hard, cold face and held the lifeless hand to my body. The grass was gone, and the sun in my life had gone out.

10

Summer, 1918, arrived without my knowing it. I didn't feel the air turn warm, didn't see the trees bloom, didn't hear the sound of the birds playing around the windows. I didn't see or feel a thing. Pearl was dead.

Somewhere in the dense fog of these days, however, a particular day stands out. It was a Sunday afternoon and the Beals must have been on an outing, because there was nobody around and it was very quiet. I was sitting on the wooden steps outside the kitchen door in the heat of the afternoon with nothing but the sound of flies buzzing around me. I looked up and saw a large-boned, barefooted Negro wearing tattered work clothes coming across the yard. It was a dangerous thing for a field slave to come up to the Big House like this. He came nearer, and then he was standing before me with his face close to mine.

"It's me, chile," he said softly, "Buck."

I said nothing.

He smiled a kind smile. "How y'doin', chile?" I stared blankly. Then after an awkward pause, he said, "I had to come up hyar because I done promised Pearl I would. You hearin' me? Yoll be seven years old now, chile. You was born June 27, 1911. Hear me, boy?"

I said nothing.

He spoke to me with tears in his eyes. I watched his mouth and his wet, dirt-lined face without interest. Then while he was still talking, I stood up, turned my back to him, and went into the house.

Summer passed and the autumn came. A new duty was given me by Master Beal. I was to hitch up the buggy for the white children to go to school every morning after I brought in the wood and lit the fires.

I did this vaguely and stupidly. It didn't matter to me what they had me do or what they did to me. I went along with it all and felt nothing, thought nothing, and said nothing.

11

The grueling days of spring and summer had passed. Autumn was gone, and winter was settling in on the plantation. I thought of Pearl continually. It seemed that everything reminded me of her. Winter reminded me that she had no shoes when she died.

I was still wearing the same shoes they had given me over a year ago, and my toes were bent and crushed in them. I wore them without socks, and I wore my only trousers and shirt night and day.

My new chore of hitching up the wagon for the children to go to school became the most interesting point of my life at this time. I decided I wanted to go to school, too.

One day I gained courage enough to ask Master Beal if I could go to school. "Please, Massuh, suh," I said in my best speech, "can I go to school, suh, please?"

Master Beal rocked on his heels in laughter. "You? You? You nigger slave boy, go to school? What would you do there?"

I was lucky I didn't get the back of his hand or the heel of his boot for annoying him with what he said was "dumb nigger botheration" and "damn uppity."

Every morning I helped the children climb into the buggy with their lunch baskets and their books. I wanted to go to school more than anything.

I would wait for them to come home in the late afternoon.

"Teach me about book learnin'," I'd beg. Thomas, who I played with the most because we were the same age, would tell me what he had learned each day. He was the teacher and I the pupil. I drank every word in hungrily.

Juanita and Virginia would play school with me, too, and once in awhile John would even join in. He was ten years old now, and his meanness was growing with each new year.

It was not long before I could count to ten and write some numbers. Juanita taught me how to write my name, which I thought was the most wonderful thing to be able to do. I would write R O B E R T a hundred times a day in my mind.

They were good days. I can truthfully say that we were close and enjoyed each other as children. I had no rights, but I enjoyed their wanting to play with me. I didn't care about their hurting me—they were playing with me right then, and I liked that.

The winter of 1918 enfolded us. Sometimes the temperature dropped below freezing and twice that winter we had snow. I would go out to the woodpile to bring in the wood with my feet squeezed into my shoes, without socks, hat, or covering for my hands.

It was during the coldest part of the winter that Daisy, the house slave who helped Harriet, died. She had given birth to her third baby, and a few days later she was working in the Big House and doing the laundry outside. Harriet tried to keep her from working so hard, and she did twice as much herself, but it was hopeless. I watched Daisy writhe in pain on the kitchen floor, and then a week later she was dead.

Since Daisy didn't have a husband, they gave the baby to another nursing mother in the quarter to care for.

I overheard the overseers in their dining room talking about her the day after Daisy died. "She woulda been a good 'nuff breeder," I heard a gruff voice say; "it's a damn shame."

Daisy had been born on the Beal Plantation and didn't know any other life than slavery. She would have served the Beals another fifty years without complaining because she didn't know any better. She was illiterate, obedient, brainwashed, and handsome. That is why she could be given the tribute of being a "good breeder." She thought that was part of life, too.

The many hours I spent each day in the kitchen were in dreaded fear of Mary Webb. She always had a bottle near her and drank heavily. The Beals never seemed to mind because they liked her cooking. Mary Webb hated me. I still carried the scars on my face of the biscuit pan she had heaved at me. Daisy had gotten along with Mary Webb. She knew how to stay out of her way.

One night while taking swipes at the kitchen floor with the long, clumsy straw broom, I muttered, "Massuh an his chillrens don't hardly care nohow thet Daisy be daid now." Big Mac heard me and whirled me around by the arm. With a hard look in his eye and in a cold, stern voice, he said, "Boy, you *stop* lookin' for someone to care about us, hyar? It's a fool nigger who can't live by hisself, you understand what I'm sayin' to you? If a white man care about a black man, it's a peculiar thing! I ain't havin' no nigger chile livin' with me who's lookin' to make a *friend* out of the white man!"

He was real angry. He had never raised his voice to me before. I was so surprised, I stood with my mouth open staring at him. "Yoll learn to care for *yo'self*, chile!"

"They ain't no place in this hyar worl' to hold a weepy nigger!" he continued. His face was tense with emotion. "Yoll learn yo'self to care for yo'self! If'n you love somebody, chile, shor 'nuff they'll take 'em from you, jes like they done with yo' Sister Pearl and Sister Margie. *Now you stop lookin' fo' mercy from the white man and start lookin' fo' Robert to be a man.*"

A hush fell over the kitchen. Even Mary Webb was silent. Harriet, who felt real bad about Daisy, suddenly picked up her head and began to sing. I stood still, staring at Big Mac, who stood glaring at me, waiting for me to acknowledge what he said.

". . . Yessuh," I said faintly.

Harriet's voice was deep and rich as she sang,

They's a comin' wi' de chariot,
Ah know, ah know,
They's a comin' wi' de chariot
To carry mah poor bones home. . . .

She was singing her last respects to a girl she loved. Mac's words had touched her, and she knew all too well "they ain't no place in this hyar world for a weepy nigger."

Ah done work and ah done sweat;
These ole bones is goin' a rest,
Ole chariot
Carry me home to Jesus.

They's a comin' wi' de chariot,
Ah know, ah know,
They's a comin' wi' de chariot
To carry mah poor bones home. . . .

When she had finished the song, it was finished in her heart as well. She would never talk of Daisy again, and not another tear for her would escape from her eye.

It was not until much later that I learned Daisy was Harriet's oldest daughter.

One afternoon when I was playing school with Thomas and Juanita, Master Beal appeared in the doorway. His eyes flashed.

"What's goin' on hyar?" he demanded.

Thomas answered innocently, "We are playing school, Daddy. I'm the teacher."

"You learnin' this nigger to read and write?"

"Yessuh," answered Thomas proudly.

Master Beal was so angry he grabbed a chair and threw it at Thomas. It just missed him.

"Git!" he shouted at me. I scrambled to my feet and fled from the room. Huddled in a corner of the porch, I could hear him shout at the children.

"If I evah catch any of you learnin' a nigger to read and write agin, I'll whup you so's you won't set down for a month!" I heard the smack of his hand against each of the children's faces, and I heard them cry. It was good-bye to school learning for me.

12

The winter months dragged slowly along now that there was no more play school for me. The children avoided me, but I knew they missed our special times every day, too. I still tried to read their books, and I practiced writing my name, but I couldn't do anymore than that. It made me sad, and I moped around the house. Harriet saw me pouting one afternoon, and she snapped, "Why's you sad in the mouth, chile? Ain't for no lil slave chile to know readin' an' writin'."

"George Murphy knew readin' and writin'," I responded.

"George Murphy was no slave. He be a free man when he come here."

I thought for a moment. "Is they really a law that say a man ain't spose to own another man?"

Harriet's face was thoughtful. "If they's a law Massuh Beal ain't knowin' of it."

"George Murphy say a man spose to git paid fuh his work."

"Humph. That George Murphy, he be big on the talkin' side."

"Harriet, what's a law?"

"Wal, I dunno zackly for shure, but I do believe it is where they put a big sign up, and everybody who see the sign got to do like what it say."

"Is that all a law be?"

"I do believe that be all that it be."

"Wal, maybe Massuh Beal ain't see'd the law!"

"Now you's talkin' uppity!"

It was very confusing to me, but I didn't want to ask any more questions. "Uppity" is what they called George Murphy.

When the children came home from school, I would be waiting to unhitch the pony. Thomas began to toss off orders at me and talk crudely to me. He grew less friendly and more mean and nasty.

John, who had always been mean, grew worse. One day he and Thomas laid waiting for me, and as I rounded a corner, carrying wood to the kitchen, they leaped at me and beat me until I was lying bloody and bruised on the ground.

Since I was not allowed to fight back, I tried to cover my face with my hands and hunched my body to miss some of the blows. Sometimes I would try to run, but they always caught me and beat me worse for trying to get away.

One warm Sunday morning in early spring, visitors arrived at the plantation. We had been preparing for their arrival for days. I watched them coming and then hurried alongside Big Mac to unhitch their buggy. They were a handsome family. The father was dressed fine, and he had dark hair combed straight back and slicked good, and the mother was stout with a round face and big hands. The three children were fat and looked very uncomfortable in dress clothes. I guessed they were around my age. Big Mac and I carried their bags and parcels up to their rooms in the Big House.

After their evening meal, the two families went strolling on the grounds outside. I heard Master call for me. "Robert! Come hyar!" I came running.

"Yessuh, Massuh Beal, suh!"

Then he turned eagerly to his sons. "OK, boys git him!" Like wild dogs the boys descended upon me, kicking and hitting and pounding. I went down immediately. They yanked me back to my feet and then with a hard blow, sent me sprawling to the ground again. The others cheered and shouted in delight.

Out of the corner of my eye I saw the faces of the visiting boys. They looked as though they were in ecstasy. The oldest one had spit running out of his mouth, and he was grinning a horrible grin. Again and again I went down with the blows, and then, finally, when I had nearly lost consciousness, they stopped. But it wasn't over.

"Oh, gim*me* a lick at 'im!" shouted one of the boys. "Gim*me* a lick at 'im!"

There followed then a series of dirty punches and pinches. One of them pulled down my trousers. Another sat on me. Again and again they hit. I cried and screamed for mercy, but it was no use.

When they were finished with their fun, they went skipping off, laughing and out of breath, to the stable to get horses for riding. Then it was quiet.

I could smell honeysuckle through the dust and blood in my nostrils and I could hear insects chirping happily in the grass. The sun was beginning to set and the sky was bright red. From the branches of a willow elm a few feet away I could hear the high squeaky singing of a cowbird.

It was many days before I could walk without limping, and each day I dragged my body through my chores, trying not to cry or faint. It was July before I could move normally again, although my body would never be normal again.

Harriet got two new girls to help her with the house, and I was given the added chores of tending the flower beds and keeping the lawn and yard clean. All other hands were in the fields.

One afternoon Master Beal announced, "Robert, you free to go to the quarter when you finished with your chores, in the evenings and on Sundays. But you better do your chores good! And you git back here by a proper time."

I was overjoyed. Oh, to play with children who were black like me! I did my chores that day happily and eagerly. I finished early and ran with a jerky limp to tell Big Mac where I was going. He grinned at me and stuck some tobacco in his cheek. "Git then," he said softly.

The squalor and filth of the quarter looked like heaven to me as I approached the rows of shacks. I walked along the dirt and mud around each shack drinking in the smells of salt pork frying and hoe cake baking in the ashes of hearths. I looked at the tiny gardens beside some of the shacks, with carrots, cabbage, and turnips growing. The boards that made up the walls of the shacks were far enough apart to lay a dog. The setting sun spread across the land in gold and silver streaks, and the sweat and dirt on the faces shone in the light. My heart swelled to see the black faces of my people. Sitting in the dirt or on the wooden plank before their doors, they were like angels—worn, beaten, dirty, stupid, beautiful angels.

"Robert!" I heard a voice call. I turned and saw Corrie Moore standing and talking with another woman.

"Robert, chile, I declare!"

I ran to her and she grabbed me in her arms. The smell of her was acrid, wet, and wonderful. She crushed me in the dirty cotton of her dress, and I pressed my cheeks against the soft nap of her head.

"Thank God!" she cried.

Soon she was calling people to come and meet me, and then I was surrounded by staring children and smiling grown-ups. Only St. Peter at the pearly gates was missing.

The time went by quickly. Before I left to go back to the Big House, Corrie took me to her shack to see Buck and one other person. As I entered the shack, I saw Buck sitting on the bed and in his arms was the other person—a tiny, newborn baby.

"We done got ourselves a boy-chile," Corrie announced.

It was a warm and happy reunion. Only for a brief moment did my mind stray back to the last time I was in that cabin when Pearl lay dying.

"Yoll lookin' a little fat, chile," Corrie exclaimed as we sat together in the few remaining moments.

"Ahz?"

"Yoll is."

We laughed heartily, I held their new little baby, and that night back at the Big House my spirits were flying.

Night after night I fled to the quarter. The days weren't so bad because I had something to look forward to.

One Sunday afternoon after the Beals had left for an outing, I went to the quarter to play with the children. "Hyar comes that *house nigger*!" one of the children spat. I was stunned.

"Hyar comes that *Tom*!"

It was the first time I was called that. It was a terrible insult. I recoiled and stood ready to defend myself.

"They feedin' you chocolate cake and tapioca up there in the Big House?"

"Whitey's favorite little niggerboy, huh!"

"Ha-ha-ha, Robert loves the paleface! Robert loves the paleface!"

I leaped at one of the boys and began to hit him. The other children joined in the fight, and I found myself wildly hitting and punching. I got hold of one of the boys who had been taunting me and pounded his head on the ground. My rage grew each time his head hit the ground. Then I felt myself being torn from him, and before I knew it I was dangling from the fist of a large black man whom I had never seen before. "You tryin' to kill somebody, boy?" he snarled. "Don't you come around here causin' no trouble, hyar? Stay up at the Big House! Now git! *Git!*"

He dropped me from his grip, and I whirled around

furiously, making words as best I could. "I ain't no Tom! I'sa black nigger slave jes like yoll! Next one call me a Tom I's gonna kill!"

I stood my ground and then slowly turned my back on them and walked toward the shacks. Nobody made a move to get me, but I knew what they were thinking. They really believed I was just a Tom, a no good Tom.

I wandered around the shanties of the quarter listening to the sounds of the people: singing, babies crying, sounds of people living too close to each other, moving, living, loving, hating; there were smells of liquor, tobacco, sweat, and cabbage cooking. The sun was hot and the air thick and humid. I knew how conspicuous I must have been, but somewhere inside I believed that it was only here that I would find friends. I refused to be a coward and run back to the Big House.

As I walked along, I looked at the faces of the people. Lined, streaked with dirt and skin oil, they looked at me blankly. But near the end of one row of shacks I saw a face that looked back at me with kindness. "Hello, honey." A woman with white hair tied up in a rag, wearing a dirty calico dress and spotted apron, sat on the ground outside her shack.

"Hello, mam," I answered.

"Whey you from?"

"I be from the Big House, mam."

"From the Big House? Ohhh, then you up thar wi' Harriet and wi' lil Daisy who passed—"

"Yes'm."

"That be Harriet's shanty right over there." She pointed to a broken-down wooden shack surrounded by grey dirt like all the others, and sitting in front were three small children—just sitting there staring. I wanted to go and talk to them, but I didn't know what to say.

"Set down, boy," offered the white-haired woman. Her eyes were warm and friendly.

I sat hesitantly in the dirt, looking across the path at the children in front of Harriet's shanty. It was hard to imagine Harriet here in the shambles of the quarter when I had only seen her in the environment of the Beal household. I had never seen her with a black baby in her arms, and these little ones in the dirt looked like they were in desperate need of a mammy to hold them.

The old woman saw me staring at the children.

"Jerry! Amos! Agatha! Come over hyar!"

The children looked up and with listless movements ambled over to where we were sitting. "Massuh done tuk me outcha field and set me to keerin' for the chillrens," the woman told me. "These hyar babies is some o' mah babies." She folded them into her arms, and they seemed to melt into her. She kissed their heads and smoothed their cheeks with her bent and gnarled fingers.

"Whatcho name, boy?"

"Robert, mam."

"This hyar be Robert, chillrens, he work wi' yor mammy up in the Big House." The children brightened somewhat.

I stayed there for over an hour. The old woman's name was Ceily. She seemed to be peaceful, and I found that I liked talking with her.

"You say yo' prayers, chile?" she asked me off-handedly.

"Prayers?" I asked, surprised. "I don't reckon so, mam."

"Yoll don't pray?" she asked incredulously.

"No mam," I answered, wondering if I had done anything wrong.

"Well, I don't reckon I know how you done lived this long," she said. "Mus' be the Lor' savin' you for the day when you will look up at 'im an' shout, Hallelujah, Jesus!"

"Huh?"

"Whey's yo' mammy?"

"She daid, mam."

"Didn't she never pray wid you, boy?"

I thought for a moment. A picture of my mother sailed through my head. I saw her fine, high cheeks, her large, sad eyes, her light brown skin. I heard her voice again singing softly in the hot, empty cabin.

I blinked and said in a low voice, "I reckon my mama done prayed, mam."

"Yoll know what ah'm gonna do ri' now?" Miss Ceily asked with a broad smile.

"No, mam."

"I'm gonna pray fo' yoll. Right now. Ah'm gonna pray the good Lor' come an' show you how He died fo' yor sins so's you kin go to heav'n when you die."

"Heav'n?" I asked. "Do they's be colored people in heav'n?"

Ceily laughed. "I spect so, chile, I spect so."

She laid her hands on me and in a soft droning voice prayed to a heavenly Father she seemed to know quite personally. I felt kind of light and happy inside as I made my way through the rows of shacks to the path leading to the Big House.

I deliberately passed the boys who had bullied me. If I ran from them, I'd never have face in the quarter. They watched me but didn't do or say anything. I passed Buck and Corrie's shanty, and they were sitting outside against the house in the heated shade. "Oh, Robert," Corrie called as I came near. "I done forgot to tell yoll!"

"Mam?"

"Yoll be eight years old now!"

13

I was not too eager to return to the quarter after the fight with the slave children. I didn't want any more trouble. I began, instead, to take long walks around the plantation. I discovered the location of the dreaded overseers' houses. To my amazement, they were little better than the shacks the slaves lived in. Thrasher's house was a small, white-washed cabin with a tiny garden growing alongside it and a small shed for his horse and tools. I saw Mrs. Thrasher hanging out clothes on the clothesline, and playing around her were some poorly dressed babies.

Sometimes in the afternoon I would hide in the tall weeds and watch the slaves in the field hoeing cotton. I saw the whip rise and fall and I heard the low, mournful voices singing and groaning as they labored.

There was never a time when I left the Big House that Big Mac didn't know it. Sometimes he would be in the yard cleaning fish or in the back kitchen putting up pork, but he always knew when I was gone. When I returned, he'd be waiting for me. "Watch yo'self, boy," he'd warn me. And if Master was drunk or in an evil temper, this was all I needed to keep out of the way.

One day as I returned from a walk in the woods along-side the far field, Mac was pulling water from the well on the porch. With one look, I knew there was danger in the kitchen. I ran from the porch and hid alongside the house, and from there I could hear Mistress beating the new house girl who had not pleased her in some chore.

The girl was about thirteen, pretty, with very black skin and a strong body. Her name was Tennessee. Mistress hated her and she hated her name as well, and took to calling her Caroline instead. Tennessee didn't like that name and refused to answer to it.

Tennessee never moved quickly and never seemed to be afraid of Master or Mistress. Whenever Mistress screamed at her or hit her, she just sneered or looked at her with cold hatred. There was nothing Mistress could do to break her.

Then one afternoon when Master was in the house, Tennessee sat down at the white folks' table and buttered herself a piece of bread. Even Mary Webb was shocked. She reached for a knife to throw, but as she did, Master entered the kitchen. "I'll handle this!" Tennessee didn't even look up. She just took a bite of the bread and sat chomping on it. Master watched her eat the whole thing and didn't say a word. I thought sure there'd be a killing. But Master Beal just turned and didn't even say one word.

Living in the house that summer was like sitting on a keg of dynamite. There were always fights. Mistress and Master fought and yelled at one another whenever they were together. The overseers fought, too, because there was a lot of rivalry and jealousy among them.

I ran to the quarter often during these months to see Miss Ceily. She was always happy to see me. I would help her with the slaves' children in her charge if I could. Tennessee brought down the large caldron of corn mush at noontime for them, and she would linger a moment to talk. Miss Ceily was so filled with compassion and mercy that even Tennessee warmed up to her.

One of Miss Ceily's seven sons was sick in bed. His name was John Henry, and he was about eighteen years old. He had worked in the field since he was eleven. The bed he lay in was only a 12-inch slab of wood with a little pile of sticks for a pillow. In the humidity and heat, the dirt floor of the shanty was wet and muddy and smelled bad. I sat with John Henry and dipped cool water on his face. He had the fever and moaned all day. Ceily prayed over him and didn't seem to be at all worried about his condition. "The Lor's healin' is on him," she said confidently.

One day when Tennessee came with the mush for the children, she had a jar of honey tucked under her skirts which she presented to Ceily. "It's for yo' son who be ailin', mam," she said.

Ceily took it, and they came into the cabin to John Henry's bedside where I was sitting. I saw John's face when he saw Tennessee. It was as though a little light went on in his eyes.

John Henry got well just like Ceily said he would and was back picking cotton in a couple of days.

Every chance Tennessee got, she would be at Ceily's shanty or else John Henry would be at the shanty where

Tennessee lived. I noticed that Tennessee was becoming a little more lively.

On a bright August morning when the slaves were all in the field and I was helping peel apples in the kitchen, I was given charge of baby Anna again. I wasn't very happy about it.

"Why can't Tennessee or one of the girls mind Anna?"

"Yors ain't to question, Robert. Massuh done gived the order."

I wanted to dislike the blond-haired four-and-a-half-year-old. I had no intention of treating her with any kindness.

"Go 'head an' climb up on Robert's lap, honey," Miss Harriet prodded.

Anna looked up at me with sparkling blue eyes and a shy smile, and then she threw open her arms and climbed into my lap. Her arms went around my neck, and she giggled softly close to my cheek.

Her face was filled with trust, and she had no mischief in her eyes.

"Robert's gonna mind yoll now, hyar?"

Little Anna giggled and seemed very pleased with the idea.

With her trusting look, happy nature, and loving personality, Anna brought back memories of my own little sister, Ella. I found myself playing the games Ella and I had played, and once again I had the love and trust of a small child.

I was embarrassed to be Anna's "maid" though, and I hated it when other slaves saw me minding her. I knew they were calling me a sissy and a Tom. It made me angry. Sometimes I took this anger out on Anna.

"Come hyar, Anna!"

"Whatchoo want, Robert?"

"I'm gonna whup yor hide."

"Ahhhhhhhhh!"

I'd scare her practically out of her wits, but then I wouldn't do anything to her. If she cried, I'd feel a certain sense of fulfillment.

One Sunday afternoon when the Beal family was gone, I went down to the quarter to visit Miss Ceily. She was praying for her son, Little William, when I got there. Little William was about twelve years old and his mind didn't seem right. He would take to yelling at the air or kicking and throwing his body around as though something invisible were attacking him.

I sat with her outside the shanty with John Henry, and I got to talking about Anna. Miss Ceily heard our talk and didn't like the part about my bullying her around.

"Child, you need Jesus."

I looked at her, surprised.

"Did you ever ast Jesus to fill yor heart and forgive yor sins?"

"Not to my rememberin'."

"Well, that's what you need to do. You need salvation, that's what you need. You is doin' an evil thing up there in that Big House wi' that chile, and the Lor' want you to repent of it and ast Him to save you so's you kin be *His* boy instead of the devil's. A man's revenge don't mean nothin', chile. It's the *Lor'* who do the revengin'.' He know how better'n any man know."

"Revengin'?"

"I want you to git on yor knees, boy, and I'm gonna teach you how to pray."

I did as she said, and I heard myself talking to an invisible person called Jesus. John Henry quietly prayed beside me on his knees.

Something happened to me that day. I knew even then that something had taken place, something wonderfully great. Ceily told me to pray every day, and she began to teach me the Lord's Prayer. I was eager to learn, and I drank in every word.

"Our Father which awt in heav'n . . ."

Cotton-picking time was the worst time of year for the slaves because they were driven so hard. After they returned to their homes late at night, sometimes not until almost midnight, they had the cooking for the family to do and the tending of their own tiny gardens. They had only a few hours in which to sleep at night—oversleeping meant a whupping.

Then something terrible happened. Ceily's boy, Little William, became an informer. He was paid by the overseers to give information about the men and women in the quarter. An informer was worse than a Tom, because an informer was a traitor. Little William would sneak around listening to conversations and trying to find out if anybody was planning on escaping or if anyone was saying bad things about the master. There were a lot more whuppings in the quarter, and everybody was nervous and angry.

I knew it was dangerous for me to be visiting Miss Ceily with Little William's eye on me. I was certain to get a few licks from the master.

"His mind is tore up," Ceily lamented. "Jesus, hepp him, hepp him."

Then, all of a sudden, Little William disappeared. Nobody knew what happened to him. Some said he escaped. He was missing for several days when finally he was found in the swamp under a cypress tree. His throat had been sliced from one ear to the other, and birds had already begun to eat on him.

When they lowered Little William into the grave, Miss Ceily said quietly under her breath, "Jesus done answered my prayer. He helped him. He's in glory now."

Autumn was on its way. It was time for the white children to return to school. I had heard about a Negro school not far from us, and I once again began begging to go to school. It was hopeless. Master wouldn't hear of it. "Schoolin' ain't for niggers!"

Having charge of Anna all day long made it almost impossible to get to the quarter. I had to stay near the Big House with her. The only time I could escape the prison of the Big House was on Sundays if the Beal family went visiting.

Thomas and John continued to enjoy their sport of jumping me. One cool Sunday afternoon they both jumped me right outside the kitchen door. I drew up with every bit of energy in me, took them both by their straight, slippery hair and with a swift surge of strength crashed their heads together. They fell to the ground, and I then pulled them up one at a time and smacked them in the face and chest with my fists. When they got up I hit John so hard he went flying across the yard. When Thomas saw that, he took off running. I knew I would get a terrible beating from Master Beal for what I did, but I had discovered I could lick both of them, and I didn't care.

Big Mac had seen the whole thing from the smoke house where he had been working. When he came into the kitchen later he was whistling, and then he hopped around doing a little dance.

Tell me, Jim, whatcha got in tha bag,
Oh Mary, Oh Mary,
Saw a nigger whup the massuh's boys,
Law' diddie, Law' diddie, Law' dee day.

> Saw that nigger done whup they hide,
> Oh Mary, Oh Mary,
> Massuh goin' whup that nigger tonight.
> Law' diddie, Law' diddie, Law' dee day.

I joined him in his whimsical dance.

> I whup em once, and I'll whup em again,
> Oh Mary, Oh Mary . . .

I was delighted to see Big Mac's approval of what I had done. It was worth the whupping I was going to receive.

It came sometime after supper. Master Beal dragged me out behind the barn and made me lie down on my belly. He whupped me with the buggy trace. I pushed my face down hard in the ground so I wouldn't cry out. As I followed him back to the house, though, I was still happy about having taken his two boys. When we got halfway across the yard, Master turned to me, and with a funny kind of gesture he said, "I don't like to whup you, boy; mind yo'self so's I don't have to do it again. I'll turn Thrasher on yoll next time."

I thought for just the tiniest second that he was trying to tell me he didn't like hitting me, not because it wore him out but because he liked me. The idea was crazy, but I kept it in my mind and I studied on it.

The winter of 1919 passed, as did the frenzied spring of 1920 with cultivating and planting. That spring Tennessee gave birth to a baby boy in her little shack by the house, and she named him Amos because she had heard that her father's name was Amos. Master moved Tennessee and the baby to a cabin away from the Big House. I think he was afraid Mistress knew the baby had a white daddy and would try to do something evil to them.

The summer of 1920 was hot and long, and I was given permission to take Anna to the creek to wade and play. "Do you gots a mama, Robert?" Anna asked me one day. I looked at her large blue eyes. "No, chile, I don't got no mama. My mama daid."

"Do you gots a daddy?" For a minute I saw white lights pass before my eyes, like lightning. The thought of my father aroused in me a sudden, unexpected fury.

"Huh?"

"Do you gots a daddy?"

". . . Ah reckon ah gots a daddy, Miz Anna."

"Do he be a nice man like my daddy be?"

I looked at her little upturned face, the round cheeks just right for tweaking. "Ah reckon so, yes, ah reckon so. My daddy be jes right nice like yo' daddy be."

I sat at the edge of the creek, my feet stretched out into the water. Anna sat close to me digging her toes in the mud.

"Robert, you knows what?"

"Uh."

"Robert, you be's my honey baby. I love you!" She threw her arms around me, laughing happily.

Anna would tell me what she learned in Sunday school each week.

"Jesus, He come down to be the Savior," Anna explained.

"Whey'd He come from?"

"He come from the heaven. He come because He want the people to love God. It say so in the Bible."

"Some day, Anna, you'll be able to read the Bible, and then you can teach me all about the Lord."

Anna sang a little song that went,

He washed my sins away,
He washed my sins away,
Now I'm white, white like snow,
for He washed my sins away.

These words haunted me. I remembered what Mistress Beal had said about the sins black people had committed that made our skins black and forever in debt to the white folk as their slaves. I wondered if there was a way for me to get my sins washed away and be made white as snow. But why would God make a sinner like me white and not Miss Ceily? She was a praying lady. Surely she would be the first one He would wash till she was white.

Miss Ceily calmed me on the matter.

"Honey, you is washed clean jes for the astin'," she told me. "When yoll ast Jesus to forgive yor sins, He does it. That means you is washed clean from yor sins. Don't mean no color of yor *skin*; it mean the color of yor *soul*. Sin make the soul full of darkness. Full of the shadowy substance. But when the love of Jesus come through and you gits forgiveness from yor sins, then you is washed clean —yor soul is white as snow."

"Uh. But a colored person ain't got no soul."

Miss Ceily reeled on her heels. "Lissen to me, chile, don't you lissen to them lies, you hear me? *Don't you lissen to them lies!* When the white man tell you them lies, yoll jes wag yor head, 'Yes'm, Nossuh, Yes'm,' but don't you pay them no mind. They's a-lyin to you!''

"Yes, mam.''

Ceily explained to me that God loved me and cared about me. It was very hard to understand, and I didn't grasp most of what she told me. She prayed over me and asked God to show me that He cared about this "poor lil ole nigger chile.''

In the shanty farthest down the line, behind a clump of trees, a party was in full swing. I could hear the music and the singing and the slapping of feet on the dirt floor. When I left Miss Ceily's, I walked toward the bleached and rotted wooden shack. Somebody had a homemade banjo, somebody else played the sticks, and there was a drum made out of a piece of tree trunk with a skin stretched across it, and above it all were the loud, exuberant sounds of singing.

I stood in the doorway and peered into the shack lit only by one kerosene lamp. I watched as the men and women stomped and danced together, laughing and hooting. Children were lined along the walls, too, as well as outside the shanty. The air was thick with the smells of whiskey, tobacco and sweat. I stood rivetted in place watching the bodies of the men and women twirl and whirl and strut and jump in the dim light of the room. It was very exciting.

There was a formal kind of dance that had to be learned when we "set the floor.'' It was done with a glass of water on the head. Then we'd do another dance inside a circle trying not to go outside the lines. I stayed until way past midnight.

The next morning I asked Big Mac if I could go to the little church that the slaves attended. He wasn't too happy about my leaving the house. He made it very clear I had to be back before Master and the family returned from the church they attended about a mile down the road.

I scrubbed my face and put on my only clothes. Harriet had shown me how to clean myself and my own clothing. I washed my clothes about once a month, and I bathed without soap whenever I went to the creek.

I walked to the meeting place with Miss Ceily and her sons, John Henry, Isaiah, Jerry-Ben, Fred, and Boot. We walked slowly and silently in the morning sun. The smell of honeysuckle was thick and sweet, and insects sang loudly along the path as though heralding us on our way. Miss

Ceily wore a black dress with a worn, lacy collar. The boys wore clean overalls and tow shirts. All of us were barefoot.

The church was a shack made out of logs with hay and mud stuffed in the cracks. There were two openings for windows with wooden boards that pulled across them when they needed to be closed. Inside were wooden benches to sit on and a pulpit for the preacher. Because it was such a lovely day, the door this morning was closed and we filed by, following a path leading to a narrow creek which flowed into the Savannah River.

There was a cluster of people already gathered by the little creek in a shaded clearing when we arrived. There were many warm greetings and embraces. The meeting began with singing. The singing went on and on. I felt elevated in the music, lifted far beyond anything I had ever experienced.

There were songs filled with ecstasy and joy, songs that were lamenting and sad. They were a part of me, a part of everything I felt and knew. In the dark and untapped places of my mind that day, I began to understand who I was and what I was made of.

There might have been a hundred of us there, I didn't know; I only knew the joy of belonging and the closeness of the God Miss Ceily had been telling me about.

I didn't get back to the Big House until afternoon. Big Mac was angry. "Massuh's been back for two hours! Chile, I ought to whup you!"

He gave me a new chore then. "Massuh tole me to have you doing it since August last. But I thought it would be too hard on ye, so's I did it for ye. Now yoll kin do it. Tomorry yoll kin carry water to the men in the field. You carry two two-gallon cans. And yoll do it every day, hyar? Now git and tend to Miz Anna."

The excitement of the morning faded as I went to find Anna and begin my work around the Big House. I wanted to tell Big Mac all about the meeting in the woods. I wanted to tell him how the Negro preacher had told us that one day we wouldn't have any more troubles and that Jesus would take all our troubles from us. He told us that God didn't like the way the white man treated us and that He would make them pay for it. I guessed that if Master Beal knew that the Negro preacher was telling us things like that, he'd have him strung up high on a tree. I prayed that the Lord wouldn't allow that to happen. And then I prayed something very strange. I prayed that the Lord would forgive Master Beal.

14

In 1921 I turned ten years old. On a starry Saturday night in September, the Beals were invited to a party at another plantation. Master Beal was now the proud owner of a new automobile.

That Saturday night when I saw Buck Moore walk through the kitchen door of the Big House, I jumped with surprise.

"Buck!"

"Hello, Robert."

"What you doin' here?"

"I is Massuh Beal's chauffeur now. He done come down and give me this new job. Even give us a cabin closer to the house so's I can be right near when he need me."

Buck and Corrie near the house! That night he chauffeured the Beals to their party. I watched from the parlor window as they drove off, and I trembled with excitement. I had never seen such a fine automobile, and to see Buck sitting up so clean and slick driving it made me very proud. He was wearing clean overalls, and he looked young and strong.

While Master Beal was at the party, Tennessee escaped from the plantation. She ran off with John Henry and her mulatto baby.

Master Beal didn't realize she was gone until late Sunday afternoon. He went crazy when he found out. The hounds were sent out after them, and he hollered for Buck to drive him to the train station in town. His friends rallied together, and the search was on. I prayed with all my heart that they wouldn't catch them.

"Please, please, can I go to Miss Ceily?" I begged Big Mac.

"Yoll ain't goin' no place," Big Mac answered firmly, and I knew I couldn't leave the Big House and would have to wait there for news of Tennessee and John Henry.

The hours went by. Juanita and Virginia, the Beals' daughters, played "tea party" on the lawn beside the summer porch. Their laughter, like tiny bells, could be heard above the oppressive silence in the house. Mary Webb was overly busy in the kitchen preparing sweet potato pies for the white folks' supper, and Harriet was down in the quarter with her children. Big Mac sat in the shadows of the kitchen porch by the well rolling Master's cigarettes.

If Tennessee and John Henry were to make it to freedom safely, it would be a victory for every slave on the plantation. We would each know a little greatness for a time. But if they were captured, their torture would belong to all of us, and we would moan on our pallets sharing their defeat. Sweat rolled down my body as I waited by the window in the children's bedroom while Miss Anna took her afternoon nap.

Evening came and Mistress Beal ate the sweet potato pie and baked ham with her children without Master. There was no word at all. Mistress behaved oddly, and I heard Mary Webb say she was drunk. When they had finished eating, she took the children into the music room, and we heard the piano playing simple two-part melodies. I knew Juanita was performing. She played haltingly, studying the music every time the position of her fingers changed.

Nightfall came. Juanita played on and on. The stop-and-start sounds wore on everyone's nerves, especially Mistress Beal's. She paced the floor of the parlor like a cat. I dressed Anna in her soft cotton nightgown and held her on my lap before putting her into her bed for the night.

"Robert," she cooed, snuggling her face against my chest, "Robert, when I get big—"

"Yes, Miz Anna?"

"When I get big, will you marry me?"

I laughed until tears came. I was afraid I might burst into sobbing and so I lifted her from my lap, set her down firmly on the floor, and said without courage, "I declare, chile!"

"Don't you love me, Robert?"

"Well, I 'spect I do."

"Then we can get married!"

I didn't answer her, and she bubbled on. "I'll have to have a pretty dress and pretty white shoes, you know. Then I'll tell my children to be very, very quiet and you can kiss me, too."

"Uhm."

"I love you, my Robert. I love you bestest in all the world. You's my honey baby."

It was after midnight when the sound of horses' hooves woke me. I sat upright, listening. The other children did not stir. Carefully, I slid out of my bed and walked across the bare floor to the window. I could see nothing. I tiptoed out of the room and down the hall to the dining room. The room smelled of stale smoke and liquor. From the window I could see the driveway plainly in the moonlight.

There were at least ten horses. The moon was full and shone on the forms on the horses. My heart pounded in my chest when I saw the riders. They looked like monsters from hell, like ghosts, apparitions of the dead. I held my breath for fear one of them might see me through the window and slay me with one evil look. They were all in white, like sails of ships that I had seen in the children's books. Their faces were covered with hoods, and they all carried rifles and sticks. It could have been the end of the world, and I wouldn't have been more terrified. So this is what I had heard about and never seen—this was the Ku Klux—the devil himself.

Shaking, I clutched the edge of the curtain. They were shouting back and forth. One of the apparitions descended from his horse and strode to the front door. I froze where I was. Who would answer it? Mistress surely wouldn't. Big Mac was sleeping in the back of the house and wouldn't be able to hear the knocking. I was the only slave around.

The knocker sounded. It was loud and unmistakable. I didn't move from where I was. The knocking continued. "Sam!" a voice shouted. "Sam Beal!"

Then I heard a sound behind me. My heart stopped. I turned slowly, without breathing. A man was sitting across the room in a straight-backed chair with his elbows on the dining room table. It was Master Beal. He must have been there when I crept in to watch out the window.

"Answer the door, boy," he said in a growling whisper.

"Yessuh, Massuh Beal, suh."

I hurried to the door and, with shaking hands, opened it.

"Where's the bossman?" asked the robed form before me. Speechless, I simply pointed toward the dining room. The form marched into the house.

"Ain't you got no lights here?" he asked angrily.

I scrambled to light a lamp. My fingers were trembling, and I could hardly hold the match to light the kerosene lamp by the door.

Seeing Sam Beal, the figure announced, "We got the man down by the hollow."

Sam Beal didn't answer.

"Do you want to hang him tonight or tomorrow?"

"Tonight! Hang the devil tonight!"

I could hardly keep myself from crying out. Caught! Lord, no!

Usually they strung up a runaway when there was a crowd to watch. They made sure the other slaves saw the proceedings in order to discourage future escape attempts. First they beat the victim unmercifully or tied him by his feet to be dragged by a horse. Then when he was half-dead, they strung him up. I had even heard where they cut the guts out of a man while he was still alive. After they hung him, they chopped off his head to stick on a post somewhere as a warning to other blacks. That was for rape of a white woman, or something like that.

I was so frightened I nearly fainted. I wanted to scream, to protest, but to do so could mean a hanging for me, too.

"I want that nigger dead," Master Beal said quietly.

When they left the house, Master Beal could hardly walk. He stumbled over his own feet in a drunken attempt to move quickly.

"We'll take my car!" he shouted.

Somewhere between the house and the hollow where poor John Henry awaited his fate, Master Beal donned his white Ku Klux regalia. I sobbed and cried out to God for mercy. When the sound of the horses and the engine of the car died in the distance, I flew out of the house, down th driveway, around the yard, and onto the path leading to the quarter. When I arrived at Miss Ceily's cabin, I found her on her knees in front of the hearth. Her face was drawn and wet with tears. She had not stopped praying since John Henry and Tennessee had fled.

She did not know he had been captured.

"Miz Ceily! Oh, Miz Ceily!" I cried when I found her.

She turned and opened her arms to me. The other boys were fast asleep, and the cabin was still. I ran to her, crying.

She held me in her long, hard arms and said, "Son, the Lord hisself jes spoke to me. He tole me John Henry will be all right."

I began to sob uncontrollably. Poor Miss Ceily. The noise awakened the other boys.

"Is John Henry all right?" Isaiah asked, frightened.

"Yes, son, yes," answered Ceily. "The Lord has jes tole me he is all right."

I cried so hard, the other boys were suspicious. "Has you heard something?" Isaiah asked finally, drawing near to me and kneeling down where I was sitting on the floor.

Between sobs, I explained that they had caught John Henry and had him down in the hollow.

"They's gonna hang him tonight!" I cried.

Miss Ceily's face did not so much as flinch.

Isaiah pounded his fist on the dirt floor. There was nothing any of us could do. There was nobody to turn to for help.

Except One.

"The Lord has done said John Henry is all right," Miss Ceily repeated. "Until they carry a dead man through this door and lay him at my feet and tell me, 'This is yor son, John Henry,' ah'm gonna believe God."

I stayed for about an hour; then Isaiah insisted I go back to the Big House. "It's dangerous for you to be here," he told me. "If they catch you tonight, they might kill you, too. There's killin' in the air!" He was right. If I got caught between the house and the quarter, I could be hung, and they'd justify it by saying I was trying to escape or I was stealing or conspiring.

I fell into a fitful sleep when the dawn was just beginning to brush across the tops of the trees outside the window. I slept only a few moments because it was time to rise and begin the day's work. I hurried through my tasks. The overseers marched in for breakfast in their dining room, and I hung around near the door to hear their conversation. Surely they would talk about the hanging last night. They didn't talk at all this morning, though, and the only sounds I heard were forks scraping plates, lips smacking, chewing, and gulping.

When they left for the fields, I was confused. Why didn't they talk about the hanging? Surely they knew!

Finally, we heard the master's car pull into the drive. Master Beal wasn't driving. Buck was. Big Mac hurried around the car, opened the door, and stood looking inside. I watched from the wooden steps of the porch.

"He's passed out," Buck told Big Mac. "I had to carry him to the car. Here, help me get him upstairs. He ain't gonna walk, that's for sure." Together the two men lifted the drunk form of Master Beal out of the car and carried him inside. When Buck and Big Mac came to the kitchen, there was nobody there but Mary Webb and me.

"Set yourself down," Big Mac told Buck. We went to the slave's table and bench. "This story you jes ain't gonna believe," Buck began. "You jes ain't gonna believe it. The likes of it ain't never happened in this world."

"What is it?"

Buck wagged his head and then began. "Las' night the master and the Kluxes went down to the hollow to string up John Henry. See, they found him jes outside of Belton walkin' along the railroad track. Tennessee had gotten on the train in Greenville and was far gone. They was no way of catchin' up with her. Poor John Henry, he had only 'nuff money to buy one ticket, so he put Tennessee and her baby on the train, and he took to walkin'. He had already walked about six miles."

"Guess Massuh knowed they'd try to get on a train, so's he went to the stations right off. Well, when they picked up John Henry, they beat him and tole him they was gonna kill him. They carried him to the hollow over by Savannah River to hang him."

"Here's the part you ain't gonna believe. Ah declare, I never see'd nothin' like it."

"Come on, man, tell us!"

"Massuh come back home to get some whiskey or some-thin' or another, and then he wake me up on his way to the hollow for me to drive the car. Well, we gits to the hollow, and I sees John Henry lyin' there on the ground. They done beat him good, and he ain't making no sound; he is jes lyin' there, quiet-like.

"Massuh sez, 'We ain't gonna hang 'im here; we'll hang 'im on the hill by my horse barn. That way all my other niggers will see 'im.' So he tells his friends to throw John Henry in the trunk of his car. They throws John Henry in, and then they gits on their horses and ride off. Massuh tells me to drive, and so I starts drivin'. 'Faster! Faster!' he yells at me, so I drives faster. 'Can't you make this devil go no faster?' he yells, and so I say 'Yessuh,' and I come down on the gas to go faster. 'Faster! Faster!' Massuh yells, and we jes rippin' up the road. I don't know where he is having me drive because we long past his farm. But we go faster and faster and he is yellin' and cursin' and drinkin' his whiskey. Then he tells me to git back, and so I turn and we rip back to the farm for to hang John Henry.

"You ain't gonna believe this now. We gits out of the car. The other men are waiting. They open the trunk, and look inside the trunk—and they ain't no John Henry in there!"

"Wal *now*!" Big Mac exclaimed.

"Thet John Henry is jes plumb gone outa that trunk! Look like it opened while we was ripping along, and John Henry he roll out. We went back to look for him, but he be long gone now."

I hooted with joy. "Hallelujah!" I shouted. "John Henry am a free man!"

"An' I reckon he'll stay free this time," Big Mac said, slapping his knee with a cackle.

"If'n he got to town, he'll be all right. No hounds'll pick him up there."

"I declare," Big Mac sighed. "I do declare, God hisself musta come an' opened that there trunk and let that boy out."

"I believe so," I said.

15

Harvest time of 1921 saw plenty of work on the plantation. The slaves were in the fields before dawn, ready to work. The work in the Big House began before dawn, too, and I was given added chores. Carrying water to the overseers in the fields was the hardest. I tried hard not to spill as I climbed the hill and walked along the uneven dirt paths the quarter of a mile or more to the overseers, but more often than not water spilled out of the pails and I would be punished.

When I arrived at my destination, breathless and dripping wet with sweat, with the heavy two-gallon buckets, Thrasher would sometimes tip them over, dumping the water on the ground, and order me to go and fill them up again. "Don't spill any this time!" he would snarl.

I would fight tears as I struggled, toting those buckets. It was a job I had for nearly three years.

I had eaten my supper one night when an awful pain in my jaw made me gasp. "You ailin', boy?" Big Mac asked, without looking up from his dish.

"I believe my tooth is ailin'."

And ail it did. In a week's time my face was swollen twice its normal size, and I was dizzy with pain. Big Mac told Master Beal about it, and he came into the kitchen to see it.

"Ain't nothin' I can do except take you to the dentist in Anderson, I reckon," he said. To the dentist! It sounded so wonderful to me, I wanted to throw my hands in the air and shout for joy. That meant a trip in the buggy, or possibly the new car! I loved going into town but had never been there since I had been bought as a slave six years before.

He called me the next morning after he had been to the field for a couple of hours. "Git in the buggy," he commanded. I hurried outside, fetched the horse, hitched her up to the buggy, and then climbed aboard and waited. Master Beal came out soon, and we started on the journey to Anderson. I stayed near him because the road was filled with holes and very bumpy. When it got really bad, I took hold of his coattail and hung on for dear life. He never did slap my hand away. This simple gesture of holding his coattail meant as much to me as a warm embrace and a kiss. After all, he didn't push me away from him, and he was taking me to the dentist! Maybe he cared about me!

The town of Anderson bristled with activity. I gazed with wide eyes at the store-lined Market Street. The sun shone on the low buildings as we drove up the sloping hill and pulled in front of a large, white corner building.

The dentist was a young white man with what seemed to be a kindly face.

"Well, where's the Hudson today, Sam?"

"My man is picking cotton," Master explained. "Need him more in the field than in the car."

The dentist smiled and nodded his head in understanding.

"What have we here?" he asked.

"This nigger of mine has a toothache, Doc, and I'd like you to fix him up."

"Sure enough, Sam. Come here, boy."

I went into a small room with a window that overlooked a grassy empty lot. "Open your mouth," the dentist told me.

"You got yourself an abscess. I'll have to pull it and let the poison drain out."

The dentist strapped my arms to the chair and then he took a strange, silver-looking instrument from his drawer, clamped hold of my tooth, and began to yank. It was a chipping and yanking and grinding process, but he finally got the tooth out. I screamed and howled and wailed miserably. Master Beal had told him he didn't want to spend anything on a pain killer because, after all, I was a nigger.

I hobbled out of the office somehow with cotton wadding stuffed into my mouth to catch the blood and pus. Master Beal did consent to some medication for me, but with great reluctance. "If he doesn't take this, the poison could spread through his body and kill him," the dentist explained.

"All right, give me the stuff. I'll see that he takes it."

Going home was terrible agony. I wept bitterly in the back of the buggy. This pain was worse than a hundred whuppings with the cow lash.

Once back at the plantation, Master ordered me to get the water to the men in the field. My face was fiery hot, and my entire body ached. I couldn't speak at all. I wouldn't even try to form words in my mouth.

Thrasher saw my face and snarled, "Somebody ought to shoot you, niggerboy, and put you out of your misery."

"Yeah," mocked one of the drivers, "why don't you shoot him right through the haid now?"

"Maybe this niggerboy would like a bullet through the head; would you, nigger?"

"Oh, come on now, Thrasher," jibed the driver. "Give him a chance! Let him at least run for his life!"

Thrasher laughed, "Yeah!" He pulled his rifle out of the saddle and cocked it.

"OK, Robert, get runnin'! Let's see if you can outrun this bullet!"

I twirled around, grabbing the buckets, and began to run with every bit of strength I had. I heard the gun fire, and I screamed and threw myself on the ground between and cotton plants, sending the buckets tumbling. The bullet missed me.

"Git going!" Thrasher shouted. I began to crawl frantically toward the buckets. I couldn't lose those. When I had retrieved them, I tried crawling in the direction of the trees at the edge of the field. Thrasher fired again. I was almost insane with pain and terror, and it was only after about six shots were fired that I realized he was shooting into the air. The laughter rang across the field. The other slaves knew what was going on. I felt like a fool. I rose to my feet and ran for all I was worth, and when I was safe in the trees, I fell on the ground and lay there until I had regained enough strength to continue back.

As I lay in the shade of the trees, I remembered Miss Ceily praying for John Henry when he was sick and how the Lord had answered her prayer. I looked up into the leaves of the trees. "Lor'," I prayed, "plee—" I wanted so badly for the pain to subside. I was dizzy and nauseous and could not form words.

A few minutes later a tiny, cool breeze blew across my face. It was so refreshing and sweet that I wanted to smile. Not long after that, I sat up, feeling a little better. By the time I got back to the Big House, the pain was almost gone.

When Master Beal came in from the field that day, the swelling had vanished from my face, and I was suffering no pain at all.

"Take your medicine, boy," Master called to me when he saw me bringing a load of clean towels upstairs. I stopped on the stairs and smiled broadly. "Oh, suh," I exclaimed, "I was in sech terrible pain I thought I was dyin' for sure. Then I looked up to the Lor', and I begged Him to take the pain away an' heal me."

Master Beal grunted.

I continued. "They won't be no need for the medicine from the dentist, suh. I got the medicine straight from the Lor'!"

Master Beal's eyes narrowed, and he drew closer to the stairs.

"Come here," he ordered. I obeyed and jumped down to where he could see my face better.

The look on him was one of complete consternation.

"Open your mouth."

In the place where the tooth had been pulled, there was a smooth, gaping hole with no sign of swelling or infection.

"Well, I'll be damned—"

"Oh, suh!"

"I'll be—"

"The Lor' done it, suh, sure enough! I prayed and asted Him to heal me! I felt a cool breeze come across me from yonder, and then He healed me!"

Master Beal shook his head and then snapped, "Well, get up them stairs if you be healed, boy, and get to workin'!"

16

The joy over the healing of my mouth remained with me for many weeks. I whistled, sang, and hopped around the house doing my chores, pleased about everything. Most of the ugliness and the pressures escaped my notice during the harvest because I had discovered that God actually cared about colored folks. Furthermore, I knew for sure that He cared about me—*me*! It was hard to believe, but I knew it was true.

That autumn Miss Anna started school. I helped her get ready on her first day. I was sure this would be the end of our friendship. At school she would learn to hate me just like her brothers and sisters had learned. She hugged me and took her lunch box which Mary Webb had packed for her.

Anna was distressed about the whole idea and wanted to stay home with me. In those early weeks of attending school, she often awoke in the morning fitfully sick. She would complain dramatically of a stomachache or a headache or a sore throat. Once she insisted she had the pneumonia. As soon as the buggy was gone, she would miraculously recover.

"I'se hungry," she'd tell me with a grin. Then after breakfast we would head for outdoors, and I would take her riding on her pony or we would catch frogs by the creek or pick wild flowers.

When Master Beal got wind of Anna's missing so much school, he ordered her to go to school, sick or not. Anna cried and wailed so pathetically, Master picked her up in his arms and cooed, "Tell Daddy what would make you happy, honey."

Between sniffs, Anna said, "I wants Robert to come to school with me!" Master was not pleased with her suggestion, to say the least.

"He kin go with you jes once, and that's all!" he snarled.

I could hardly sleep that night. I finished my chores

well before daybreak the next morning and had my breakfast with Big Mac in the kitchen while it was yet dark
out. I was given a chunk of corn bread for my lunch,
which I wrapped up in a piece of brown paper. Big Mac
didn't realize that I thought I'd be going *inside* the school.

I scrubbed my face and put on my trousers and shirt
and then waited for the children to wake up. Harriet was
not at all happy about my going with them.

"They's gonna treat you bad, boy," she warned me
in a whisper. I was too happy to consider bad treatment.
God had shown me He cared about me, and now I was
going to school!

We climbed into the buggy at last. I sat in the back
on the end. Anna talked and giggled in front with her sisters. The ride was slow, and the early smells of the day
were fresh and clean and sweet. I breathed in and felt
good. The bumpy road was lined with dogwood, wild violets,
and Joe-Pye weed. Before long we drove up to the school-
house.

It was a small, red building, well built with even boards,
and it had windows with glass and a door with hinges and
a knocker. There was a hitching post for the horses.

I walked up the path with Miss Anna. She wore a blue
dress and a white pinafore. She had white button-up shoes,
which weren't quite buttoned up. Her blonde, curly hair
looked uncombed, even though it had been carefully
brushed and put into place, and it blew in wisps in her
face and eyes. She stayed close to me, and we neared the
big door.

At last we were inside. I stood staring, my heart
pounding loudly. The room was so clean, so neat, so polished. The wood was deep brown and it shone brightly.
The rows of desks were clean and orderly. The walls were
wood-panelled with many things hanging on them. In the
front of the room was a wooden platform and on it a large
wooden desk. A white lady was sitting at the desk, and
she smiled at the children as they took their seats. When
her eye caught mine, the smile on her face faded.

"I'm afraid you're in the wrong school, boy," she
said coolly.

"Oh, uh—I come wi' Miz Anna—"

"Anna, dear, take your seat," the lady instructed.

Anna obeyed happily after depositing her lunch box
with the others against the wall by the door.

I stood awkwardly by the door holding my corn bread wrapped in brown paper in my hands, digging my toes into the cracks of the wooden floor. The children took their seats and were quiet. The teacher rose to her feet. She was a stout woman and wore a blue dress with puffy sleeves and a black shawl over her shoulders. She peered at me over her glasses.

"Are you going to stand there all mornin', boy?" she asked.

"No, mam."

"Well, you know you can't stay here, don't you?"

Somebody in the room started to giggle. I searched for Anna with my eyes.

"I uh—"

Somebody else began to giggle and then others joined. Soon the room was filled with laughter. I couldn't find Anna. Helplessly, I looked at the teacher and tried to explain. I couldn't hear myself above the laughter. The teacher grew angry and pounded the desk to quiet the children. There was an empty seat near me, and I inched toward it. The teacher sprang at me. She shouted something, but I couldn't hear her with the noise of hooting and laughing. Then I felt the sting against my face. She had struck me across the face with a hickory stick. The class screamed with laughter. The teacher pointed to the door. I thought she was going to hit me again. I cowered against the desk that I still wanted to sit down in.

Finally the teacher screamed, "Who is responsible for this?" After what seemed like ages, John said, "He's ours."

"Get him *out* of here!" the teacher shouted. John stood and walked slowly toward me. "Didn't you hear Miss Roland? Git, nigger!"

"Coloreds are not allowed in this school!" the teacher said. I moved toward the door with my eyes on John.

"Coloreds not allowed!"

"Out!"

"Get out, black thing!"

The side of my face burned. Standing by the buggy, I could hear the laughter still going on inside the school.

I spent the day sitting at the edge of the piney woods by the school. When the children came outside to play, I hid behind some trees so they wouldn't see me. I didn't want to be laughed at anymore. I saw Anna, though, and she ran all over the schoolyard from one end to another looking for me. When the children went back inside, Anna was the last one on the wooden steps. She lingered there for a brief moment stretching and looking with her hand cupped over her eyes. She was worried about me and wanted to know where I was, I could tell. I remained unmoving in my hiding place.

That evening at home, I wanted nothing to do with anybody. I swore I would learn reading and writing one day, and, furthermore, I'd put in a book all that the white man had done to me and to my people on this plantation.

I knew I should forgive Master Beal like Miss Ceily had told me to, but I couldn't help wanting to get back at him. I chose stealing as my revenge. I stole little things at first—food, small coins, trinkets. I would bring these down to the quarter and give them away. On one of my visits, I met two brothers, much older than I, named Mitt and Waxy Edwards. They enjoyed my gifts and suggested a deal.

Whatever I brought that was worth something, they'd give me cash for. Then they would, in turn, sell the stuff to sources outside the plantation, so it would never be discovered in any of our possessions.

It sounded like a good idea. I told nobody about it, especially not Miss Ceily, who would talk me out of it, and Big Mac, who would probably whup me for it.

One day I stole a pretty vase, the next day a silver pitcher. I stole a watch, a ring, handkerchiefs, and money.

The money I made from stealing I tucked into the drawer of my little dresser. I had no idea what I would do with the money, and I really didn't care about it, but I put it into the dresser drawer anyway. Maybe someday I would give it away.

One sunny morning I was upstairs cleaning the master washroom when I heard a commotion coming from downstairs. Not paying any attention, I continued my cleaning. The commotion became louder. Soon I heard Mistress Beal's shrill voice call up the stairs.

"Roberrrt, get down hyar!"

I hurried down the stairs, and Mistress walloped me across the face without warning.

My head spun. Then she hit me again across the ear, and I felt something pop inside my head. My ear burned and a ringing sound remained. Again she hit me on the head.

"You been stealin', huh!"

"No, mam—" I lied.

She ordered me into the children's room. She opened my dresser and pointed at the box of money I had collected. Also, there was a paperweight in the corner of the drawer that I had gotten off Master's desk and hadn't sold yet.

"If that ain't stealin', boy, what is it?"

My head ached, and the ringing in my ear was deafening. I didn't dare answer her. I could be killed for this. I remembered what they had planned to do to John Henry, and I began to cry.

"Lor', have mercy—"

Mistress Beal was furious. Her face was bulging with red blotches, and her eyes were little fiery holes in her head. She found a belt of Thomas' on the floor by his bed and picked it up. She struck me again and again on the head and shoulders with it; then she ordered me to sit on the chair by the door until she returned with the master.

I was dizzy with fear and the burning pain of the belt's lashes against my skin. My ear and head ached terribly, and the ringing noise seemed to be worse.

I wanted very much to pray, but I was afraid God wouldn't hear me. I had been bad, and now I was going to be punished for it. Maybe they'd hang me, or tie me to a fence post and let me starve to death. I thought of running away, but that was impossible. I'd be caught and tortured to death. I was helpless in my predicament and frightened out of my wits. ". . . Lor', have mercy!" I pleaded again and again. I was sorry for stealing, truly sorry, but I knew there was nothing I could do to make up for it, and I'd have to take my punishment.

The day wore on. I was still sitting on the chair by the door when the children came home. Big Mac had to unhitch the pony and put the wagon in the barn for me. I didn't dare move.

When Big Mac heard what I had done, he wouldn't even look at me. His face held disgust and contempt. Mary Webb clucked like a hen, "He's ruined it fuh all of us, that chile, ruined it fuh all of us. They ought to dress him up good and if'n the white mens don't, the niggers ought to!"

The talk in the kitchen was noisy. I could hear the angry voices from where I sat. There was arguing, cursing and bad words, and tempers were riled up good. The Beal children gloated over me when they heard what I had done. Virginia stood before me, hands on her hips, and sneered. "How could you steal from my daddy, Robert, when he's been so good to yoll?"

"Yeah," added Juanita. "Daddy took yoll in this hyar house when you wasn't nothin' but a pickaninny baby. He's done tuk care of you, fed you, and put the clothes on yor back. Even carried yoll to the dentist when you was ailin'. Now yoll go and steal him blind!"

"You ain't nothin' but somethin' bad, Robert. Youse jes plain bad!"

"My daddy has treated you like one of his own children, Robert. Yoll even sleep in the same room with his children. Yoll thank him by stealin' from him!"

The only one who didn't participate was Anna. She seemed detached from everything going on and stayed in the music room by herself trying to pick melodies out on the piano.

The hours passed and I sat on the chair waiting.

The pain in my ear became so bad I wanted to cry out. It was evening when I heard the sound of Master Beal's heavy boots in the hallway. He smelled of whiskey.

He stood in the doorway, and at his side was Mrs. Beal. She was scowling and waving her finger in my face. "There he is, the devilin' thief! I told him to sit there and wait for you to come and punish him."

"I oughta kill you, boy," he growled. "I oughta kill you. You ain't only a damn thief, yor damn dumb!"

Mistress Beal opened the drawers of my little dresser. "Look what he's stolen, Sam. He's been stealin' yoll blind!"

Master Beal looked in the drawer with all the money and the paperweight I had taken from his desk. He turned to me, eyes narrowed. "You steal this from me, boy?"

I lowered my head and whispered, "Yessuh, I done it, suh."

Grabbing my face in his hands, he said, "What were you figurin' on doin' with all this money, boy?"

"I dunno, suh. I didn't have nothin' figured."

He hit me hard on the cheek. "Yor lyin'! Now you tell me the truth, or I'll cut you up till I get it from you!"

I was frightened and I told him the truth. "I'd give it away, suh. Ah'd give it to the folks who is hongry, thas what I'd do!

Master hit me again, harder. "You never took this money from me, boy, 'cause I ain't never missed this much! You been stealin' from mah house and *sellin'* stuff to somebody. Now who you sellin' to?"

I trembled from head to toe. I couldn't tell about Mitt and Waxy! I couldn't! I just couldn't!

"No suh, they ain't nobody else, suh—"

He struck me again on the face, and I tumbled off the chair. He picked me up by the collar and hit me again. "Yoll tell me the truth, boy!"

He hit me again and again, but I couldn't tell him the truth.

"I have been missing many things," Mistress said. "I just didn't suspect Robert. I thought maybe it was the new girl, Rosalie, or the chauffeur, Buck—"

Master grabbed hold of my head and pulled me by the uninjured ear through the house and into the parlor. We passed Big Mac, Harriet, and Mary Webb, who were in the kitchen. Their faces were cold and indifferent, and none of them turned to look at me. Rosalie, the new girl, was in the dining room sweeping the floor, and when she saw me pass, she nearly dropped the broom. She stood staring with her eyes wide and filled with fear. Maybe this was her first experience seeing a slave tortured. The pitiful expression on Rosalie's face suddenly made me feel older. I would hold out and not tell Master about Mitt and Waxy even if they killed me.

In the parlor, Master told Mistress to put the poking irons in the fire. "Mebbe I ought to burn that lyin' tongue outa yer, boy!" he snapped. Then he brought out the cat-o'-nine-tails. The whip cut the skin, and the lead balls tore it up. He ordered me to stand against the wall. Then he called, "Rosalie! Rosalie!"

After a minute or so, Rosalie came slowly into the room. "You damn slow, nigger!" Master cursed. "Cain't you move no faster!"

"Yessuh, Massuh Beal, suh."

"Go git Big Mac an' bring him in hyar! An' git a move on!"

"Yessuh, Massuh Beal, suh."

I was so filled with fear, the pain in my ear was hardly noticeable now. What did he want with Big Mac? Oh Lord, have mercy!

Big Mac entered the room. His face was hard and his

eyes cold. He stared unmovingly at Master Beal. Master Beal wiped spittle off his mouth with the back of his hand and rasped, "This hyar nigger stole from me, Mac."

"Yessuh, I know, suh." The scar on his face glistened in the yellow light.

"You does, huh? Well, mebbe you know who he's sellin' the stuff to?"

"Only Robert knows that, suh, if'n it's so, suh."

"Well, he won't tell me, nigger, and I aim to find out!"

"Yessuh."

"Take yer shirt off!" he yelled at Big Mac.

Big Mac slowly drew the grey shirt from his body. Master moved to the fireplace where the poking irons were red hot. He held one in his hand.

"Turn around, nigger!" He laid the end of the poking iron onto Big Mac's back. I screamed in horror.

Master whirled around to me and said, "Niggerboy, you tell me who you sold my stuff to, or I'm gonna fry this hyar nigger up till he ain't nothin' but a pile of ashes!"

"No! No!" I screamed. "Don't!" Master pressed the poking iron onto Big Mac's flesh again. Big Mac moaned in agony. I screamed, "Stop! I'll tell! I'll tell!"

Master held the poking iron poised at Big Mac's neck. "Please, suh!" I screamed. "Please, Massuh, suh, I'll tell!"

"I'm listenin', niggerboy, I'm listenin'!"

"It was Waxy and Mitt Edwards!"

Master stood still for a moment, then walked slowly to the hearth and carefully replaced the poking iron. Big Mac was bent over in pain.

"Mac," Master said in a low voice, "next time I give you a niggerboy to learn, you better do a better job than you did on this one! Now git!" Big Mac straightened painfully, his face twisted. Then, without a glance at me or Master, he left the room.

"Waxy and Mitt . . . Waxy and Mitt Edwards . . . Wal, niggerboy, yoll gonna take me to them and point them out."

I stared at him in unbelief. Why, it was unthinkable! That would be Uncle Toming in the worst sense! My life would be worthless. "And if you don't show me, niggerboy, I'll lay that iron on Big Mac till his face is nothin' but cinder. You hearin' me?"

Master Beal sent for two of his white drivers to come with him and dragged me down to the quarter. When we reached the edge, some of the children I played with ran around behind shanties to hide. Everybody was afraid when they saw Master come. They knew it never meant any good when he showed up in the quarter. He had me lead the way. We walked along the path right in front of all the shanties so everyone inside could see me walking with Master Beal and the drivers. The shame and the dread was almost more than I could bear. I longed to die right there. If only Master would kill me!

Finally, we came to the Edwards' shanty. Master nodded and I went inside. The family was seated on the floor eating. The cabin smelled of poke salad cooking over the open fire.

Tears streamed down my face. "Miz Edwards," I blurted, "Miz Edwards, the massuh done foun out that we been stealin'—"

"Who been stealin'?" she asked, surprised.

"I been stealin' from the massuh, an'—"

Waxy and Mitt stiffened.

"An—an—"

"Wal, what is it, boy?" asked their father. I was shaking violently. "Waxy an' Mitt done take the stuff from me and sell it—Massuh, he outside—"

Mrs. Edwards rushed to the door. Mr. Edwards turned to his sons. "Is this true? Have you been sellin' stuff from the Big House for this boy?"

Waxy and Mitt lowered their heads. "Yessuh," they confessed.

Mr. Edwards accompanied his sons out of the cabin to face Master Beal. It was a dreadful scene.

"Well, Robert?" asked Master Beal.

"Uh, uh—this hyar be Waxy and Mitt," I answered.

"Wal, what about them?" asked the master. "I already know their names."

"Wal, they be the ones who was sellin' stuff from the Big House—"

"Are you tellin' me that these hyar niggers been sellin' mah stuff from mah house, Robert?"

I looked down at my feet. "Yessuh, Massuh Beal, suh, they be."

A picture of Little William, his throat slit and the crows gnawing on him, sailed across my mind.

Master Beal hoisted himself up tall and said loudly, "Wal, good boy, Robert. You done real good to *inform* me about these two thievin' niggers. You're gonna get a nice little reward for this, boy."

I felt every eye in the quarter on me. "You boys gonna pay for this real good," Master shouted. "Tie 'em up, boys!" he ordered the two men with him.

Mrs. Edwards began to cry. "Oh, have mercy, Massuh Beal," she cried. "They good boys! They good workers! They never done nothin' bad before!"

"Auntie, they ain't never gonna do nothin' bad no more!" spit Master.

Taking me by the shoulder, Master Beal strutted back along the same path. We led the way, and the two prisoners followed behind between the two field drivers. I was sick with fear and shame. "This hyar will be jes fine!" Master shouted. We had stopped right by a large chestnut tree with low hanging branches. People peered from the doorways.

"Oh, God, no—"

Waxy and Mitt didn't make a sound. Mrs. Edwards had been following behind, along with Mr. Edwards and the rest of their children. She was crying loudly and pleading with Master Beal. "They good boys, they good boys!"

Slowly the slaves encircled us, surrounding us like a long wall of grief.

"Yes, Robert, you did right good by bringin' me down hyar and showin' me these two nigger thieves! That's what I call a good nigger!"

I shrank from him, but he grabbed me by the arm. "Now you can tie the rope around their black necks!"

A high-pitched wail pierced the air, and Mrs. Edwards threw herself on the dirt ground. She kicked her feet and screamed until dust flew up all around her. Master was taken aback by her demonstration.

"Mind yo'self, Auntie!" he snarled after he watched for a few seconds. "When a nigger steals from his bossman he got to be punished!"

"Take me instead!" cried Mr. Edwards. "Take me! I'm old and my days of usefulness to you are numbered. These boys is young, and the strength is still in them!"

Soon the air was filled with weeping and wailing. Mrs. Edwards threw herself at Master Beal, sobbing loudly. Others were moaning, praying, and pleading.

Master turned angrily to the two boys. "Strip off their clothes!" he ordered. Then he made them squat down naked, and he whupped them with the cat-o'nine-tails. Then he had them lie down flat and he whupped the bottoms of their feet.

When it was finished, Master wiped his mouth and turned to the people. "Any of you niggers steal from me again, there'll be some dead niggers around hyar." Then he turned to Mrs. Edwards. "OK, Auntie? I didn't hang 'em."

He gave me a shove, and we left the quarter. Back at the Big House, Big Mac was stretched out on a bench in the kitchen with leaf poultices laid on his back and shoulders. Master stood looking at him. "Huh! You ain't so tough after all, eh, Mac?" Big Mac did not move or turn his head to acknowledge his boss.

Master sighed and then growled, "You carry this thievin' niggerboy outa this hyar house and set him to work in the fields tomorrow, Mac. You hear me? I don't want to see his thievin' nigger face round this house agin!"

How long I had wanted to hear these words, and now they were my death warrant.

"Give him to Thrasher and set him to work with a mule and a plow!"

I didn't sleep that night, and when I arose before dawn, the bed was wet with tears. I wanted to take a last look at Anna, maybe feel her soft little arms around my neck once more and kiss her round, smooth cheeks again, but when I saw the iron-jawed face of Big Mac in the doorway, I didn't dare do anything but follow him.

There was a big slab of cold corn bread and a hot cup of sassafras tea waiting for me on the kitchen table. I ate and drank in a daze. Then Big Mac handed me a small brown sack. "This is to eat at noon."

"Thank you, suh," I said softly, longing for a smile from him, some sign of tenderness. There was none.

He walked slowly and deliberately. I followed him, crying miserably. "Mac—" I whispered. He stiffened and refused to answer. "Big Mac—I'm sorry, I'm sorry." There was no answer.

"Kin I fetch the wood before we go? Kin I—"

It was no use. Big Mac would not answer.

His agony was intense. Since I was five years old he had watched over me like a father. He had loved me like a son.

We reached the quarter, and I could see dark forms emerging from doors to line up for the fields. Big Mac brought me to a shanty in the center of the quarter. We went inside. There was a man and a woman there.

"Massuh done sent this hyar nigger to live. He'll be

put to work today plowin' with a mule," Mac told them. The man and the woman stared at me. Their expressions were cold and unfriendly.

Then, without so much as a glance at me, Big Mac turned and left the shanty. I ran after him. "Mac!" I sobbed. "Big Mac!" He wouldn't turn. "Please, Big Mac, don't leave me!" I held onto his shirt sleeve. I saw the caked blood on his neck and back that had soaked through his shirt. "Please, please—" I sobbed. Big Mac would not look at me, and I saw in the dim light of early morning that his scarred face was covered with tears.

17

The lines of workers were already streaming toward the toolsheds and fields. I had no idea of where to go, and so I followed behind a young man heading toward a toolshed. I walked along in the darkness feeling cold and sick. My ear still ached from the blow Mistress Beal gave me. Master had put me out of the house and sent me to the quarter, knowing they would kill me just like they had killed Little William.

I pictured Big Mac's face in my mind. There was no person so dear to me, but I understood why he wouldn't talk to me or show me any compassion. He knew I was a dead boy.

We stood in a line at the shed, and I saw the forms of the overseers up ahead. There was no mistaking the hulking form of Thrasher atop his clumsy horse, Trigger. The boy ahead of me brought a steel walking plow out of the shed. Thrasher saw me as he clopped near us on his horse.

"I knowed yoll 'ud be hyar this morning, Robert," he gloated. "Yoll git yonder with a plow. Tomorry yoll git yer mule ready to go by the horn! Jed! Git him ready!"

The boy named Jed showed me how to hitch the mule to the plow and tie the reins over my shoulders. He helped me get a firm grip on the handles of the plow and showed me ridges between water furrows where I was supposed to run the blade of the plow. I was completely dumfounded by everything. To make matters worse, there were women behind me with bags slung around their necks filled with cotton seed. They were to drop the seeds into the place where I had plowed. And to make it even worse than that, there were more workers behind these women with heavy wood farrows for covering up the seed. All this to plant a row of cotton.

Naturally, if I did a poor job, the whole line of us got the lash across our backs. This made the other slaves so furious, they'd be fit to kill the slave who was at fault. This was one of the ways the overseers made sure the slaves did their work well.

I blindly began to manipulate the plow, my head swimming with pain. I made an awful mess. The mule knew I didn't know what I was doing, and I couldn't get him to obey. It is a wonder I didn't get killed that first morning. The lash came down again and again on our backs. Some of the women were nursing mothers, some of them grandmothers. It was so cruel to make them pay the vicious penalty for my blundering.

By noon the sun was high overhead, and it baked our bodies as we labored. I had no covering for my head, and the constant beating of the sun's rays made me nauseous. Then came a lovely sound—the horn that announced noon eating time. The workers left their places and moved slowly to shady spots at the edge of the field for their meal.

I began to follow them, but found I couldn't walk. Then I saw a grey wall coming toward me. I fell broadside into its cushion-like softness, and all was black and very quiet. When I awoke, I was lying beneath a tree at the edge of the field. Someone sat near me. I opened my eyes and saw Corrie Moore.

"Oh Corrie, mam," I moaned.

"Robert, you is with the fever for sure."

"Whey the mule and the plow is?"

"I drug yoll here, Robert, and Thrasher done put another man on that plow."

"Ohhh, Lor'."

"Buck 'n me heard what fix yoll is in, and we thinks mebbe we kin work it so's yoll live with us till the air clears. 'Sides, you bein' with the fever ain't no good nohow."

"Corrie!" I gasped. "It don't make no difference. I is a dead boy. Jes leave me be an' let it happen."

"Wal, we'll jes see about that, Robert. We'll jes see. Now come on wi' me. I done got permission from Thrasher to git you offen the field."

I tried to get to my feet but I couldn't. The grey wall came at me again, and once more I entered its very black and quiet interior.

Corrie managed to drag me to her cabin while I was unconscious. Often I have marveled at her strength. She was a little woman, and yet she had the strength of a grown man. I awoke long enough to drink a swallow of warm water.

Corrie had lifted me onto their bed. I lay there, unaware of where I was, when through the darkness I saw a face.

I heard laughter. The face came closer to me. Bathed in sunlight, smooth and lovely, it was Pearl. She smiled and reached out to me. Eagerly I ran to her. But I could not reach her. The harder I ran, the farther away she was. "Pearl! Pearl!" She looked wonderfully happy and radiant. Farther and farther away she moved and then she was gone. I stood alone calling her when suddenly I heard a voice beside me. I recognized it but couldn't immediately identify it. It was as beautiful and sweet as the smell of honeysuckle. "Honey," the voice called. I turned. The sight was so glorious I cried out in joy. "Mama!" I ran to her, but she put up a hand to stop me. "Honey," she repeated, "everything is going to be all right." Her words were no sooner spoken than I felt a cool balm cover my body. "Everything is going to be all right."

Then she vanished, but not before I saw the small figure beside her—Ella, my Ella! And she was gone.

Later, when I opened my eyes and looked around the darkened shanty, the memory of the dream was fresh in my mind. The bed against the rough wall, the crunch of the shucks in the mattress, the wash bucket on the table and a low fire in the hearth—all was in sharp contrast to the peace and bright beauty I had just seen. "Mama," I said in the darkness. "Oh, Lor', Ella . . . "

Crawling from the bed, I groped along the wall to the wooden table in the center of the room. Then slowly, across the wet dirt floor, I moved to the hearth and lifted the tea kettle from the wire hanger which hung across the dying coals. I set the kettle down on the table and stood trying to catch my breath. Then I filled a tin cup with the hot water, drank a swallow, and returned to the bed.

There was a piece of fatback hanging from a hook by the hearth and a bag of cornmeal in the corner. Since there was no garden near the house, I knew this was their only food. I was hungry, and I saw near me the brown paper wrapper Big Mac had wrapped my lunch in. Opening it I found corn bread and a—could it be? Maybe my sickness was making me peculiar in the head. Right beside the corn bread was a slab of chicken! I ate it slowly, enjoying every bite. The thought that Mac had done such a wonderful thing for me made me feel better. I fell asleep then and didn't awaken until much later when Buck came home.

The fever had not subsided, and the pain was terrible in my ear and head. Buck poured some salt in the water from the kettle. He mixed it up and then poured some of it into my ear. Then he took some ashes from the hearth, wrapped them in a palmetto leaf and, dampening it with hot water, he told me to lie with my head on it.

I knew something had burst or broken in my ear when Mrs. Beal hit me, and Buck's remedies didn't help.

Buck and Corrie's weekly allowance of cornmeal and fatback barely fed them and their little boy. Now there was me to feed, too. They never complained about me being there, though, and they shared what they had without a second thought.

I prayed daily for the Lord to heal me. He had already healed me miraculously once with the abscessed tooth, and now I begged Him to heal me of the terrible pain in my ear.

In about a week's time, the pain began to subside. To my dismay, however, I discovered I couldn't hear well out of the injured ear. I never did regain the hearing in that ear. Now I found myself with two disabilities—slurred speech and one almost-deaf ear.

Buck decided to try some more cures. Once he poked some axle grease inside my ear, and another time he squashed an enormous bug on the table and squeezed its blood and insides into my ear. Every night I slept with my head on the ashes wrapped in the palmetto leaf. Once we even put a few drops of urine into my ear thinking it might open it up. Of course nothing worked. I was feeling stronger, though, and it was time for me to get to the field, with or without my hearing.

The first summer as a field slave was the longest summer of my life. Each day was grueling misery. I could not get the knack of handling the mule and plow.

One day after work, I was putting the mule back in the barn, and I remembered that when the hot weather came, I was always a year older. I knew I had been eleven, but I didn't know what came after it. "Mule," I asked the mule, "is you eleven or eight? I been a studyin' and I believe I am twenty years of age, now."

Corrie informed me, however, that my birthday was June 27 and that I was now twelve years old. "It was Pearl's wish that yoll know when you was born, and that yoll know yor age. You is now twelve years old, chile."

While hoeing cotton, I was able to think about being twelve years old. I felt the whip on my back often because I'd plow right into the cotton plants, which were now about a foot high. It didn't help much to be twelve—I still was no good in the field—good only for the lash.

Every night I fell asleep weary and aching. I slept on the floor of the shanty, wrapped in a dirty, lice-infested blanket. Buck made a wall of cardboard out of several smaller pieces and stuck them together as a partition so he and Corrie and their little boy could have some privacy. I had my own private room for the first time in my life. It was only a corner without windows and only one blanket on the floor, but it was mine.

Saturday night was payday. We didn't get paid but it was still called payday. I kept my head down though I tried to get a glimpse of Big Mac. I couldn't find him. I saw Miss Ceily's son, Isaiah, out of the corner of my eye. I wanted to ask him about Miss Ceily, but I didn't dare draw any attention to myself. Isaiah worked a different field than I, and I never saw him. When I had received my provisions and was heading back to the shanty, he took hold of my arm.

"Robert," he said flatly. "You enjoyin' bein' a field slave?"

"Shure. It's fine. Jes fine."

"Yeah. It's fine, jes fine all right."

That's all he said to me. He turned his face away.

"Isaiah," I urged quietly, "please tell yor mama, tell Miz Ceily that Master woulda killed Big Mac if'n I hadn't brought him to Mitt and Waxy—"

With a quick jerk, Isaiah turned away from me.

I knew it was useless to try to defend myself. What I had done was my fault and my fault alone. There was a price to pay for making mistakes, and I had to pay mine.

The days were endlessly long and the nights far too short. Sometimes we wouldn't be finished working until way past midnight. Then we would drag our bodies from rest at 4:00 a.m. to begin all over again. There was constant muttering and grumbling. Hatred, bitterness, and suffering were all we knew. The parties in the quarter, with energetic dancing and noisemaking, gave very little relief.

Master Beal supplied whiskey to his slaves, but even in drunkenness there was no relief. There was nothing to help forget the anguish and torture we were bound to. Sometimes the hopelessness became too much to bear, and the mind of the tormented slave would crack. Violence and suicide were often the result.

I could not understand how any of the older slaves had

lasted through the years. Day by day I felt the heart within me turn cold and bitter. All this good land to grow crops enough for all. Yet the black people had to plow with their own blood; they hoed, chopped, picked with empty bellies to make the white man fat. Then the harvest came and they carried the cotton and the corn, the soybean and the tobacco, and their own dead babies. Dead babies, dead mamas, dead brothers and sisters—beaten till they couldn't bleed anymore, broken till they couldn't move to pick any more cotton. O Lord, O Lord, they's got to be a just God.

Toward the end of the summer the cotton fields were like broad white carpets, and I had to learn how to pick cotton. I was as bad at cotton picking as I was at plowing. With my long sack strapped around my neck, and holding the mouth of the sack chest high, I would drag it along the ground beside the rows of the five-foot high cotton plants, pulling cotton from the bolls. At the beginning of each row there were baskets; we emptied our sacks into these baskets. At the end of the day, the baskets were weighed.

Jed tried to teach me how to pick. "Don't put yor fingers all the way into the burr, just put them in about halfway. Then pull the lock out." He showed me how to stoop down, too. "Yoll bend this way so you don't git tired. Sometimes you carry two rows." Then he told me with a laugh, "Some o' these old-timers can pick 200 pounds before noon!"

The cotton pickers moved down the rows of cotton, pulling the blossomed cotton from the bolls. The unopened bolls were left for another picking. My hands were clumsy, and I broke branches as I handled the plants. This was a serious offense and warranted a lash of the whip because cotton will not bloom on broken branches. I just couldn't seem to get the knack, and I envied those who did it so well. Their fingers moved with skill and precision, whereas mine were troublesome and awkward.

Weighing-in time was at the end of the day. In my sack they would always find dry leaves or a piece of boll, and the penalty would be another lashing. I didn't pick enough cotton to satisfy the overseers, either. The other slaves picked 200-400 pounds a day. I could never reach that quota. Not once.

On Sundays we didn't go to the fields. I stayed near Buck and Corrie's shanty, not wanting to go near the quarter. There had been no attempts on my life yet, but I thought every morning might be my last.

One Sunday afternoon I was alone in the shanty and was startled by a shout at the door.

"Robert Sadler!" a woman's voice called. I sat absolutely still, not knowing what to do. "Robert Sadler? Are you in there?" the voice called again. Finally, I decided to answer and moved quietly to the door. There was a young black woman standing beside the shack peering inside. She wore a cotton dress wet with sweat, her hair pulled up beneath a straw hat, and she held a paper bag at her side.

When she saw me, her eyes grew wide and she cried, "Robert! Robert, is that you, chile?"

I stared at the stranger coldly. "Robert," she whispered, in a warm but frightened voice, "come on out here and let me see yoll." I didn't answer her, and I didn't move. I just stood staring at her.

The woman put her bag down and held her arms out to me. "Robert, honey—I'm your sister Margie."

Margie.

I squinted. *Margie.* Something inside my head blew into a million colored pieces. I saw a horse-drawn buggy and a terrified twelve-year-old girl sitting in the back. I heard the long-ago-lost voice of Pearl, "No, Lor', don't take Margie! No! Please, Lor', bring Margie back!" Margie!

"Robert . . . honey . . ."

I moved out the door, my heart beating wildly. I stumbled toward her, and as the burst of sunlight hit me, I fell into her arms.

Vaguely I heard the Beals' chickens clucking and crowing in the yard, and I could hear the dogs barking, yet there was nothing around us, nothing and nobody. It was not happiness that I felt, and it was surely not hope—merely a numbness. The dead had come back to life.

Margie held me tightly. "I swore I'd find you again some day, Robert, honey—I swore—"

"Pearl—Pearl's dead," I sobbed.

"I know, honey. I done found that out when I come here the first time."

"Come here the first time?"

"Chile, I been here at this ole farm three times lookin' for yoll!"

I straightened.

"First time a white chile ran me off. I come around the back and come to the door, and a lil white child come and say, 'Whatchou wantchere?' I told her I was lookin' for my brother, Robert Sadler, and my sister, Pearl Sadler, who was bought by Sam Beal seven years ago.

"That lil old chile lift up her lip at me like she was fixin' to take the hickory to me herself. 'Pearl's daid!' she hollered at me, and then she told me to git or she'd call her daddy on me. So I couldn't do nothin' but leave. It done broke mah heart, and I never found out where you was that time."

I closed my eyes. That little chile must have been Anna...

"So I come back agin," Margie continued. "It's a walk that takes the whole day nearly. Figger 10 or 12 miles. Then I was runned off the place two more times. Oh, I know that I ain't allowed here, but I had to come anyhow."

She smiled at me. "Ah brought yoll some things." For a crazy second, looking at her in the sunlight, I saw my mama again.

"Here's some trousers I done sewed for ye, not knowin' yer size or nothin'—and a shirt ... " Then she pulled out some vanilla wafers, cold pork chops, and a cluster of grapes. There was also a jar of vaseline.

I stuck a vanilla wafer in my mouth, and she lowered her eyes. "Yoll ain't eatin' but a handful a day, are ye?" I didn't answer her.

Then she told me of her escape from the family in Hartwell, Georgie, who had bought her from Tom Billings.

"One day Janey come and carried me offa that place."

"Janey?"

"Yes, chile, our *sister*, Janey."

I could remember no sister by that name.

"Well, chile, she be third from the oldest, and she found out where I was and she come lookin' for me in a big ole car! She tuk me to Anderson to live with her."

I listened as though I were listening to a story that the white children might make up before they went to sleep at night.

"Janey tole me," she continued, "that the only way I could stay free would be if'n I got married. Tole me if'n I was married, the white folk couldn't come and carry me back to Hartwell. So they done fixed up a weddin', and I got married to a gittar player they found who was willin' to go through with it.

"Been trouble ever since." Margie sighed, then took a breath and said, a little brighter, "I gotta be movin' along, chile. I'll be back agin." She kissed me on the cheek, held me tightly for a moment. "They beatin' on you, honey?"

"Naw, they ain't beatin on me."

When Margie had gone and I was alone again, I thought maybe I had dreamed the whole thing. But a paper bag filled with wonderful things was evidence that I had not dreamed it all. A stranger named Margie had been here.

18

I was sure glad when the cotton picking season was over. I was given chores such as chopping wood, cleaning the barns, feeding the hogs and mules, and painting and fixing. I did all that I was told to do with very little concern or care. I spoke little, and even when I was with Buck and Corrie and their little boy, Adger, I had nothing to say.

Margie came to visit me once more, this time bringing Janey. They brought food and clothing. We sat by the hearth in Buck and Corrie's shanty talking.

Janey was a large-boned, striking girl with high cheek bones and flashing eyes. Her broad smile was bright and showed beautiful, white even teeth. She was obviously some-one who wouldn't be held down. I eyed her with interest.

Janey didn't say much to me, but she seemed to be genuinely concerned about me. She told me about a brother of ours named Johnny, who lived in Anderson.

I could not remember a brother named Johnny. Then she told me that I had another brother named Leroy who lived near the Beal farm. She told me Leroy owned his own little farm. It was shocking for me to be hearing things like this, and I could not relate in any way to the news. Strangers who called themselves my sisters telling me of a free world outside and about brothers of mine owning farms—it was just too much for my one good black ear to bear.

"I won't be back for a while," Margie told me. "I's gonna have a baby." The words meant nothing to me.

When they left, Janey said to Corrie, "Kin yoll teach him about washin' and sech? He stinks terrible. 'Sides that, he's got bugs so bad they's crawling all over his face!"

Corrie worked from sunup until late at night, but she squeezed in time for me as well as for her child and husband. I had forgotten all that Miss Harriet had taught me about keeping clean. Corrie showed me how to wash myself like Janey had asked. She showed me how to wash my teeth with a stick and reminded me to wash my clothes.

Soon the winter would descend upon us. Even though the South Carolina winters are supposed to be mild, the temperature does get below freezing, and there is an occasional snowfall. The cold weather doesn't last long, but when there is no heat, shoes, or warm clothing, it is agony. The clothes Janey and Margie brought really helped. In fact, I doubt whether I could have survived had it not been for their gifts.

With the harvesting finished, the pressure was not quite so heavy on us, and I felt myself begin to loosen up a little. I began to notice things again, like plants and trees. I noticed faces and sunsets, and I noticed animals. One day when I was through working in the barn, I took a walk down to the creek that ran through Beal's land. I stood on the bank watching the water for a minute or so, and then got down on my knees and stuck my head in the water. I scrubbed at my scalp and then dried off with my shirt. When I stood up, it occurred to me that I wasn't alone. I turned around and saw a young man standing not six feet from me. "Hi," he said with a friendly voice.

"Hello, Thomas," I answered coldly.

"Whatcha doin' down hyar, Robert?"

I smiled sarcastically. "I'm taking a bath, suh, whatch yoll doin' hyar?"

"I'm takin' a walk, that's all," he snapped. "'Sides, it ain't none of your business."

I shrugged and climbed back up the bank to begin the walk back to the barn. Thomas Beal ran after me.

"Robert!" he called. I stopped. "Robert, yoll doin' OK?"

"Jes fine, Thomas," I answered without looking at him. A July sun flashed across my mind, and his chubby face was covered with mud; we were children and playing in the rhododendron in the yard.

"Well, it's jes that I know it must be hard for yoll bein' in the field when you been in the house all those years."

I didn't answer him.

"Listen, Robert—"

I took loud breath indicating my disinterest. "Robert, I just wanted to say—that is, listen, I gotta tell ye somethin'—"

"Thomas, if you got somethin' to say, say it."

"Well, first of all, I want to tell you I'm sorry for the

hard things I've done and said to you—"

I looked at him hard, wondering what he was getting at.

"And then I wanted to tell you about—well, about that stealin' business."

I turned away. "Well, I don't care to talk about thet there subjec', Thomas. 'Scuse me, I gotta go back to mah work."

"Wait, Robert. I think you ought to know something! Mitt and Waxy, the boys you was givin' the stuff to and they was sellin' it?"

"Yeah."

"Well, they was sellin' the stuff to—"

"To another plantation, Thomas. They had a way. I knows all about it."

"Robert, they wasn't sellin it to anybody on another plantation."

"Huh?"

"Robert, they was sellin' that stuff to—Thrasher."

My mouth opened in spite of myself.

"I swear I'm tellin' you the truth."

"Thomas, you is plumb crazy—"

I rolled my eyes and began to laugh.

"Daddy went down to the quarter when he got drunk one night and went to the Edwards' place, and he told Mitt and Waxy they could leave the plantation."

I didn't believe him.

"You're crazy, Thomas. They is good men. Master Beal need strong men. They ain't enough strong men on this farm!"

Thomas looked at me sadly. "There ain't enough of nothin' on this farm, Robert, and that's the God hepp me truth."

That night I told Buck and Corrie what had happened. "Ah declare," Corrie said, wagging her head. "I been hearin' that Massuh's drinkin' is causin' him to ruin . . . mebbe it's true."

"Why would he turn out Mitt and Waxy?"

I had to find out for myself, and I cared little enough for my life that I went down to the Edwards' place that night. I called inside. When Mr. Edwards came to the door, he looked surprised.

"Whatcha want hyar, boy?" he asked.

"I come to find out if it's true that Master turn out Mitt and Waxy for they freedom."

"They is free, all right. But they is still workin' the land share croppin'."

Mrs. Edwards called from inside. "Come on in, boy."

Mrs. Edwards smiled at me. "Robert, I'm so glad you come by. I been wantin' yoll to know that we don't hold no hard feelin's for yoll. Come on and set yerself down hyar." Mrs. Edwards told me, "Son, bein' a slave they want you low and mean and like a animal. But we ain't no animals. We is people, an' we gotta remember thet. Don't let 'em make you a dog when you is a man."

I nodded.

"Yoll prayin', son?"

"I reckon not, mam."

"Yoll better not forgit *Him*, hyar? He's the answer to all this. He's the *only* answer. If you don't gots the Lord, you gets a festerin' and all tore up on the inside. Nossuh! Lett'um tear us up on the outside, not the inside. Son, don't you *evah* forgit the Lord!"

"Mitt and Waxy's place ain't no better than this one, but they call it theirs," said Mr. Edwards.

"Do the master pay 'em?"

"He done give 'em tools an' seed, a few chickens an' a hog. They keeps half the crop and the other half goes to Master."

"Lor'!"

Mitt and Waxy farmed like they always had, but now instead of being called slaves, they were called share-croppers. At least they were out from under Thrasher's whip.

One Sunday afternoon Master Beal found me standing by the door of Buck and Corrie's shanty, and he motioned to me.

"Robert!" he shouted. "Come hyar, boy." I ran to his side. "Yessuh, Massuh Beal, suh."

"Go get me some whiskey at the store yonder." I was shocked. He might as well have told me to take a little jaunt to glory. I wasn't sure I heard right. Buck wasn't around. Nobody was around to tell me if I heard right.

"You hear me, boy? Run up to Jube's and get me some whiskey. You's the only nigger around. Take the horse and git."

Take the horse! What was he saying? Then I looked at the horse he was pointing at. It was Trigger, Thrasher's horse.

It must be a trick. They're wanting to kill a nigger

today. I'm the one. I'm gonna git killed.

"Suh, Massuh Beal, suh, yoll mean I should git on *Trigger*, suh?" I was so scared I almost called Trigger "suh," too.

"Get on that horse, Robert, and get up yonder *now*! Don't you know Thrasher's dead?"

Dead? I stared at Master Beal with wide eyes. He rubbed his chin with a dirty fist. "That's right, the Thrasher is dead. He got hisself stabbed in the gut while he was sleepin'. Now, get me thet whiskey."

Thrasher dead! As easily said as "today is a nice day" or "tomorrow it might rain." Thrasher is dead.

The narrow dirt road was lined with trees, and you could see the ironwood, fire pink, and asters growing wild along the sides and in the clearings.

Never in my wildest dreams had I imagined I'd be sitting on Trigger—*Thrasher's* horse! The horse was as demonized as his owner was, and I was glad that I got back without getting hurt. A few days later someone poisoned that horse.

The slaves were still scared of Thrasher after he was long dead. They thought his ghost might come back and torture them. Some said they could hear Trigger going up and down the quarter at night looking to do devilment. There was talk like that.

19

Another year went by, and I labored and prayed and grew stronger, but never better at being a field slave. I couldn't plow, hoe, cut stalk, or pick cotton right. It was misery twenty-four hours a day. My only relief was in the winter months when I was put to other chores before plowing time would begin again. I missed Big Mac. There was hardly a day went by when I didn't think of him.

The summer of 1925 I turned fourteen years old. I had grown large, with broad shoulders and thick arms. The other boys didn't want to fight me because I could beat them. Jed, who still worked the same fields as I did, often teased me. "One of these days thet mule gonna plow *you*, Robert."

Jed told me his real name was Zephaniah. The white master had it changed to Jed. "They find it too hard to say. So they shorten it up an' call me Jed." A Jeremiah was called Jerry, a Josiah would be Joe, and a Delilah Lee was changed to Lu. I thought of Tennessee, who refused to allow her name to be changed and wouldn't answer to Caroline. I smiled and said a quiet prayer for her right there in the field, for her and for John Henry.

It was on a Saturday night in the middle of the summer that Buck cleared his throat and told me, "Boy, we's leavin' this hyar place." When it had sunk in, I jumped up and down. "Buck! Buck! Don't leave without me! Promise me yoll won't leave without me!" Buck promised.

That night there was a dance going on down in the quarter and they were "settin' the floor," but I didn't go. Though my life was no longer in danger in the quarter, I wasn't welcome and everybody stayed away from me. I walked slowly across the yard, past the chicken coop, and up the hill to the barn where the mules were.

My mule, Jim, was standing quietly eating hay. "Mule," I said softly, "I has done plowed you fo the las time."

The words startled me. I held my breath. "I has done plowed you fo the las time," I repeated.

I stroked his head and then left the barn. The night

was hot and the air thick. My body was wet with sweat. There was something inside me like a fluttering bird. "I is leavin' this hyar place," I whispered. "Yes, I believe I is leavin' this hyar place."

I walked back to Buck and Corrie's but was too excited to go inside and go to sleep, so I walked up the familiar path which led to the Big House. I had walked that path for nine years, and I knew each lump and crag to it. When I reached the Big House, I stood by the wooden steps leading up to the back porch. Taking a breath, I opened the door and went inside. I could get an awful beating for what I was doing, but I wanted to see Big Mac again. It was quiet inside. Mary Webb was rolling dough on the big table in the center of the kitchen. She didn't see me standing in the shadows. The kitchen looked exactly the same as it did two years ago, except a little smaller and dingier. I heard voices and hid behind the door. Mistress Beal entered the kitchen with Harriet from the dining room.

"Harriet, we'll be visitin' tomorrow, and I want those crinolines pressed right nice. I want an extra pinafore for Anna, too, hyar?"

The smoothing irons were heating on the cookstove, and I heard Harriet's bare feet brush across the kitchen floor.

I wondered where Miss Anna might be and if I could catch just one more look at her. I peeked around the corner. Mistress Beal had left the room, and Harriet was testing the smoothing irons on the stove. I was afraid if Mary Webb saw me she'd start to screaming and throwing things, so I remained hidden. After nearly an hour went by and Big Mac didn't appear, I crept back across the porch and back out the door.

I had a longing to see Big Mac, and it was like a tight fist in my stomach. I searched the grounds around the chicken coop, the smoke house, the well, woodpile, toolsheds, and barns for him, but I didn't find him. I returned to Buck and Corrie's shack that night feeling sad and uneasy.

Nearly every day when Buck had returned from the Big House, I had asked him about Big Mac, and he always answered the same, "Big Mac be fine, boy, jes fine." This is all I had to carry with me for the rest of my life because I never saw him or heard from him again.

Buck and Corrie were in bed. I passed their bed quietly, but I wanted to talk to Buck. "Ssst," I whispered. "Sssst."

Buck grunted.

"Buck, don't forgit me, please don't forgit me."

"OK, Robert, we won't forgit you. Now go to sleep."

I fell into a deep sleep, and I awoke Sunday morning long after daybreak. I lay for a moment or so in the stillness of the cabin, glad that we didn't have to go to the field.

Then in a sudden panic I jerked up from the floor and ran to the partition. Climbing up on the woodbox, I peered over the top, not believing what I saw. The cabin was stripped bare. There wasn't a pot or a rag left. Everything was gone—in fact, it didn't look as though anyone had ever lived there. Black, dirty, empty, and damp. They were gone, gone without me. They were gone!

I leaped down from the box and ran to the door. The sun was shining and it must have been at least 8:00 in the morning. I ran frantically across the yard and through the brush to the road. It was hopeless. There was nobody in sight and no way to find them.

I walked slowly back to the shanty, but I didn't go inside. I walked on to the barn and stood beside my mule. "Jim," I said, "they done gone without me." The mule acted as though I weren't even there. I filled the water tub, and as I stood there in the heat and the buzzing flies, I heard the sound of my own voice. "I has done plowed you fo the las time," I heard.

Without even being aware of making a decision, I turned and walked out of that barn, walked down the dirt path toward the Big House, walked right past the Big House, past the circular drive, and onto the road leading to the highway.

The road was narrow and hot—the pebbles had barely cooled during the night before the morning sun began to bake them. I heard the insects in the grass, smelled the honeysuckle and azaleas. The road wound through the thick, green clumps of trees, and the sky overhead was a deep, rich blue with thin trails of clouds scattered across it.

I walked along the road with my heart pounding loud in my chest. I could be tied up, I could be thrown into the back of a buggy and beaten. I could be strung up, I could be dragged by my heels—I could be—"Oh Lor', hepp me. Hepp me now."

I reached the place in the narrow road where it met a wider dirt road, Abbeville Road. This is the road which led to Anderson. I took a breath and began to walk toward town. As I walked, the fear began to leave me. I had the feeling that I wasn't alone—that there was someone walking alongside me very close, so close I could have touched Him.

"Jesus," I whispered, "I know you're with me, and I want you to know, I'm thankin' yoll."

I passed a little cabin nestled behind some tall poplar trees. There were wooden chairs on the porch. I noticed the woodpile, the well, and the iron kettles out in the yard for washing clothes. There was the sound of birds singing everywhere. I walked kind of hunched over, never letting my eyes leave the house in case someone would take a shot at me or come running out after me. To my amazement, I saw a black woman with two little children walking up a path by the cabin, and as they entered the cabin, she paused and waved a friendly "hi" to me. Then a tall man in overalls and a T-shirt followed the family into the house. He waved at me, too. I didn't wave back. They could be some of Sam Beal's people, and I hoped they wouldn't guess what I was doing. I didn't know they were free people.

I walked for several hours. Many cars passed me, but nobody seemed to take any notice of me. One or two buggies passed by, too, drawn by white people, but there wasn't a word said to me as they passed me. I couldn't understand it. I was fully expecting to be caught and dragged back to the Beal Plantation.

Soon the plowed fields on either side of the road gave way to an occasional house, then more houses, some stores, and I was in town. It was midday, and I was very tired, hungry, and thirsty.

I walked along a road with a graveyard surrounded by barbwire along one side and houses on the other. There were black children playing in the street and in the yards. I stopped by a group of young men who were leaning against a stone wall opposite the graveyard. Remembering what Margie told me about a brother, I asked in a parched voice, "Do yoll know where Johnny Sadler live?"

"Sure," one of the boys replied, "right down yonder, two blocks and turn to your right. It's the end house."

Johnny Sadler, I was sure that was the name my sister had given me. Johnny Sadler, my brother. Breathless and feeling shaky, I walked up the quiet, hot dirt road to the end house on the right, two blocks down.

The unpainted house was set up on concrete blocks. There was a small wooden porch lined with pots of blooming plants. All around the dirt yard were rich, green trees, and wild shrubbery and flowers.

I walked cautiously up to the porch. When I arrived at the door, I called, "Johnny Sadler!"

A woman came to the door. She wore a cotton dress, an apron, and her hair was tied up in a bandana.

"Is this where Johnny Sadler live?"

"Yes," she answered, a puzzled expression on her face.

"I be his brother, Robert Sadler, and I be runnin' away from the Beal Plantation where I—"

"Oh my Lord!" she cried and, throwing open the door, she swept me inside.

"Johnny! Johnny!" she called. "Come in, honey. Come in and set down. Johnny!" I heard noises from another room, and in a few minutes a figure just awaking from sleep appeared in the doorway, smoothing his hair.

"Johnny!" the woman cried very excitedly, "this here is yor brother, yor brother Robert!"

The man's mouth fell open, and his hands froze in mid-air. "Rob—" He walked over to me, looking at me with wide eyes. "Is you really Robert?" he asked.

"Yessuh," I answered.

"How'd you git off'n that farm?"

"I done walked. I done walked off this mornin'."

"Oh, Lord A'mighty!"

The man and the woman looked at one another with alarm on their faces. Finally, the woman said, "Honey, you must be hungry. I'm gonna fix us all somethin' to eat."

She fixed a feast beyond anything I could imagine—eggs, grits, bacon, biscuits, and hot coffee. They watched me eat with eyes so wide they were as big as the fried eggs on the plate.

"Didn't you never learn how to use a fork, honey?" the woman asked.

"No mam," I said, pushing the food into my mouth with my hands.

Johnny said, "Robert, you wasn't nothin' but a baby when I las' saw you. I didn't think I'd ever see yor lil ole face agin."

He told me he had a job in Anderson working in a textile factory and that he had been working there a long time.

Over and over again he asked, "You mean yoll jes *walked off down the road?*" He shook his head and repeated, "Impossible, that's impossible . . ."

"Well, I done it."

He explained that it wouldn't be safe for me to stay in Anderson because Sam Beal would be sure to be around looking for me. They decided to take me to the train station and put me on a train to Belton. From there I could catch a train to Greenville.

I grew frightened. The train station was where they caught John Henry.

"We got a cousin there yoll can stay with. Name Bessie. Bessie Watts." He gave me a few dollar bills and folded them carefully into my pocket. Then the lady packed me a box lunch.

They took me to the station in a car. "Git down on the floor," Johnny told me. "An' stay there." They were plenty scared as we drove, and they dropped me off about a half block from the station. I walked inside and did as they told me to do. I purchased a ticket to Belton and waited outside because I didn't see any colored people in the station. They warned me to be careful not to sit where there were white folks. There was a special place for us. They drilled me about the bathrooms and drinking fountains, too.

I boarded the train without incident, though my heart was pounding wildly. When the train arrived in Belton, I still held my lunch on my lap untouched. I got off and went into the train station. The noise of the train, the newness of a depot and people, and the strange town made me nervous and excited.

The colored section of the station was easily recognized. It was a narrow room like a hallway that nobody bothered to clean. I saw a man and a woman and a child sitting on the bench in the back. I gasped at the sight of them. Buck and Corrie!

They were startled at the sight of me. Buck sprang to his feet and ran to the window. He hurried to the other side of the hallway and looked out the door.

Corrie began gathering things together and held her son to her heart. "Did you bring him, boy? Did you bring him with you?"

"Bring who?"

Buck hurried back to the bench. "Robert," he said gruffly, taking my arm and holding it hard, "did you come hyar with Master Beal?"

"No, Buck!" I answered, surprised. "I done run away, too."

"I swear, boy, if you done brought him, I'll—"

"Buck, I didn't bring nobody. I done run away, too!"

Finally he let my arm go. I slumped down on the bench with them. They sat still, staring at me. I was quiet and did not look at them.

It was not until we were almost to Greenville that Buck could speak to me. "Robert, chile, we has been walkin' all night. We took the desert way."

"The desert way?"

"That's right, boy. Through the woods, the fields, the back roads . . . We ain't slept a dot—"

"Why didn't you wake me, Buck? Why didn't you take me with you?"

Buck looked at me sadly. "Son, if'n they'da caught us, they'da hung us, and I couldn't do that to you."

"But you promised!"

"Son, I couldn't get ye killed."

We wept together then, and I shared the lunch Johnny's wife had prepared. There were apples, raisins, corn bread, and some candy bars.

Buck and Corrie were exhausted and dirty. Their clothes were stained with mud and sweat. They had carried their belongings packed in boxes and blankets and toted six-year-old Adger over twenty miles through the swamps and woods of South Carolina to Belton, but they would not rest until they reached Greenville. They sat rigid, with their eyes darting up and down the aisle of the train, expecting any minute to see Sam Beal come bursting through the door to take them back.

We did not notice the rolling hills and the lush forests of the up country pass by the train's window. We hardly saw the moss-draped oaks, the tall pines, or the flame azaleas and the mountain laurel in bloom. Our hearts beat in time with the clashing of the wheels of the train, and we would not rest until we reached Greenville. And even then, once in Greenville, there was no guarantee that we would be safe.

PART II

Freedom

20

Cousin Bessie's house in Greenville, a white-washed wooden structure set on brick supports, had a narrow, sloping porch and three wooden steps leading up to it. The dirt yard was broken up with two or three small bushes, and two wooden boards laid in a crooked line served as a walkway from the dirt road.

I was made welcome and given a small room of my own with a bed, a glass window that went up and down, curtains, and a rug on the floor. There was a closet for hanging clothes and, wonder of wonders, sheets on the bed. Bessie had me take a bath in the large tin washtub outside in the backyard with some special soap. I had arrived covered with lice.

Each day was shocking to me as I learned what it meant to be a free man. Bessie's husband, Jake, was a porter in one of the hotels in town. He told me, "When you goes for a job, Robert, be sure'n say yessuh, nosuh, an' act respec'ful." He drilled me on how to act in town and on the streets. Smile real big and never look at a white woman. Never look at a white man for too long, and never act smart or like you knows any sense. He bought me a pair of shoes, a shirt, and overalls. I strutted around the house like a peacock in my new clothes.

"How old you, boy?"

"Fourteen June las'," I answered.

"Tell them you sixteen."

I didn't know a thing about working out, but I walked into a factory, asked for a job, and I was hired as a window washer. I worked ten hours a day, six days a week. I got up at 5:30 a.m., walked to work, and started at 7:00 a.m.. I didn't dare ask how much I would be earning, and on my first payday when I received my wages of $3.00, it was like discovering Fort Knox.

I spent that first paycheck almost entirely on candy. I pointed out almost everything I saw in the candy case to the grocery clerk. I also bought a quart of peach ice cream and a pocketknife, and gave the rest to Bessie.

I ate the candy almost all at once and then ate the ice cream. My stomach hurt and Bessie scolded me. "Don't eat till you sick, boy!"

"I had no idee," I said weakly.

Cousin Jake drank a lot of whisky, and one morning after he'd been out all night, someone poisoned him. He managed to get himself home and into his bed. He lay there moaning and complaining, and Bessie thought he was drunk. He died while she was in the kitchen fixing him some coffee.

Nothing was done about the murder. The police came, asked Bessie some questions, and then left. We never heard another thing about it. When Bessie asked her friends what to do, they advised her to do nothing. "It's just another nigger murder, honey. The whites don't care if'n it ain't one of them."

I continued at my job, and the day after the funeral Bessie went back to her job cooking for a white family on the other side of town. Then she started drinking, too, and pretty soon she was drunk every night. She even went to work in a drunken state sometimes.

One afternoon toward the end of the summer of 1925 Buck paid me a visit. I was delighted to see him. "Man! You doin' OK!" he exclaimed when he saw me. "Them bones is sure fatter than when I saw yoll last!"

He told me about a job opportunity in Florida he was all excited about. "They needs workers!" he told me. "They's asking for men to go and work, and they'll pay the fare and take it outa the wages later on."

It sounded like a good deal, and it was an opportunity to get farther away from Sam Beal. I finished the week at my window washing job, said good-bye to Bessie, and boarded the train with Buck to Vero Beach, Florida.

The train was crowded. The car we rode in was jammed with Negro men of all ages going to Florida where, the promotion told us, was our chance to get rich. Our hopes were built up big. For us, who had never hoped for anything at all, it was a new and exciting opportunity.

Vero Beach was one big undevelopment. Forest, swamp, sand, and ocean was almost all there was to it. Our job was to clear the land for development.

I stayed close to Buck and wherever he went, I went. One day we got separated, though, and I was sent to a different section of land to work. "Watch out for those rattlers!" a worker warned me. I grinned and said, "Yessuh," but I honestly didn't know what he meant. I took my scrub hoe and began digging up palmetto trees. I was in a spot all by myself when I heard a rattling noise. I turned and saw the biggest, longest, and fattest snake I had ever seen. Its fangs were ripping, ready to dig into me. I screamed frantically, and some of the men came running. They tore at that snake with their hoes and killed it. Then they dug up its hole and found about twenty little baby rattlers which they killed too.

"Thank you, Jesus," was about all I could say. I was so scared that I didn't know what to do with myself. I was too scared to work because of the rattlers, and I was too scared not to work. I was so backward and naive that I didn't dare open my mouth.

On payday we found that the train fare had been deducted, which was a violation of the agreement that said they would wait to deduct the fare for at least three paychecks. Buck was furious.

"Come on, Robert," he growled. I followed him to the highway. He said he had had enough of Vero Beach and getting rich; he was going back to Corrie and his boy. "Reckon yoll stay on hyar or come on with me, Robert?" Naturally, I would go back with him.

We hitchhiked some, but mostly walked. Day after day we walked. A white man in a Ford sedan picked us up outside of Sebastian and carried us to Melbourne. He had a greasy face and eyes that kept rolling back and forth from us to the road. He asked questions about sex and black anatomy from the time we got into the car until we got out. It made me sick, but Buck said it was nothing unusual. "Them white mens, they think all us Negro mens is studs, and they want to know all about it."

We slept outside by the roadside at night. We walked over sixty miles and reached Daytona Beach worn out and hungry. We went to a house near the highway and asked for a meal. The lady, white, and in her early twenties, said, "Sure! Set youselves down on the porch and I'll be fixin' yoll some food."

She served us chicken noodle soup, white bread with butter, and black coffee. Then she gave us both a piece of blueberry pie. I had never tasted blueberry pie and gobbled it up practically without chewing. When we had finished eating, she sat down on the porch with us. She had a smile on her face.

"Yoll look plumb tuckered."

"Yes, mam."

"Best linger on the porch awhile and rest yourselves."

"Thank you, mam."

"I just want you to know that I'm all for you folks."

"Huh?"

"I believe all the trouble with the Ku Klux Klan is a crying shame, I do. All that fuss because families want to be free. Killings, hangings, tarrings, whuppings, brandings, tearing down property—it's a crying shame."

"Yes, mam."

"I think Mr. DuBois has the right idea, if you want my opinion. Oh, you people have such talent, too! I have a victrola and I listen to records. I listen to Oliver's Creole Jazz Band; I listen to Louis Armstrong and the Hot Five, Bix Beiderbecke—of course, he's white."

"Yes, mam."

The young woman, who had very green eyes that looked directly at a person, paused for a moment. Then she said brightly, "You know, I just loved reading *Uncle Tom's Cabin.* I just cried and cried."

"Oh."

"I just want yoll to know that I'm all for you folks." She sighed and stood to her feet. Turning, she said, "I want yoll to know it has been an honor to have you eat on my porch today."

"Thank you, mam."

"Now yoll just rest, and I'll be taking my leave."

When she went inside, I looked at Buck and he looked as scared as I felt. We were too tired to go anywhere, though, and we fell asleep in the cool shade of the porch, leaning against the steps. When we awoke, there were about six little white children standing and staring at us. It might sound crazy for two grown men to be terrified of a few small children, but we were. They were staring at us and when we opened our eyes, one of them squealed, and another one jumped up and down, acting foolish. The woman came running out of the back door.

"What do you think you're doing?" she demanded, waving her arms at us. "You molesting these children?"

" . . .No, mam!"

One of the children smiled at me and stepped toward me, holding her hand out. I smiled back at her.

"Ginger Amy! Don't you touch thet nigger!"

Buck and I recoiled against the porch. "Don't you make a move, nigger," the woman said, pointing her finger at me. She was very frightened. The veins in her forehead were standing out and her face was red.

"And to think I cried when Booker T. Washington died!"

"Mam, we didn't mean no harm—"

Just then there was a man's voice from inside the house. "Rosemary, what's going on out there?"

Buck jerked away from the porch. "Thank you kindly for the meal, mam," and he turned and headed for the field adjoining the house. I followed behind on his heels.

We could hear the man's voice from the porch. "My *gawd*, is that *niggers*, Rosemary? You havin' trouble with *niggers*?"

Later that night as Buck and I lay on our backs looking up at the stars, I asked him, "Why for that woman be so kindly and then change and act so poorly to us?"

Buck studied on it. "The way I sees it, Robert," he said, "is that she be big on the talkin' side but short on the bein' side."

We got out of Daytona Beach and walked until we reached Ormond Beach. There we found a place on the sand near the water to rest our feet. There wasn't a cloud in the sky, and the sound of the ocean rolling upon the shore was soothing and calming, like a sweet lullabye.

A Negro family in a pickup truck picked us up and carried us to Saint Augustine. From there we walked to Jacksonville. We had very little money left, and Buck decided we would have to find jobs and get some money up before we could make it the rest of the way back to South Carolina.

"With two of us, it won't take no time hardly at all," he said confidently.

But it took two years.

21

Jacksonville's downtown district is set in a bend of the St. John's River where the river turns eastward to join the Atlantic Ocean, some ten miles away. Buck and I walked the crowded hot streets, and then we turned into a building that a taxi driver told us was an agency hiring laborers. We climbed two flights of wooden steps and entered a small, hot waiting room with several benches lined up in rows, behind which were low swinging doors and some desks where a white woman and two white men were sitting. There were no other men in the waiting room, and so Buck and I stood quietly waiting until one of the men called out, "Either one of you done cement work?" Buck answered quickly, "Oh yessuh, yessuh, we has." I was surprised at his lie, but went along with it. For the next two years we worked mixing mortar for a building contractor.

We rented a couple of rooms in a rooming house in south Jacksonville. Every weekend there was always a party going on. I was very shy about being around people, but Buck encouraged me to go to the parties. "Come on, Robert, you needs some fun!"

"I don't want to go to no party nohow."

"Boy, you is crazy!"

"I don't want to go to no party, Buck."

When Buck would persist the argument, I'd flare with frustration. "Buck, I been locked in a white man's house most mah natural life! I been in *prison* in thet big house! I was put out to the field an' live like a animal—How's yoll spect me to act right around wimmin and parties!"

"Jes watch ole Buck, thas all. Do like I does an' yoll be fine."

He would go to the parties, and I usually stayed in my room. Occasionally I would walk around south Jacksonville to get out of my room. The palm trees were beautiful, sweeping the sky with their long, slim leaves, and the air was sweet and fresh. I enjoyed just looking around. I bought ice cream almost every day and I would have lived on ice cream alone if I could have.

I thought of Mary Webb making ice cream for the Beal family. I was forbidden to go near the bowls of sliced peaches and the huge pans of cold, creamy ice cream. I could remember the sick longing for just one tiny drop on the end of my tongue, and now here I was, eating peach ice cream to my heart's content.

Bananas sold for a nickel a bunch, and I would buy them and eat as many as ten at once. I had never tasted most fruits, having only gotten fruit once a year, at Christmas time, on the plantation, and then only hard oranges and soft peaches. I went on an all-out eating binge. Peanuts, candy, apples, oranges, pears, peaches, pineapple, pastries, and ice cream. Whatever I saw that looked good, I bought and ate. While I worked on my job I dreamed of the good treats that waited for me when I was finished.

There was a young white clerk in a grocery store on Atlantic Avenue who waited on me one afternoon. He was a college student, I believe. I heard him laughing as I was leaving the store.

"Man!" he clucked, "it sure don't take much to make a nigger happy. Just give him some candy and some ice cream and he thinks he's in heaven!"

I happily discovered clothing stores, too. I bought some shirts, pants, socks, underwear, a leather belt, a green cap, and a ring with a shiny blue stone. Buying certain things for the first time sometimes brought consternation to the store clerks.

"Lemme have one of them red shirts."

"Which shirt do you mean?"

"Anyone. Jes so it's red."

"All right, what size do you wear?"

"Uh, I don't know."

"—You don't know?"

"No. I'll take any one."

I needed some shoes and went shopping for some. In the white stores Negroes weren't allowed to try anything on so I chose the shoes that looked the shiniest and nicest. They were much too small for me and pinched my feet terribly. When I got back to my little room, I practiced tying the laces until I had it right and then wore those too-tight shoes until they were worn out. They left painful bumps and corns, but I didn't know any better. I didn't know that shoes weren't supposed to hurt you.

Buck and I talked about getting back to Anderson, but

every payday the money went out, and we never had enough to last from week to week. Buck became quite popular with the girls, and there were always one or two chasing him.

There was one girl in particular named Beulah who had Buck thinking he was the finest man on earth. I never cared for her, and she didn't like me too well either. Beulah hung around Buck all the time, and when Buck got to trusting her, she ran off with his paycheck and every stitch of his clothing. She even took his frying pan and his hair creme. His room was stripped bare by the time Beulah was finished.

"Serves you right, you fool!" I laughed. "Parties and wimmin! 'Jes watch ole Buck'!"

Debts, foolish spending and running out of money kept us from getting back to Anderson. Finally in September of 1927, two years after we arrived in Jacksonville and three months after my sixteenth birthday, we boarded a train for South Carolina. We had two five-dollar bills between us. I was sixty pounds heavier and as round as a grapefruit. Buck was lean, strong, and handsome, and sure didn't look like a slave.

We rode in silence, and my mind went back to the Beal Plantation. I thought about Big Mac and wondered how he was doing. I tried to imagine him at work in the smoke house or in the kitchen cooking for the hired hands. Buck saw the look on my face.

"Robert, where you is?"

"I's jes thinkin', Buck."

"Look like you studying on it mighty hard."

"Uhm."

I remember Big Mac's delight when I beat up the Beal boys that afternoon. 'Law diddie law diddie, law dee ay . . .' Oh, Lord, some things are so hard to think on, a man would almost rather have the whip on his back than suffer certain remembrances in his mind.

"When you last see Big Mac?" I asked Buck suddenly.

"Huh?"

"I ain't never laid eyes on him, Buck, not after they put me outa the Big House."

"Don't trouble your mind, Robert—"

"They gonna be a day I gonna see him agin, Buck. I *has* to see Mac agin!"

Buck was very serious then. He put his head down and

said in a low voice, "Robert, they's somethin' I never done tole ye. . ."

I held my breath.

"I jes couldn't tell ye, what with you bein' in the bad spot you was in. I mean, we didn't know if you was gonna be alive one sunup from the next. . ."

"Say what you has to say, Buck."

"Wal, Robert, ye gotta understand that you was sech a young feller—hardly nothin' but a chile. . ."

"Buck, say it out."

"Big Mac is dead, boy."

"Lord!"

"I couldn't tell ye!" Buck struggled to speak. "After you was sent out to the field, he jes died. They say it was of a fever. He had some bad burns on his body, and he was an old man. . . ."

There are certain feelings you get when your world is so low it hardly seems it could get lower. It's like when your nose is broken so many times you'd almost look forward to breaking a foot. Or when you've done so much crying that laughter becomes pain. I didn't speak again on the way to Greenville. If Buck spoke to me, I didn't hear him. I looked out the window and saw only a black furrowed face with a long, silver scar along one side.

In Greenville, Buck hugged me good-bye, and I watched him run down the hill toward town, past the bars and cafes, and around the bend along the twisting road to town. Corrie would be waiting. I stood alone on the platform for several minutes. I was sixteen years old, I couldn't read or write, I had no place to go and no one to go to.

I walked slowly toward town with my grip in one hand and a paper bag of Florida oranges in the other. I walked until the paved streets ended and the dirt ones began. You can always tell, when the pavement is behind you and the dust of the road hits your face, that you're in the black section of town.

I walked to Cousin Bessie's where I had stayed before, but when I got to the door a stranger answered. "Bessie done moved to Charlotte," a pleasant, round-faced black woman told me. "Her husband died and she just up and left for Charlotte. Who're you?"

"I'm Robert Sadler, Bessie's cousin."

"She gots a sister, Gertrude, livin' right down yonder," she told me, and so I picked up my grip and oranges and walked in the direction she pointed.

Cousin Gertrude was a thin young woman with cinnamon skin. She wore a cotton print dress with an apron tied around her middle. I explained who I was, and she invited me in with a bright smile.

"Yoll must be plumb tuckered!" she exclaimed, and fixed me a meal of fried fish, greens, corn bread, and hot coffee. "Eat aplenty now, hyar?"

Cousin Gertrude was an avid church member and an enthusiastic Christian who believed in getting a person saved and sanctified immediately. She let me stay there and preached night and day to me. I listened politely, respecting my memories of Miss Ceily and the wonderful experiences I had worshipping God with the slaves at the Beal Plantation. I remembered Ceily's genuine love for God and her intensely personal relationship with Him.

"Robert, you needs to be saved! You come over to church with me to the meeting and get saved before it's too late."

I experienced the same feeling in her church as the day I sat by the water's edge with Miss Ceily and the other slaves on the Beal Plantation. The exuberant singing, the earnest and powerful prayers ringing through the air, the happy faces and swaying bodies—it all touched me deeply. I felt again the sweet presence of a living God, a God who cared and who was a giver of love and justice. I began to sing along with the rest of the people. Soon I was weeping. The next thing I knew, I was on my knees at the wooden altar at the front of the church.

There was much celebrating over me that night as the people sang and prayed over me. As I prayed, I felt the chains of bitterness and fear begin to slide away from me, and by the time we arrived home, I was feeling happy, relieved, and at peace with myself and the world.

I helped Gertrude with the housework, doing things like washing floors and keeping things clean. The rest of the time I stayed by myself sitting on the porch smelling honeysuckle and watching the sun rise and set. The winding dirt road was peaceful and quiet in the heat at any time of day.

When I'd run an errand to the store, I'd pass the close-together wooden shanties, the people sitting on their porches, and I'd hear the friendly hellos. I'd smile back and I'd hear the birds and children's voices at play. Outwardly the neighborhood was peaceful and quiet. But inside the heart of the neighborhood was a different story. Most of the wooden shacks had a mother and a bunch of children with no father. The grandmas and grandpas living with them were supported by the breadwinning woman who washed clothes or scrubbed floors for white folks six days a week for fifty cents a day. Their diet was mainly salt pork, corn bread, and greens. With their sweat they built the fancy homes of the white folks in town, and with their sweat they continued to keep them clean and running, while their own homes were shacks unfit for human habitation, and their children ran untended and naked. Where was the freedom in freedom? I wondered.

I needed a job, and Gertrude suggested I go to Winston-Salem, North Carolina, to her brother Caldojah. He was a preacher on weekends and a factory worker during the day at John Reynolds Tobacco Company. He might be able to get me a job. I packed my grip on a Saturday morning in late October and boarded a Greyhound bus for Winston-Salem.

Counsin Caldojah met me at the station in Winston-Salem. He was a heavy-set young man with deep-set eyes and huge hands. He welcomed me wholeheartedly and took me into his little shanty with his wife and seven children and treated me as though I were one of his own sons. The day after I arrived he brought me to the employment office at John Reynolds Tobacco Company, and I got a job in the lumberyard stacking lumber at $10.00 at week.

Caldojah couldn't read or write, but he sure could preach. The first Sunday I attended services at the little shack that had been converted into a meeting hall. A large woman they called Mother Shepherd swooped me into her arms and kissed me on the cheeks. "Praise the Lord!" she shouted in a voice that could have brought the roof tumbling down upon us.

"Yes, mam," I said weakly.

"Jesus is wonderful!" she boomed.

"Yes, He is, mam," I answered, smiling faintly.

"Honey, we're on our way to glory!" She gave me a squeeze, and if it had been any harder I would have departed for glory right then.

When I had caught my breath, I found a seat on one of the benches, and Mother Shepherd brought the people over to meet me one by one. I was made to feel very important and special. I loved Mother Shepherd at once.

The meeting was wonderful. The joy and love I had experienced and cherished before was here, too; in fact, it flooded the little shack. Caldojah preached with power and authority on Bible verses he had memorized, since he couldn't read. He concluded his message with, "This hyar world gonna pass away, but Jesus, He gonna last forever!" The tiny congregation burst into singing. My faith was assured, I felt strengthened from heart to toe, and I thanked the Lord for bringing me to Winston-Salem.

Mother Shepherd knew I was a new Christian and told me with a broad smile after the service, "Honey, I gonna teach you God's mo' excellent way."

Mother Shepherd became my closest friend. After work in the lumberyard I would go home, get me a good little wash-off right quick, change clothes, and go to her place. Usually there would be others there, too. We would talk about the Lord most of the night.

Mother Shepherd had a friend about seventy years old named Sister Agnes, who was blind. She would often be at Mother Shepherd's, sitting straight as a stick in the wooden chair, and you could hear her strong, throaty voice a block away singing and praising the Lord.

On Saturday and Sunday afternoons Mother Shepherd and blind Sister Agnes would go out on the streets and hold street meetings. When they asked me to go along with them, I was both delighted and terrified. We must have made an amusing picture as we inched our way down the street. Mother Shepherd and I walked on either side of Sister Agnes, holding her arms and carrying Bibles which we couldn't read. Sister Agnes would begin singing before we had even stopped anywhere. It didn't matter where we were, she would begin a hymn in her deep, throaty voice whenever she felt so moved.

The teenagers in the neighborhood made fun of me with these two old ladies and they'd tease me. "Why, Robert, you lil old granny, you!" When they followed us, laughing and making deriding remarks, Sister Agnes would stop in her tracks, turn in the direction of their voices, and sing, "Ole Devil Gonna Take You Soul" loud enough to be heard in Asheville.

Then Mother Shepherd, never missing an opportunity, would follow with a hair-raising sermon on the "mo' excellent way." Sister Agnes would shout loud amens at nearly every sentence, and sometimes she'd lift her heels and commence to dance.

I loved those meetings with all my heart. I was not aware of how ridiculous we must have looked, and I didn't mind the other teenagers teasing me. We prayed for each of them beforehand, and I was quite confident that the Lord was going to help them and save them.

One afternoon as we stood on a street corner, four of the teenage boys came up to us and said soberly, "Show us how to know Jesus and that mo' excellent way, like you talkin' about." That love Mother Shepherd had was the love of God. She led those boys to the Lord right there on the street.

Mother Shepherd loved to pray for people. When she laid hands on them, sick people got well, people who were bound by demons were set free, and sad people became happy. I watched it all with admiration swelling in my heart. Mother Shepherd really *knew* the God she talked about. She knew Him like a true friend and trusted Him to do what she asked of Him. He always seemed to answer her, too. I prayed that I could know the Lord like Mother Shepherd knew Him.

When May came and roses bloomed in the yards and along the highway, and the smell of tobacco covered the city, I knew it was time to head back to Greenville. Mother Shepherd wept when I told her, and the day I left they had a little party for me. Sister Agnes, though she was blind, was still a good cook, and she made fried chicken, rice, corn bread, and my favorite, poke salad. Mother Shepherd baked sweet potato pie. There was hot coffee and iced tea to drink. We kept our conversation happy and light.

Mother Shepherd embraced me as I left, and kissed me. We both knew it was probably the last time we'd see each other. Tears stung my eyes as I walked up the dirt road toward town and the bus station. I could hear Sister Agnes and Mother Shepherd singing, their voices low, mournful, and sad, mingled with the sunshine and dust in the air,

Bye and bye, when the morning come,
All the saints get together,
In our new home,
Tell the story of how we overcome,
We'll understand it better
Bye and bye . . .

22

Back in Greenville I lived with my Aunt Julie who was cousin Gertrude's and Bessie's mother. She was a kind woman, short with coal black skin. She wore her hair corn-rowed or tied in a rag, and I never saw her with a pair of shoes on her feet except for the coldest days of winter. She worked in white folks' homes around the town, washing and ironing. She walked to and from work every day, leaving her children to care for themselves until she returned late each night.

Aunt Julie's husband had died two years earlier of the pneumonia, leaving her with a broken-down house and the care of five of their thirteen children. The oldest children, including Caldojah, Bessie, and Gertrude, were married and had families of their own. Four were dead and that left five at home, the youngest not yet three years old. "Before now, I don't hardly ever recollect being without a baby in my arms or on the way," she told me in her low, soft voice.

I got a job at a cotton mill for $8.00 a week. They said they were looking for men to run machines, but they gave me a job cleaning toilets.

At night Aunt Julie would sit in a big chair in the middle of the big room, or on the sloping porch with the children all around and we would talk. Aunt Julie was a wonderful talker. She had a captivating way of telling stories, and I looked forward to these times together.

"You know, Robert, I fought with yor daddy about selling you. I woulda takin yoll in myself, but he wouldn't hear of it," Aunt Julie told me tearfully. "He wanted thet money."

With a sharp, burning sensation, I wondered what it might have been like to grow up in a home with my own people.

"You been under slavery, chile, but we been under it, too," she said. "They didn't sell us, but they had us. If we fought, they killed us; if we didn't fight, they killed us in another way."

I thought about Mother Shepherd's more excellent way. She said that anger and hostility only produced more anger and hostility, and black folk had had enough of that. There was a lot to think about.

When Aunt Julie discovered that I couldn't read or write, she set aside a learning time for me every night after supper at the kitchen table.

With the plates cleared and the table washed, we would sit down together and she would write big letters on a brown paper bag with a pencil, and I would try to copy them. She taught me how to print R O B E R T S A D L E R and how to count to twenty. I don't know where she got her education. I spent most of the day of my seventeenth birthday learning to write my full name. I worked hard at each assignment she gave me.

Aunt Julie taught me from the Bible, too. She taught me how to find Matthew, Mark, Luke, and John. And how to find verses. She taught me words like GOD and JESUS and LOVE. As I ran my hands over the smooth pages of her worn Bible, I thought of the Bible at the Big House on the plantation. It sat on the shelf in the parlor. I heard Mistress read from it several times, and Master occasionally read aloud. I remembered hearing the words, "And it came to pass. . . ." I thought they were thrilling words.

"Aunt Julie, show me where it say, 'And it came to pass. . . .' "

After some searching, she found those words, and in another couple of days I could write R O B E R T S A D - L E R and I T C A M E T O P A S S and 1 2 3 4 5 6 7 8 9 10 11 12 13 14 15 16 17 18 19 20.

The winter passed and I continued to work at the cotton mill, giving most of my salary to Aunt Julie. I joined Aunt Julie's church and faithfully attended, and yet something inside of me wouldn't rest.

The restlessness in me is hard to explain. I was a free man but I had nowhere to go, nowhere to belong. I couldn't live with aunts or cousins forever. I didn't know how to be a free man.

I had studied plenty on freedom. Black men rode in the back of the buses and drank from separate drinking fountains than the whites. They walked with their heads down on the streets, and they got jobs cleaning toilets or doing hard labor for less money than it takes to feed a family. I had seen plenty of free black people who had come up from slavery. Many became drunks and alcoholics; they lived lives of poverty and powerlessness, and died in bars and jails and on roadsides. I didn't want that. Lord, I didn't want that.

I was moving with an ache, like the kind you get when you've broken a leg. It's always there, you just move a little different with it. I finally decided that if Sam Beal would take me back, I would work for him—why, I'd break my back for him. Then I'd sit down with my feet in the dirt and my head in the grass and I'd watch the sun go down. Freedom was strange and frightening. I didn't know what was coming next. As a slave, I knew what to expect.

Maybe going back to the plantation was the answer and maybe it wasn't. I wasn't looking for an answer. Maybe I just needed something a little familiar. I decided to return to the only place in my life where I had ever belonged. I announced to the family that I was going back to Anderson.

"But why's you wantin' to leave, son?" Aunt Julie asked.

"Wal, for one thing, I'm going back to Sam Beal's."

Aunt Julie's eyes grew wide, and a loud wail escaped from her lips. "You is goin' *where?*"

"I'm goin' back to the plantation. I wants to see Sam Beal agin."

"Robert, they'll keep you there and you'll never get offen that place agin!"

No amount of pleading dissuaded me. I was determined to go back. In the spring of 1928, three years after my escape, I boarded a bus and headed back to my old master.

23

I took a taxi from the bus station in Anderson to the Beal Plantation. The spring air was hot and sweet with the smell of honeysuckle. Flowering dogwood bloomed along the roadside, and spotted irises and violets grew wild in the woods and ditches. The air was filled with the music of the starlings, the jays, and the finches. My heart beat wildly with excitement and fear underneath my new red knit shirt. My grip sat on the seat beside me.

As we neared the plantation, I could actually sense the oppression in the air. It was something unexplainable. Even the Negro taxi driver grew agitated as we neared the place. I heard him cursing under his breath, and when we arrived at the Big House, he refused to pull up in front of it.

"Git out here, uncle," he told me flatly. "I ain't drivin' up there."

The sounds of the taxi driving off, the barking of the dogs, and the clucking of chickens surrounded me as I stared unbelievingly at the grand old plantation home I had left just three years ago.

It was a junkyard, a shambles. It sat bent and wounded against the sky like a defeated and broken soldier. My mouth dropped open. "Lord, have mercy."

I walked quietly around the side of the house through weeds, broken wheels, cans, and pieces of lumber to the kitchen door. There was no answer when I knocked, so I left my grip under the porch and began walking across the huge, cluttered yard. I walked through the weeds to Buck and Corrie's shanty. It was empty, dark, and mice ran squeaking through the hay scattered across the floor. The partition was still there that Buck had built.

I continued walking. The path to the quarter was nearly grown over with weeds. As I walked along, I heard workers in the field. Looking up and shielding my eyes from the sun, I saw several figures bent and plowing in the field.

"Lord a'mighty!"

It was John Beal doing the plowing! And Thomas! And

behind them spreading seed were Juanita and Virginia! I ran to the edge of the field. Could it be true? Was I dreaming?

It was true all right. The Beal children were plowing and planting. I ran on to the quarter to look for my friends. There was no sign of anybody. From shack to shack I ran— all empty. I couldn't get to Miss Ceily's shanty fast enough. There wasn't a shred of evidence that she had ever been there. Some wooden boards slapped together over a piece of dirt—that was all there had ever been, but now the life was gone, and it was ugly and terrible. I felt sick and sat down on her step to catch my breath.

On my way back to the Big House, Thomas saw me from the field. He dropped the handles of the plow. "Ho there!" he shouted. I stopped and looked at him, unmoving. He shouted again, and it was obvious he didn't recognize me.

I walked slowly out to him and he walked toward me. John and the girls stopped to watch. Thomas' mouth dropped when he recognized me.

"Rob-Robert? *Robert!*" I thought for a second he was going to run to me and embrace me, but he caught himself. "Robert!" he repeated.

"Hello, Thomas," I said. "What has happened? Why you out in the field plowin'?"

"Robert, we've lost everything. All the land we have left is what you see right here. Everybody and everything is gone." He looked heartbroken.

"Your father?"

"He's in the house, sick . . . very sick. He's dying."

"Where are the slaves?"

"All gone. All set free."

"Praise the Lord," I said. "I'm sorry for you, Thomas, but I'm glad they're free."

"Why did you come back, Robert?"

"I wanted to see your father again," I answered. "In a funny way, he's my father, too."

Thomas' eyes were riveted to mine. "Uh huh," he said quietly.

I left him in the field and walked back to the Big House. I walked up to the back door again and knocked loudly. There was no answer, and so I opened the door and walked in. The kitchen was a stinking mess of garbage, dirty dishes and pans, opened boxes and jars of food left on tables, dirty clothing, greasy walls, mud-streaked floors, and flies and bugs everywhere.

After standing at the door and surveying the room for a few stunned moments, I turned and walked out. The well on the porch was still there, and I drew the bucket up for a drink of water. I wondered if I had been the last one to sweep the porch—it was piled high with pieces of wood, old furniture, broken machinery, straw, rags, and layers of hardened mud on the floor hid the wooden planks. There was the acrid smell of the dogs.

I heard someone coming into the kitchen just then, and I put the bucket back into the water and hurried to the doorway. "Hello!" I called.

A fat, unkempt woman with uncombed grey hair shuffled toward me in worn bedroom slippers. "What do you want?" she demanded.

I stared in disbelief. "Miz Beal..." I breathed. She eyed me suspiciously.

"Mam, it's me, Robert."

Her eyes narrowed. "—Robert!"

"Yes mam."

She pulled herself upright and snapped, "What do you want, Robert?"

"Please, mam, may I see Master Beal?"

"No, you may not!" she spit at me.

"Oh please, mam, just for one minute—?"

"No, Robert, you ain't seein' Master Beal. Now you can just git off the place."

"Mam, please?"

She paused for a moment, as though she were considering my request. Surveying me she said, "Gawd, boy, you gained some weight. You is positively *fat*!"

"Yes, mam," I said. "I been eatin' good."

She laughed. "I can see that, boy. I can see that. Yoll growed up since you left hyar!"

"Yes, mam. I'll soon be eighteen."

"Uh huh. Same as Thomas...."

"Yes, mam."

She had seemed friendly for a flashing few moments, but then anger flew across her face again. "Well, you can't see Master Beal. He's ailing, and he don't want to see nobody. It won't do you no good to plead with me, I ain't lettin' you see him nohow. Now git off the place, Robert."

I turned to leave, but I made one more request. "Mam, how is Miss Anna?"

"Miss Anna be fine," she answered crisply.

"Mam, could I see her?"

Outraged now, Mrs. Beal shouted, "You may not see

Miss Anna, and you may not see Master Beal! Now get off this place before I get the shotgun!"

I walked back to Anderson with my grip, taking the same route I had taken four years ago. I was like hundreds of other blacks who had grown up under slavery. I was set free in a world that had no room for free blacks, and I didn't know who I was or where to belong. I knew in my head that I belonged to the Lord and that He loved me, but I had little understanding of what love meant, and the only real belonging I knew about was being owned as a slave. I was no longer a slave—but I wasn't free either.

24

I found my sister Janey's house on Fant Street, and she let me move in with her. Margie was living there, too, with her two little boys. Her husband had left her after she had the second baby.

Margie was overjoyed to have me near her. In these first weeks she fussed over me more than her own children. She washed my clothes, cooked for me, sewed me things, and tried to help me the best she could. Janey didn't like the special attention given me—it irritated her. Already cold toward me, Margie's affection added to her annoyance.

"You makin' that boy a old lady, Margie."

"I is carin' for him, Janey, and I'll do as I please."

Janey's house was anything but peaceful. She often had temper tantrums; she got drunk, brought boyfriends home whom she fought with, and if it wasn't the boyfriends she fought with, it would be Margie or me or even the children. She thought nothing of beating Margie's boys, and this infuriated Margie. The oldest child, Alan, was four years old, and the baby, Walter, was about two and a half. The way Janey treated them reminded me of the way our stepmother, Rosie, had treated us. I was glad when I got a job on a small farm outside of Anderson and was gone from the house most of the day and night.

I went to work at plowing time for a white farmer named Wheeks. He was very kind and had a stout, friendly wife who was as kind as he was. They often invited the hired hands to eat lunch with them. Mrs. Wheeks would fix pig hocks, boiled cabbage, corn bread, custard, and fresh fruit pies. I never knew white folks so nice.

Mr. Wheeks showed kindness in other ways, too. I had to walk two miles to and from work each day, and there were times when I showed up late. He would have my mule hitched up for me and ready to go by the time I got there, and he never said a word about my being late.

I made mistakes and did things to earn dozens of whuppings, but Mr. Wheeks never raised a hand to me, or to anybody else. I never heard him curse or call any man a bad name. He helped his men buy homes as well as send their children to school.

One day I heard him telling Mrs. Wheeks someone named Hoover was elected President. I didn't know what president meant, and I sure never heard of elected.

At settling up time I cleared $100. That was one Christmas that there was plenty of food and fresh fruit for everybody. After I bought a few things for myself, I gave the rest of the money to Margie. When Janey found out I had given money to Margie and not to her, she threw us both out of her house in a rage. Margie found another place for us, a tiny, one-bedroom shanty on Johnston Street for $22.50 a month.

Janey eventually felt bad for throwing us out. Attempting to make amends, she decided to throw a big family reunion party at her house. She invited my brothers Johnny, Leroy, and Harvey, their wives and children, Margie, her children, me, and lastly, my father.

My heart beat fast and my tongue became thick at merely the thought of seeing him again. Deeply printed in my mind was my last sight of him—driving away in the buggy, leaving me in the dirt of Sam Beal's driveway. I could still see Pearl jumping in the dirt, shouting at him, "You evil man! Selling you own chillrens! You is an evil man!" And Pearl, my Pearl—her miserable death when only a child, ending an even more miserable life. Yes, my father was one person I had never wanted to see again as long as I lived.

The day of the reunion arrived. Except for my brief meeting with Johnny, I didn't know my brothers at all. They told me that we had another sister named Ada, who was the oldest, but she was working in Roanoke, Virginia.

When they brought my father in, I was startled at the sight of him. Thirteen years had paid a heavy toll on him. He was bent, tired, grey, and much thinner than I had remembered him. His blue-black skin was furrowed with deep lines, his tall body no longer proud.

Margie was the one who presented me to him. "Dad," she said in a flat voice, "this is Robert."

He stared at me for a few seconds and then said in a timid voice, "Hello, son."

I cringed and could not reply. He looked at the floor and said softly, "I don't blame ye for hating me. I been sorry for what I done since the day I done it."

I could not answer. The years of bitterness and despair in a forsaken little boy seemed to hit me all at once. I prayed silently for the Lord to help me. Finally I managed, "How's Rosie?"

"We ain't been together for las' ten years. She quit me." I moved away from him. I had nothing more to say to him.

Janey was all dressed up that day. She wore her long black hair pulled back and sleek. She had high cheekbones and enormous eyes, brightly painted lips, and a long, slender body wearing a shiny black satin dress. Margie was beautiful in a different way. She was plump with nappy hair, and the dress she wore was white and pink cotton. Her beauty was the kind that made you want to know her and be with her, and she made you feel warm and happy inside.

My brother Leroy, who owned a small farm near the Beal Plantation, told me how Sam Beal had come to his house with his Ku Klux friends looking for me after I escaped.

"They come across the field when my beans was up about like that and my peas up like that. They come across the field at night, and they come up the road by day. They come a-lookin' for yoll, Robert. I told him you wasn't at my place, and I didn't know where you was nohow. That Sam Beal always feared you'd run away, and he feared that yor daddy would come and take yoll back. Thought you'd come running to my house, but I didn't even know yoll."

I listened with grave interest. "When did the plantation go down?" Leroy gnawed on a chicken neck, spitting out the small, knot-like bones as he talked. "He jes plain lost everything. Oh, that place is cursed, cursed, I'm tellin' you. God is a just God!"

"But what happened to all of the slaves? Where did they all go?"

"Oh, I see some of 'em around—right here in Anderson. You'll find 'em shor nuff, they's here and they's there. . . ."

Big Mac never made it to freedom, I thought. But how about Miss Ceily? The Edwards family? Miss Harriet? Jed? Leroy said he thought they all were in Anderson except Jed. "Ah think he went up north."

I noticed that my brothers and sisters didn't have much to do with our father either. They hardly spoke to him or paid him any attention. He struggled to get out of his chair and nobody offered to help him, and when he spoke, nobody listened. Margie was the only one who showed him any courtesy.

"They hates him for sellin' his chillrens as slaves," Margie explained later.

"Well, you the one he sold, girl, how come you be's the one who treats him nice?"

Margie looked at me sadly. "He done paid for what he did, Robert. He'll always be payin' for it, and I don't reckon I need to punish him anymore."

"God is a just God," I said. Margie smiled.

In the autumn of 1928 Margie's baby, Walter, took sick. She called the doctor, but he didn't give us much hope. Said there was some poison in his kidneys spreading through his little body. I remembered how Mother Shepherd prayed over people who were sick, and they would be healed. I did the same. I held little Walter in my arms and asked the Lord to heal him. In fact, as the days wore on, I *begged* the Lord to heal him. His little face grew more and more sickly, though. Margie cried her heart out every day caring for him. It seemed the world just stopped during those days. We took turns sitting up nights with him, and even Janey came and helped out. He grew worse, and finally, around the first part of November, he died.

The weeks after little Walter died were sad and dark. Even though I knew the Lord had a good purpose for taking him home to be with Him instead of healing him like we asked, we grieved over it.

I joined the Zion Temple Holiness Church located at the end of Fant Street in December and began going to the meetings regularly. Margie never came along with me and told me right out, "I am not one of them who goes for religion, Robert." So I began to pray for her.

Finally one day Margie came with me to the little church, and as the people were praying and singing, Margie began to cry. She went up the altar and gave her heart to the Lord that night. She never took it back as long as she lived.

One of the first prayers I ever heard her pray was, "Lord, I jes want to thank you for takin' my baby home to heaven. I'm sorry for actin' selfish and droopy. I ain't gonna act that-a-way no more." And she meant what she said.

I got a job in the winter of 1929 at the Calhoun Hotel in Anderson, washing pots and pans in the kitchen. I bought the first raincoat I had ever owned when I received my first pay, and you'd think I'd just bought the hotel.

"Can't get near yoll in that coat!" Margie laughed.

One night when I came home from working at the hotel, Margie met me outside the dirt road. "Robert," she said anxiously, "Dad is inside."

"What you talkin' about?"

"Dad. That's what. Dad. He's inside and he's—he's come to live with us."

"Girl, you lost yor mind?"

"No, I hasn't. None of his children would take him, Robert. He don't have no place else to go, 'cept here with us."

A cold chill gripped my heart and began to spread through my chest. I looked at my sister, bewildered.

"I jes don't know if I can live with that man, Margie." I felt Ella's smooth cheek next to mine. We were huddled underneath the house clinging to each other as Father heaved a blow at Mama. I heard Mama fall to the floor, and Ella was crying softly. Her tears were warm and wet against my face.

"Robert," Margie pleaded, "what else can we do?"

"I tries not to hate him," I said lamely.

"God will have to help us, thas all. Give us love for the man."

My father moved in with us, and the first month was terrible for me. I avoided him as much as I could and never spoke to him. When I had to address him, I called him Jim.

"Don't call me Jim, son," he told me in a firm, steady voice one morning as I was buttoning my raincoat, preparing to go to the hotel. "Don't call me Jim no more. I is yor *father!*"

I whirled around. "You are not my father!" I snapped. "*Sam Beal is my father!*"

Stomping out of the little wooden shack and up the dirt road to the hotel, I grew more and more angry. I fussed all day over it. He had some nerve telling me to call him father! By the time I got home, I had built myself up for a real storm.

He was sitting on the porch waiting for me. Before I could say a word, he said quietly, "Sam Beal is dead, son. He died three months ago."

The words were like a blow to my stomach. I looked at the old man's greasy, crumpled face. He was bent over in the wooden chair like a folded rag.

"I know it's too late, Robert," he said in a cracked voice, "but I's sorry for what I done—I's sorry for what I done—" Tears rolled down his cheeks and his wide shoulders trembled. I felt a tinge of compassion for him.

"How much did you get for me, Jim?" I asked in an unsteady voice.

"No!" protested the old man. "Don't ask me that, Robert. Please—"

"I want to know, Jim. Now you tell me. I am going to tell folks my story one day, and I wants to know how much I was sold for."

He began to sob loudly. "Oh, Lord, have mercy!" he cried, "I got about eighty-five dollar for you."

In the summer of 1929 I began to get restless again. I was well liked at church, and I began to spend my hours after work in the church praying and teaching myself to play the piano. The desire to go to school was still very strong, and I talked about it to Margie.

"I thinks you should go to school, Robert. I'll help yoll."

I was elated when Margie took me to the Presbyterian school about a mile away. I talked with the principal about enrolling.

"How old are you?"

"I is eighteen, suh."

"Eighteen? But where have you been all these years? Why haven't you attended any school?"

"I been a slave on a plantation outside town most my life, suh."

"A *slave*!"

"Thas right, suh."

"Robert, that is against the law! It's—it's not *legal*!"

"I know it's against the law, suh, but I was a slave anyhow. I could take you to the place today." The man was shocked.

I told him of my escape and of my burning desire to go to school to learn how to read and write. He accepted me for fall enrollment, and I shouted with joy. "Thank you, Jesus!" I doubt if my feet touched the ground when I walked home that day. When I arrived at our unpainted shack on Johnston Street, I saw the old man asleep in the chair on the porch, took a breath, and called, "Dad! I is going to school!"

He stirred, opened one eye and said, "What'd you say, boy?"

"I said, I is going to school—Dad."

The old man grinned from ear to ear. "Thas fine, son, thas fine." The barrier was broken.

September came at last and I started school. I was in the first grade and sat in a classroom with six-year-olds. I loved every minute of it and was hardly even aware of how ridiculous I looked.

I was much too big for the desks and had to sit sideways in them. The children giggled at me, but they were never cruel. We got along fine. During recess I threw the ball to the children and played with them.

When we did our arithmetic, Mrs. Garner, the teacher, gave us problems to figure out. One morning she told us that we were going to learn Roman numerals. I was deeply disappointed because I had wanted to learn American ones.

Storytime was a favorite time for me. I loved the stories as much as, if not more than, the little children did. One of my favorites was *The Little Red Hen*.

Summer came and the principal told Margie and me about a boarding school in Seneca that was all black and free. I applied and was accepted for the summer. This meant I had to leave Margie and live on the campus.

Before I went away to Seneca Junior College, I asked my dad to go to church with me. He did, and he gave his heart to Jesus. He wept and prayed, and it was the most touching thing you ever did see. I hugged him and actually was able to say from my heart, "Dad, I forgive you."

There was one more wonderful thing that happened before I went away to school. I had a long talk with Janey about her soul. She went to church by herself the Sunday night before I left and gave her heart to the Lord. She came by the house and told me what had happened, and Margie, Janey, Dad, and I talked and enjoyed one another into the early hours of the morning. I didn't want to leave them, but another major part of my life was about to begin in Seneca, South Carolina.

25

"Have a seat, and we'll have one of the students show you to your room," said the small, bird-like woman in the school office. I sat timidly by the window. From there I could see the brick dormitories and the three-story, brick classroom building that had the dining hall in the basement, along with the log cabin library, and the dirt paths lined with English ivy. The grounds were spotlessly groomed, and the grass looked as though it had been shaved with a straight-edge razor. There were colorful flower beds, oak, ash, and sweetgum trees, and rhododendron grew along the buildings. And I was experiencing a new feeling: excitement about the future.

A young man about my age, thin and slightly built, came through the door. He smiled, "Hello, I'm Bo Brocke. You must be the new student I'm supposed to show around."

I stood up and smiled back. "Uh huh. My name is Robert Sadler." He put his hand out to shake mine. It was the first time anyone ever had done that to me. I didn't know why he held his hand out, but I figured it was to hold mine, so I gave him one of my hands. I would have given him my other hand, or possibly my arm or leg, if he had given me a chance. I was thankful the Lord had Bo be the first person I met at school. He was soft-spoken and likable.

Bo showed me to my room and told me about mealtimes and what time I was to show up in class. "And lights has to be out at 10:30," he said. "They be very strict about that." He told me where to report the next day for job duty. My job was to be in the kitchen.

Each of the students worked for four hours every day at the school, and the jobs were rotated at the start of each new quarter. Bo told me his job was cleaning the classroom building. He had only two years of school left, he told me, and then he was going to go on to college. "I'm thinking about being a lawyer," he said with a hint of pride in his soft voice.

I didn't even know what a lawyer was. "Oh!" I said nodding my head. "A lawyer! Yes, a lawyer!"

He told me he was going to summer school to try to graduate early.

"The more credits I take, the faster I'll be in college!"

"Yoll make it, yessuh, yoll got what it takes."

When he was gone, I looked around my room and sat down on the bed that was assigned to me. The springs creaked and my body sank deep into the center to within inches of the floor. I chuckled. "I can see whey I'll be sleepin' on the floor!" The room was small, with two single beds, two small desks with chairs, and a long chest of drawers along the wall.

It was better than the plantation, better than Cousin Bessie's, better than the boarding house in Jacksonville, better than Cousin Gertrude's, better than Cousin Caldojah's, better than Aunt Julie's, better than Sister Janey's and Sister Margie's—it was better than anything. It was school. At last I was at school.

The summer on campus gave me a chance to get used to the school before the fall came when the place filled with students again. My roommate was gone for the summer, and so I was alone in the room assigned me. The classes weren't crowded, and I worked out many fears and backward ideas with the help of the instructors.

My speech problem was back, for one thing, and I often got words mixed up. I had never been taught how to say words, and so sometimes I made dreadful mistakes which brought a lot of laughter.

"I don't care much about classified music," I said seriously in class one day. "I feel I is standing on a firm soundation singin' jes plain music."

Another time I confided I didn't know how to "mangle and co-mangle with people." Mistakes like this were common. I did improve a little, but I still have trouble with words.

September came and my roommate arrived. His name was Luke Small, an ironic name because he stood about six feet, four inches tall. When he looked down at you, his shoulders seemed broader, his legs longer, and his long black arms tougher than anyone you'd ever seen. You had to decide whether to pick a fight with him or admire him. I chose to admire him.

Most of the other students at Seneca chose to admire Luke Small too. He was the football hero, the basketball hero, and the dance floor hero. He had most of the girls crazy about him and most of the guys jealous of him. He had hardly even glanced at me when Bo Brocke introduced us. Of all people to have as a roommate! He was slick, sharp, and popular. I was backward, practically illiterate, fat, and on top of that, I had a speech problem.

If Luke asked me to hand him the talcum powder, I would freeze before the row of bottles and cans on the dresser, not knowing the talcum powder from the toothpaste. I remembered the bottles of pretty-smelling things that Mistress Beal always kept on top of her dresser, but nobody had ever told me the names of them or what any of them were for.

Luke seemed to like me, though, as time went on, and even encouraged me to try out for the football team. I did try out, and I made it because I was so strong. I played left tackle throughout all my school years.

I loved my classes and I loved studying. I had never owned a book before and I loved everything about books. I loved the smell of the paper, I loved the feel of the edges of the pages when you fanned them, I loved the print, the binding, the textures of the covers. At last I was learning how to read and write. Every night before going to bed I got on my knees and thanked Jesus, and every morning before going to my job in the kitchen, I did the same. "And thank you for givin' me such a nice roommate as Luke Small, Lord. Please help him, Lord. He need a Savior!"

The whole school would assemble for chapel one hour a week on Wednesday morning, and the dean of students solemnly warned us, "*Remember*, when you are off this campus, you must conduct yourselves in an orderly manner. *Never* be caught off campus after dark. Watch yourselves and keep your noses clean; then with a prayer and a friend beside you, you might make it OK. *Always* have a friend with you when you leave the campus!"

The boy beside me sneered, "Yeah, Whitey is jes waitin' for one of us to stick our black necks in his noose! They hates this school. They hates it because they don't think niggers got any brains for learnin'." I nodded, and quietly said to myself, "I done come this far . . . I done come this far."

Football was the big thing during the fall quarter. Being on the team and being a friend of Small's, the girls hung around me. With my schoolwork, football, and new social life, I hardly had time to sleep.

The football coach was a short, stocky man named Rufus McGovern. He was also a preacher, but he wasn't the Lord's preacher.

Rufus loved to party. He could really whoop it up. He influenced many a boy in the ways of sin and ruin.

Sometimes Rufus would be so drunk after partying on a Saturday night, we'd think he'd never make it to his pulpit in the A.M.E. Church on Sunday morning, but he never missed a service. Many a Saturday night the boys carried Rufus to his door, their last glimpse of him being his rubbery body sliding into a heap on the floor inside his door. But on Sunday morning at 11:00 sharp he'd be standing behind that pulpit, with his wife playing the organ right beside him.

It bothered many of the boys in school. They didn't mind his partying, but they sure hated hypocrisy.

Luke Small had at least four girl friends all the time, with four more waiting in line. It was still hard for me to be around girls, or to know how to act around anybody, for that matter, but I was trying to learn. I discovered that I really liked people and so it wasn't so painful learning how to get along.

Small received big packages of food, clothing and personal items every week from his home in Bellaire, Ohio. He never told me who it was who was sending them. I received packages from home, too. Every now and then Margie sent me delicious pound cakes covered with almonds and filled with walnuts, along with stick candy and new clothes that she had made for me. I swelled with joy at these loving packages from her. I knew how dearly she paid to make a pound cake for me—she couldn't afford to make a cake like that for herself and her son, Alan. I earnestly prayed that the Lord would make me a blessing to her and that one day I'd be able to repay her for all she was doing for me.

Several months after I had arrived at school, I received a letter addressed in a childlike scrawl. I opened it carefully.

Dear Robet
Holy greeetin in Jesus name amen. We are well and hop
the same to you. I writing this myself. I thank the lord
is so wounderful he has did so meany things for me. I will
be glad to see you when the day com. Close with love.
MARgIE

I could hardly believe my eyes. Margie had written a letter! Now where did that girl learn how to write? It was a puzzle to me. I read the letter again and again, often with tears in my eyes. Had she known all along how to read and write?

Bo Brocke wasn't on the football team, and it seemed he was always studying. There wasn't really anybody as intent on his future as Bo was. I admired him for his dedication. I wanted to be like him. We would have long talks, and he would tell me of his vision to help black people. "When they's trouble, they's all kinds of law on the side of the white man and none for the black man. Nobody represents the black man when he's in front of the judge. I'm gonna be that one, yessuh. I'm gonna be a lawyer, Robert." I respected Bo more than any other boy on campus.

Bo seemed to enjoy me as much as I enjoyed him and we became good friends. I was in his room one night when a couple of the guys came by to tell us about a party off campus that night.

"It sound like it gonna be a real nice party," they told us. Bo wasn't interested. "I've got to study," he said, "and I really don't want to go to no party tonight. Especially off campus." I didn't want to go to the party either, but the guys convinced both Bo and me that we should go.

At 9:00 Bo and I were outside the dorm, sneaking down the path to the road.

26

When we were past the gate of the school, we were met by a gang of boys. Standing in the middle of the boys was Rufus McGovern. Something inside me told me to stay away from that party.

"I'm not going to no party," I said. "I'm jes not risky tonight." But before I knew what was happening, I was being pushed along with the rest of the boys, and we were all running down the side of the road toward the woods. We ran through the trees in the dark, stumbling over brush and undergrowth and branches. Finally, winded and breathless, we stopped and Rufus pulled out a bottle of moonshine. The boys cheered, and they began to pass the bottle around, each boy taking a swig. There were probably about ten of us. Small was there, too. The bottle came to me, and I took a drink. So did Bo. We looked at each other uncomfortably. When the bottle was finished they threw it on the ground, and Rufus told us to follow him.

"Now, ain't nobody gonna see us if we stay in the woods hyar and outa sight. Jes foller me."

We followed him, a little less fearful because of the quart of moonshine we had gulped down. Some of the boys were being kind of loud, and it made me nervous. They were laughing and joking, glad to be out and having a little fun. We stopped after a while, and Rufus pulled out another bottle. This time we all sat down in the trees and drank. A couple of other boys pulled out bottles, too.

I don't know who heard them first, but the first words I heard were, "There's niggers in there! Niggers!" We all scrambled to our feet.

"Niggers, Jim!"

"Oh my God, there must be a hundred!"

"Help! Help!"

I heard running and then other voices. Apparently, a pair of young lovers had been in the woods, too, and they saw us and panicked. Before we knew it, there were flashlights beamed on us and car headlights coming toward us from the road.

"There they are! Niggers!"

"This ain't nigger territory!"

"No, it ain't! They's comin' fuh trouble!"

"Help! Help! Oh my God, it's the niggers!"

Rufus shouted, "Come on!" We tore through those woods like a bunch of rats, keeping our eyes on Rufus. None of us knew where we were going except Rufus. We ran so hard, we were gasping and choking for air. I was afraid my lungs would explode. I tried to locate Bo as I ran, but I didn't see him anywhere. We reached the street, and Rufus led the way to a little house with a fence around it. "Here! Here! In here!" The boys charged toward the house, leaping the fence. There were sirens in the distance. I still couldn't see Bo. Oh, Lord, help us. I sure hope nothing happens to us tonight. We just wanted to have a good time, Lord. I turned, trying to find Bo. I ran back towards the woods to find him. "Bo!" I called, "Bo! Where are you, man?"

I heard the voices coming closer. Oh, Lord, where is Bo? "Bo! Bo!" I ran into the thicket, straining to see in the dark. If those white men caught Bo, there's no telling what they might do. "Bo!"

"I heard one of 'em, Mike!" a voice called.

"You, nigger! Stop! We heard you!"

I fell to my stomach in the thicket. I knew I was too close to them to try and make a run for it. I hoped Bo was hiding somewhere, too. When they got past us, maybe we could make a run for that house.

Then the sirens became louder, and there were more voices. A car pulled up to the edge of the woods, its lights beamed across the top of my head. Oh, Lord, the place is crawling with white men!

"Whey'd they go, Jim?"

"I heard one of 'em!"

"Hey! Look! Over there! Someone runnin' around Lily Spotter's house!"

"It's a nigger!"

"My God they're tryin' to git in Lily Spotter's house!"

"That whore'd love to git herself a nigger!"

"She's bringin' the niggers over here now!"

A woman's voice cried. "My God, none of us'll be safe!"

Someone asked, "Did you bring your gun?"

"Yor damn right I did! We'll show them niggers!"

"Bill's got his gun! I got mine, too!"

"Them nigger bastards think they kin take our wimmin and git away with it!"

"We oughter castrate 'em and then kill 'em!"

"Hey! Mike! There's about a hundred of 'em! Call the sheriff!"

"Call the marshall!"

"There they go!"

Gunfire split the air. Voices screaming and shouting followed. I heard running and then, "Wait! Hey! We got one! We got one!"

Somebody ran across the thicket where I was hiding and nearly stepped on my head. There was struggling. More feet running.

"We got a nigger! Mike! Here's one!"

I heard a terrified cry. "Noo! I ain't done nothin'!"

Dear Lord, they got Bo.

"Watchou gonna do with 'im?"

"Hang the bastard!" a woman screamed.

"You after some white wimmin tonight, nigger? Izzat what you after?"

"No! No!"

I heard the smack of a fist and something tumble to the ground. Then I heard blow after blow being laid on Bo.

"Hey! Look!"

"More niggers! Gettin' away!"

"Git over there to Lily's place! Surround the place!"

There was more commotion, more gunfire, more screaming.

"They got away! Damn! They got away!"

"Oh yeah? Well, they's gonna be a burnin' tonight! We'll show them niggers to stay away from our wimmin!"

"Oh, God, what's this world coming to?"

"Hang 'im! Hang the nigger!"

"Mike, Lily wasn't home! The house was locked up and nobody home!"

"Locked from the outside?"

"Yeah."

They were so close to me I could hear their heavy breathing. It sounded like a huge crowd.

"What yoll say we hang this nigger?"

"I'm innocent!" I heard a small voice plead. "You can't hang me without provin' I'm guilty!"

Bo was hit again. "Oh can't we, nigger! You tellin' *us* what *we* can do? Huh, nigger? Tell us about how you come over here to git some of that nice white lovin'!"

"No! I didn't even know where we were goin'—"

"*We*? Boy, who's *we*?"

"Yoll better speak, boy, or we'll tear yor arms off!"

"Who're yor friends, boy?"

"Speak!"

"He ain't talkin'. OK, Jim, git his arms."

"Break his legs!"

"String the nigger up!"

"A woman ain't safe in her own home nohow!"

"Talk, nigger! Who're yor friends?"

"He ain't gonna talk!"

"That's yor las' chance, nigger. Break his arms, Jim!"

I heard scrambling and struggling.

"I got a crowbar in my trunk!"

"Well, git it, dammit!"

"Damn! This nigger's got tough bones!"

Footsteps came running. "Here's the crowbar!"

Crack! Bo screamed. *Crack*! He screamed again, and then I heard him squealing and tumbling through the leaves in pain.

"He's tryin' to git away!"

"Look out! He's tryin' to break away!"

Pheee-ak!

"Why'd ye shoot 'im, Bill? We wuz gonna hang 'im!"

"He ain't dead yet!"

"Naw! Got 'im in the gut!"

"You rotten . . . cowards. . . ."

"You hear that? That nigger coon bastard called you a coward, Bill!"

"Yor all rotten . . . dumb—"

There was a slap. Then another blow.

"Aw, Jim, ya killed 'im!"

"We wuz gonna hang 'im!"

"He ain't dead yet!"

"Git the rope!"

"Hurry!"

There was more running, a car door slammed, and the footsteps came running back.

"Got the rope, Mike!"

"Throw it over that tree!"

"Nigger, we gonna hang yor dirty black hide from thet tree! You an' yor kind jes don't know when to stop, do ye? Think 'cause ye got yor freedom yoll can call a white man names and rape his wimmin, huh!"

"Let *me* hit him!"

"Turn the lights on him! We can't see! We want to see the black bastard hang!"

I heard scuffling.

"He's dead, I'm tellin' ye!"

"Naw, he ain't! He's jes unconscious! 'Sides, these good citizens come out to see a coon hangin' and that's what they's gonna see!"

"Tie the bastard's hands!"

"What fur? He can't move 'em!"

"Gawd, this is a messy hangin'!"

"Hold 'im up!"

"Git the car!"

Within seconds, the bright lights of a car were coming toward me. I lay still, unable to move or to get out of the way of the car. As it approached, it swerved slightly to the left and missed running over my legs by less than an inch. As it passed, I pushed farther into the thicket, down into a ditch. Nobody was standing nearby it, and I pushed myself into a deep part of the ditch, pulling the branches and gnarled vines over me.

"Got him up, Jim?"

"Got 'im!"

"OK, nigger, git on yor knees!"

"Yeah! Say yor prayers now!"

Cheers went up all around. I heard another siren in the distance.

A voice nearby said, "That nigger is dead. We is hangin' a dead man!"

"Let er rip!"

The roar of an engine and the cheer of a crowd.

The car backed up directly over the thicket I had been lying in.

"Mary! Did you see that? Thet nigger didn't even jump!"

"Watchou mean, honey?"

"Well, the las' nigger I saw git hung, soon's the bottom got pulled away, he was hangin' thar by his neck and he jump around in the air—funny like."

"Aw, this one didn't!"

"No, he didn't! Daddy, how come the nigger's body didn't jump around?"

"I don't know, honey. Let's git on home now. I ain't et mah supper yit, and I'm as hongry as a bear."

27

I lay motionless in the ditch until the sounds were gone. I knew it would be useless to try to make a break for it for several hours. There were bound to be people out all night searching for "niggers." The whole town was probably alerted. Poor Bo, poor Bo. He hadn't even wanted to go out tonight.

I didn't crawl out of the ditch until the sky was beginning to turn pale yellow in the early morning. The birds were chirping in the distance, just as if nothing was wrong. I could hardly move, my body had been cramped for so long. There was no feeling in my feet. I crawled on my knees up the sandy ledge and over into a grassy patch near a tree. Slowly, with an icy shudder, I lifted my eyes up.

There he was, right where they had left him. Not even swaying, just hanging there—still. Still. He was soaked red with blood, and beneath where he hung was a big puddle of dark red. I was stunned and sickened. I thought I'd throw up or pass out.

Lord, I've got to get him down. Tears stung my eyes. I staggered to the tree, my legs and feet tingling with feeling coming back. I tried to climb the tree but I couldn't do it; the tree was too wide, and I couldn't catch hold. Frantically I looked for something to stand on. There was nothing. Just trees. Oh Lord, I can't leave him hanging here like this! I ran back and forth crying and looking for some way to cut him down. When I heard the purr of a car engine, I stopped in my tracks. A car was cruising slowly along the edge of the woods. They're still patrolling for niggers!

I didn't know which way to run, but I knew I had to get away from the road. I had to leave Bo hanging there. I ran into the trees praying I'd find my way back to the school. I ran until I could run no more. The morning sun peered through the trees, and the darkness lifted. I cut in a diagonal in order to avoid the edges of the woods where I might come out in a white neighborhood and tried to aim in the direction I thought we had come. I stopped to wipe my face and catch my breath, and looking down I saw an empty whiskey bottle. Yes, this is the spot. Here's where I stood, and there is where Rufus was—Bo was right here next to me . . . O Lord, Bo.

I began to run again. Now I was pretty sure I knew the way back. When I saw the school on top of the hill, I ran out to the road and climbed the hill.

Inside the dorm, I was met by one of the students rushing to his first-hour class. "Man!" he whistled. "You musta had *some* time las' night. You better hurry, loverboy, 'cause you is gonna be late for class!"

I found the dorm counselor, and, weeping, I told him what had happened and how they had hung Bo. He was shocked and ran out of the office in a rage.

Within an hour three members of the faculty drove to where Bo was, with police consent, and they cut him down. They brought his body back to the school until his mama came to claim it. She came the next day, a thin little lady wearing round glasses and a flowered hat. I wanted to say something to her, tell her how her son had died a hero.

The funeral was held in the church Bo had attended as a boy. His mama looked at me with tragic eyes, her thin, stiff face struggling to remain calm. "Son," she said quietly, "did you see my boy die?"

"Well, mam, I was there, but I couldn't see—"

"Did he pray before—before—"

"Mam," I answered quickly, "when a good man is killed for no reason, the Lord is there. The Lord was there, mam, with his arms around Bo. I know. Because God is a just God."

She wept softly.

"Mam . . ." I stammered, "I want yoll to know . . . he didn't get on his knees for them. And he wouldn't give the names of his friends . . ."

She blinked back the tears. "Well, ain't that somethin'? I always knowed he was a lot on the brave side. . . ."

Life at the school after Bo's death became very difficult for everybody for a while. The students were not allowed off campus, and we knew we were in danger. Nothing was done about Bo's murder, in spite of the protests and influence of the faculty. There was talk of Rufus being kicked off the faculty, but that's all it was—talk. Rufus stayed on.

Rufus had made it back to the school safely with the other boys that night. His lady friend, Lily Spotter, had decided not to have a party after all, but went to a movie instead. Rufus seemed more upset about her not being home than he was over Bo's death. "You live and die," he said. "Bo was a good man, but it's the livin' we got to think about. It's the livin' who count in this world, not the dead."

When Christmas vacation came, I stayed at the school and worked for some extra money, which I sent home to Margie. I withdrew into myself after Bo's hanging and became dedicated to my classwork and job. I think somewhere inside me I wanted to take Bo's place and finish what he had dreamed of doing. When spring break came, I got a job off campus painting houses, and I rented a room two blocks away from school in the home of a widow lady named Mrs. Black. She was about eighty years old, wore her teeth only on Sunday, and believed shoes were a sin to your feet. She cooked my meals for me, and every night when I came home after work, she'd be waiting by the window for me.

September of 1931 was as busy as the fall quarter the year before. Small was my roommate again, and we would talk on into the night about sports and girls. I was recovering from Bo's death.

It was right before Christmas vacation when another incident happened that alarmed the school. There had been some more murmurings around town that some black man had raped a white woman. Whenever a rumor like that was started, every black family had to be extremely cautious. One of the first-year students got careless, however. On a sunny Monday afternoon, whistling and singing as he walked back to the campus after running an errand, a car stopped beside him on the road. There were three white men inside. "Hey, boy! Can we give you a lift?" The unsuspecting student thanked them and got into the car.

The men drove him to a garage some distance away and castrated him. Then they drove him outside of town and dumped him at the side of the road. A black farmer found him later that day and took him to the hospital in Walhalla. He was in critical condition for several weeks and never came back to school again. We learned later that he committed suicide.

I went back to Anderson for Christmas vacation that year. Margie was thrilled to see me, and it was a wonderful vacation. In the evening I read the Bible to the family as they sat around the wood-burning stove in the center of the room.

"You know, Robert," Margie told me smiling, "Jesus make it all worth while."

"Yes, He do," I said softly.

"God is a good God, Robert."

I took her hand and stroked it. "Margie, you know, being at school is—well, it's givin' me more than book learnin'. And one thing I know is that the Lord can carry a man through anything. It ain't that He takes all the bad away and puts all good in its place; it's that He gives you strength to take the bad as well as the good—you understand what I'm talkin' about?"

"I understand, chile, I surely do."

"And sometimes the bad is—really bad. . . ."

"That's the God hepp me truth."

Back at school I was making some new discoveries. For instance, I discovered that a black man named George Washington Carver made hundreds of things out of peanuts and became very famous, and even the President came to visit him. I also learned about a man born as a slave named Frederick Douglass, who became one of the greatest orators in the country, holding political offices and speaking everywhere against slavery. I learned about another black man named Matthew Henson who went to the North Pole with Commander Peary, and Robert Smalls, who had been a slave in South Carolina and became a representative from the state to the U.S. Congress.

Then there was Booker T. Washington, who had been born a slave and had hungered to go to school, the same as I had. He worked hard to get his learning, and he founded the world-famous Tuskegee Institute in Alabama. He taught that black people should stick together, work hard, and improve themselves by education and effort before trying to integrate with the white people. He organized the National Business League.

All this new information made my head swim. I had been taught that Negroes had no souls, that they were born only to serve the white man. Now I was learning about talented and brilliant Negroes who were history-makers and great world leaders.

I especially loved to read about the abolitionists like Sojourner Truth and Frederick Douglass. They had been slaves, too, and devoted their lives to putting an end to slavery. Mr. Douglass taught that whites and blacks should have equal rights and work together side by side.

I was beginning to break loose from the prejudice and hatred that had formed my thinking and attitudes as a child. For the first time in my life I was seeing my people with hope—not only in their own camp, but in the world. I was learning that I could be and do anything—even be a lawyer like Bo Brocke wanted to be.

It had been seven years since I escaped from slavery.

I would not talk about it or tell anyone that I had been a slave. I was ashamed of it. To tell my schoolmates that I had been a slave would have been unthinkable.

28

In November of 1932 Roosevelt was elected president. I knew a little more now about presidents, but not much more about elections.

I dedicated myself to studying that year. I spent every spare minute reading and practicing my writing.

In the spring I went to visit Mrs. Black. I found her in a field near her house picking dandelion greens. She smiled a broad, toothless grin when she saw me, "Robert! Ah declare!" We went back to her house, and she put the greens on to boil with a hunk of salt pork, and then she dipped the yellow tops in batter and deep-fried them. With warm corn bread from the oven and cold buttermilk, it was a delicious meal. "Robert," she asked me after we had eaten, "how much room do the Lord have in yor life?" I nearly fell from my chair when she asked me that.

"Huh?"

"Give Him room, son, give Him room."

"Well, I—"

"You gots thet worried look about ye, and they ain't no good to worryin'. That's what we got a Lord fer so *He* can do the worryin'."

When it began to grow dark, I kissed her good-bye and headed back to the school.

"Yoll come back, and we'll pick us some poke salad!"

I did go back, at least once a week, until the month before summer break in 1933. Mrs. Black was like tonic on a wound. I could hardly wait to get an outside job and rent a room at her house again.

It had been a month since I'd seen her. It was a hot afternoon when I walked up the road to her little wood-frame house on the hill. I felt good, and I was glad the hot weather was here again and glad for the chance to work and make some money to send home to Margie. I looked forward to the quiet evenings with Mrs. Black, her good cooking, and the warm, loving friendship we shared.

I mounted the wooden steps and noticed the door was closed and the curtains drawn across the windows. I knocked loudly and waited for the sound of her bare feet padding along the floor. There was no answer. I knocked again. When there was no answer I went around to the back. The back door was closed, too, with a padlock nailed on the outside. I never knew her to lock anything. I picked up my small grip and went back around to the front to wait. Maybe she was visiting. I had waited for over an hour when a heavyset woman carrying some packages in her arms came walking up the hill. She looked up at me and called, "You waitin' on Miz Black?"

"Yes, mam."

"Honey, she done died." I sucked in my breath and my throat tightened. "They found her las' week in that house. She had been dead for almost a month and nobody knew it. You a kin o' hers?"

"—Uh—a kin? No . . ."

"Well, they didn't have no funeral on account o' she didn't have no kin and nobody to give her one, so they took her out and buried her. I see they ain't boarded the place up yit. Well, they oughta. People gonna break in there and—"

The woman stood by the steps and talked for what seemed like forever. I hardly heard a word she said.

Finally I interrupted. "How did they find her?"

"Insurance man come by. Insurance man knocked on the door and smelled somethin' terrible. He peek in and there she was—on the kitchen floor. Half-rotten, they say. Insurance man never did get his money."

I rose to my feet and picked up my grip. "Ain't that a shame?" the woman continued. "No kin to cash in that insurance money or to get this house—"

I walked for hours, around in circles I think, unaware of the beautiful summer day. Sometime in the late afternoon I came to the familiar clearing where the neighborhood variety store was. It had a gas pump outside, and inside was a little bit of everything, including groceries, dry goods, and a counter where food was served. I opened the screen door and went inside. Met by the lazy drone of a fan and a "Hiyoll" from the Negro lady behind the counter, I sat down on a stool, took a deep breath, and ordered lunch.

29

I spent the summer of 1933 painting houses and doing handyman jobs around town. I rented a room from a family three blocks from campus. I was able to save over fifty dollars, which I put in an envelope and took home to Anderson for Margie at the end of the summer.

It was wonderful to see Margie again. She seemed more worn and tired than the last time I had seen her but her spirit was high. I asked her how she learned to write. She told me that after I went off to school, she had prayed and asked the Lord to make it possible for her to learn how to read and write.

"Chile, it wasn't two days later but they was a knock on the door and a lady standin' there tellin' me about free classes in readin' and writin' jes two blocks yonder. I thought she was a white angel. You think they's any white angels, Robert? Hee! Hee! Praise the Lord!"

The vacation ended all too soon, and before I knew it I was getting ready to catch the bus back to Seneca. Margie watched me pull the strap closed on my grip. "Honey," she said with a low voice, "yoll take care of yo'self and don't get into any trouble, hyar?" From the look on her face, I knew she meant more than what she had said.

"Now what you tryin' to say, girl?" I asked.

Margie's chin quivered. "And another thing, *don't forgit me.*"

"Huh?"

"Now thassall. Gimme a kiss."

Sitting on the bus with the dry, pungent smells of upholstery and cigar smoke nipping my nostrils, I thought of Margie's face. Even though she was tough, fearless, and strong as a mule, her thirty-three years seemed more like sixty. She acted as though I was never coming back. I leaned my head against the window. Only dying could keep me from her, I thought. And Lord, I sure don't want to die.

Back at school, I found a new interest in the extracurricular activities. Luke Small was a big influence on me. "I'm fed up with this place," he would grumble. "I's leavin' this hyar place." I didn't pay any attention to him at first, but as the weeks went by, I found myself agreeing with him. "Yeah," I grumbled along with him, "this place is strifling."

Late night hours and a poor attitude caused me to get behind in my school work. Soon I began cutting classes and piling up unexcused absences.

In late October, after I had been at school almost four years, I was coming from the small log cabin library and walking toward the men's dorm when Small came running from across the lawn toward me.

"Sadler," he said with a large grin, "you and me is leavin' this hyar place tomorrow."

"Huh?"

"Thas right, man. We is leavin'."

"Watchou mean—*we*?"

"You and me, brother. You and me. We is hoppin' the ole freight and goin' on to Ohio!"

I felt a tinge of excitement streak through me. "O-Ohio?"

"We'll hobo to my house in Bellaire. Howzat sound?"

"Well—I—"

I thought of Margie and the money she had worked overtime to be able to send to me so I could get an education. "Uh, I donno, Small—"

Before I had a chance to say anything more, he was waving and jitterbugging down the path toward the dining hall.

That afternoon, instead of doing my studying, I left the campus and walked along the dirt path which led through the wooded area onto a winding dirt road I knew well. Tiny houses and shanties were scattered along the edge of the road, and I walked slowly, kicking pebbles and looking at the shacks. How many of the blacks in those houses could read? I wondered. How many of them could write numbers and figure out if they were being cheated or not on their groceries or their rent receipts?

I could read and write pretty well now, and I was proud of my book learning. If I stayed at Seneca, I could graduate and go on to college. Maybe be an engineer or a lawyer—an important person to help my people.

A little black child about three years old ran to the edge of the road. "Hi," I called. She smiled shyly. I looked beyond her to her mother hanging wash on the line. Wearing an old cotton dress, wet with perspiration, barefooted, her hair tied up in a rag, she paused for a second to look at me and then continued her work.

She lived over here in a shack, sweating and struggling to make enough food for her family, and I lived over there across the road up in the big school being educated so someday I wouldn't have to live like her. And maybe if I made it through I'd be able to help my people so others wouldn't have to live like her either. The love of learning was wearing off, and I was becoming critical and restless. Oh Lord, what'll I do?

When I arrived back at school later that afternoon, I was met by the dorm counselor. "Sadler," he said, taking me by the shoulder, "you already been on probation once; you ain't going to get much mercy if you keep skippin' classes."

"Oh . . . yeah . . ."

"By the way, how you doin' in your classes?"

"I uh—OK, I guess. Jes fine."

"In other words, you're failing."

"Yessuh."

"Man, Sadler, you gonna get yourself the title of First Man of the Year to Be Expelled."

I sucked in my breath. *Expelled!* Out of the corner of my eye I saw Small leave the building. I chased after him. "Small!" He turned. "Listen, Small, you still fixin' to leave tomorrow?"

"Uh huh."

"OK, it's a deal."

He smiled, pulling his shoulders back. "OK, Sadler. I'll tell you when."

I went back to my room and began packing my things. I could still hear the voice of the dorm counselor, "First Man of the Year to Be Expelled." I had no choice. I might as well leave before they kicked me out.

When I had my things packed in boxes, Small insisted we send everything to his house in Bellaire, Ohio. I agreed, even though I didn't like the idea, and we carried the boxes to the post office, addressed to his house. I paid for the postage because Small had no money.

We carried nothing with us. By the time we got to the railroad tracks that night, I was so scared my knees trembled.

"When you grabs on, you throws your body out like

this here," Small told me. "You gots to be careful, but once you gits hold of that handhold and you swings your feets on up on the rung, you're OK. Got it?"

"Small, I never done this before. What if—"

"Listen! Here she come! Now watch how I do it, and then you grab on right after me! Git ready!"

The train was moving slowly out of the station toward us. We would jump on just before it picked up speed. My Lord! I didn't realize how loud a train could be up close! Jesus, help me! The wheels were like death, powerful crashing steel against the rails. There goes Small! I saw his body fly out exactly as he had told me, then his knees curled under him, and he was safely on the ladder. Here it comes. The swaying boxcar rumbled past me, and holding my breath, I ran alongside, grabbed the cold metal handhold, and threw my body out like Small had instructed, hanging on with all my strength. When I felt my feet underneath me on the rung and the cool night air whipping at my face, I knew I was safe. I had made it. I was leaving the solid South and on my way to Ohio.

Small crawled along the top of the car to me, and we rode in the blind. "This here is the passenger train," he shouted. "We'll take it to Atlanta, Georgie, and then we'll take a freight!"

I nodded vigorously without knowing what he was talking about. "Then we take the freight to Knoxville! We gets into a coal car and covers ourselves with coal. That way the cops won't find us."

"Cops?"

"Sure. These trains is loaded with them. Each stop they inspect the cars, lookin' for hobos."

When the train began to slow down, Small explained that we were stopping for water. "Now listen, hang on right where you is until you see a cop comin'. When you see the cop, cross over to the other side of the car and hang on till he pass. That way he won't catch you."

I didn't know what he meant. When the train stopped, I hopped down and landed smack into a cop. Before I could say anything or do anything, he grabbed me. He wouldn't let me get back on, and the train pulled out without me. I watched the train rumble into the distance, and when its sounds were gone I stood alone in the silence of the countryside. I didn't have any idea where I was. I began walking along the track hoping another train would come along before the day was up. When it grew dark, I slept in the weeds alongside the track. I awoke when I heard the whistle of a train. It was going north so I knew I had to get on it.

Remembering Small's instructions, I ran alongside the cars, but they were going a lot faster than the other time. Groaning, I grabbed the handhold, threw my body out and hung on for dear life. Finally, I got my legs under me, and my feet were on the rungs of the ladder. I had made it. I climbed up to the top of the ladder and got on the roof of a boxcar and sat down. I didn't know what was shaking more—me or the train. After a while, though, I began to feel pretty good up there, and I began to sing and clap as the train clacked along. It wasn't long before I heard someone shout and, startled, I looked down into a man's face. "Hey you!" he called. "Git offa the roof!" I stared at him, frightened. "I ain't no cop!" he shouted. "Git offa the roof!" He beckoned me to follow him, and hesitantly I climbed down and followed him to the car in front of us. It was an open empty coal car.

"Look!" the man pointed. I looked up and saw we were entering a tunnel. I would have been killed if I had been sitting on the roof. There was no headroom. "Got a rag or somethin'?" my mysterious friend asked. "Yeah," I answered, pulling a handkerchief from my pocket. "Cover your face. You'll strangle to death in the smoke if you don't."

At Atlanta I climbed off the train and got on the one my new friend pointed out. "It'll take you to Knoxville. From there, catch the train to Cincinnati. Then you're on your own." I was grateful to him, but before I got a chance to thank him, he was gone.

I made it to Knoxville—cold, exhausted, dirty, and hungry, and without a penny to my name.

I got confused at the trainyard, and couldn't find the train to Cincinnati. I walked up and down the tracks ducking behind cars every time I saw someone coming. It soon became clear to me that I wasn't going to find the train to Cincinnati, and there was nothing to do but to find something to eat and somewhere to sleep in Knoxville.

Tumble-down shacks and heaps of old junk spread along the trainyard edge. I looked beyond at the Smoky Mountains in the distance, beautiful and blue in the grey sky. The downtown district was hilly with narrow streets and low buildings. As I climbed and dipped with the hills, I could see church spires reaching upward behind the hills and along the building tops. I found a small park and stretched out on the grass. It was two weeks before I got back to the trainyard.

Panhandling, bumming, cooking outside over an open fire, sleeping on the grass in the park until the police kicked me out, and then dropping to sleep in doorways, back alleys, and empty lots was the way I spent those two weeks.

Then one rainy afternoon I met a fuzzy-faced old hobo huddled under a tree in the park. We got to talking. "Yeah-suh," he drawled, "ah reckon ah'm goin' to take me a trip to Cincie." I was delighted. "If yoll wouldn't be mindin', I'd like to tarry along with yoll." We headed for the trainyard in the rain and hopped the right train with no trouble. The ride was smooth-going all the way. I slept that night in some wet weeds on a bank of the Ohio River and the next morning hopped the freight to Bellaire.

When I arrived in Bellaire, I didn't know where to go to find Small, but I did remember he said he lived on Noble Street. That was all I knew. I began to walk. I asked directions from several people, and I wearied myself trying to figure them out. "Lord, show me the place," I prayed. Finally, I found myself standing in front of a two-story brick house with box hedges around it. I stared up at it. I didn't even know if I was on Noble Street or not. I walked up the stairs and rang the bell. A middle-aged, brown-skinned woman, grey hair smoothed into two buns on either side of her face, answered.

"Afternoon, mam, I'm coming from Seneca Junior College, and I'm a friend of Luke Small—"

"A friend of Luke's!" the woman exclaimed. "Come in! Come in!" The Lord had answered my prayer. The woman took my arm and ushered me into a small, cozy living room. "Nancy! Come on in here." A young pretty woman hurried into the room, her eyes wide, a little smile on her lips.

"How is Luke? Is he with you?" the older woman asked.

I stared back dumbly. "He ain't here yet? We left school together nearly three weeks ago. I lost him before we got to Atlanta."

A little boy about three years old bounced into the hallway and stood grinning at me from the door. The older woman smiled. "This is Eddie," she said. "Luke's son. Eddie will be so happy to see his daddy again." Then indicating the young woman she said, "This is Nancy, Luke's wife. I'm sure Luke has told you all about *her*." Then laughing she added, "And I'm Luke's mother."

I stared at Luke's wife, my mouth hanging open dumbly. "I'm uh—Robert. Robert Sadler, mam."

Luke, you dog!

They fluttered around me asking questions about their "Luke," and I just kept staring at his lovely little wife in amazement. Small's son pulled at my pant leg and grinned up at me, wanting to play.

Luke Small, you dog!

I thought for sure Small would arrive home any time, so I stayed in their home for a week, but he didn't show up. When I heard they were hiring in Dayton, I said good-bye to Small's family and hopped a freight. I got a job there as a sandwich man in a country club. I kept in touch with Small's mother, who was a sweet and kind lady, and month after month rolled by without any word from her son. Finally, after six months had gone by, Small arrived home. I never did get a chance to see him.

The job at the country club lasted about seven months. I would have stayed longer if it hadn't been so lonely there for me. I had a room at the club and had to spend most of my time there with hardly anyone to talk to. The most exciting thing that happened to me in those months was that the Ringling Bros. Circus came to town. I walked into Dayton every night to see it. I love the circus so much that I tried to get a job with them. There were no openings, but that didn't discourage me. I'd wait. The days went by and still no openings. Finally it was time for the circus to move on to Detroit, and I hadn't gotten a job with them yet. I was so enamored of Ringling Bros., I left the country club and followed them to Detroit. I hoboed on the same train.

There was another hobo on the train with me, a white man from New York who told me he was a barber. He had all of his tools in a bag alongside him. I was very impressed and would probably have asked him for a haircut once we got to Detroit if three robbers hadn't jumped into the car with us. They stole everything from us that they could. They took all his barber's tools, and though I didn't have much money, they took what I had. So I arrived in Detroit without a change of clothes, a penny to my name, or a haircut.

30

It was hot and the busy, noisy crowded streets of Detroit were strange and frightening to me. This was up north now, and black people walked on the same side of the street with the white people. They weren't in love with each other, but they walked next to each other, sat next to each other, and talked with each other. There were black and white bums in the park, too. They ate together, panhandled together, robbed together, and slept in the same park together under their respective newspaper coverings.

I arrived in Detroit in August of 1934, the year Hitler became dictator of Germany. The Depression had hit America, and jobs and money were hard to come by. Ringling Bros. didn't need any more men, and so I had no choice but to sleep in the park and panhandle. I slept and hung around downtown in Grand Circus Park, a round little park with fountains, several statues, flower beds, and ten streets fanning out from it. There were so many people who stayed in that park that we called it the Grand Circus Hotel. Whole families slept on the benches and on the grass. It wasn't a safe place by any means. Night after night I heard screams for help. A person got used to it.

I learned how to beware and watch out for danger. I had to be careful which alley I entered because a person could get beat up and killed for as little as 25¢ or a pair of shoes.

Living in this hopelessness and seeing nothing but hunger and desperate people everywhere, the worst happened and I started drinking. At first it was just because there was nothing else to do. It wasn't many weeks before I was stealing to pay for my wine, just like the others. I never became an alcoholic, but I drank a lot and stayed drunk much of the time. Many nights I landed in the jail on Gratiot Street.

I am thankful that I never mugged anybody—and nobody ever mugged me. Those days in the city were some of the loneliest of my life. I would walk the streets of downtown along Randolph to Cadillac Square, and I'd stand and stare at the City Council Building with its tower reaching for the sky. I'd sit and look at the massive, looming Penobscot Building and the J. L. Hudson Building. I'd walk south of Michigan Avenue to the heart of the business center and panhandle. I'd walk north of Michigan Avenue on either side of Woodward Avenue and panhandle where the shopper traffic was. I was falling fast and far from the Lord and everything sweet.

Nearly every day I went to one of the missions for a free bowl of soup. I had to sit through the meetings before I could get the soup, and I sat there with my head lowered, ashamed of myself and ashamed to look up. The men and women in the missions were very kind, and they seemed to genuinely care about the men who came there. When October and the cold weather began, I slept in the mission.

It seemed like there were hundreds of us panhandling and looking for a handout. The streets were lined with bums and derelicts. I looked and acted no different than the rest of them. At night in the mission meetings, I struggled not to cry, but the tears would slide down my unshaven, dirty cheeks as shame and self-disgust flooded my heart.

It got worse, though. A couple of men had an apartment where they ran some illegal gambling and other illegal things. But when they asked if I wanted to live there in exchange for keeping the place clean and acting as a bouncer, I agreed gladly. I was so eager to get off the streets, I didn't care where I went.

It was like moving into the first floor of hell. The parties went on continually all day and all night. I saw things there that I never dreamed people could do—orgies, drunks, dope peddling, prostitution, and all forms of perversion went on in that place. Many nights I never got to bed because someone would be in my bed—often two men or two women.

Those days and nights have blurred together in my mind. The men who rented the apartment bought me new clothes, and I had a fancy cigarette case and lighter, a big, shiny ring on my finger, polished shoes, and I grew a mustache. At the age of twenty-three, I was caught in a terrible trap of degradation and sin, but I was fed, clothed, and too scared and dumb to get out.

One day when I was running an errand for my bosses, I stopped at a bar and ballroom nearby and discovered they needed a janitor. I begged them for the job and, surprisingly, got it. That night I moved out of the apartment and moved into a room in the house of a widow lady and her young, pretty niece, a college student. We fell for one another in a big way.

I was thankful to be out of the apartment, but my life didn't change much. Every cent I made went for liquor and foolishness. I stopped paying rent because the landlady had hopes I'd marry her niece, and she treated me like I was already her son. She didn't know I had about four other girl friends just as eager as her niece.

I wrote a letter to Margie and asked her to come to Detroit. I hoped that if Margie came to Detroit, we could get a place together and I would straighten out then. I told her that wages were better and how good things were up north.

In 1935 I got a job on the WPA. I had to stand in line from 12:00 midnight until 9:00 the next morning to get in. That's how it was. When I got to the front they gave me a pick and shovel.

Lord, I didn't want to work with a pick and shovel! I had seen enough pick and shovel on the plantation. I could hear Thrasher's whip whistling through the air as we dug a ground so cold and hard that our hands often bled before the ditches were dug. I went to work though—by day with a pick and shovel, and in the early morning hours cleaning at the bar and ballroom.

One day the foreman at WPA asked if any of us men were interested in learning cement finishing. I jumped at the chance to get rid of the pick and shovel. Soon I was working as a cement finisher, putting curbs in streets and driveways and earning $10 a day. I wrote to Margie again begging her to come to Detroit.

Margie finally answered me and said she couldn't come and leave Dad, who was down sick. Then she said that Janey was making plans to come to Detroit.

Janey arrived all smiles and done up pretty, toting a lot of boxes and grips. She rented herself a house, which she later bought. She moved me into it with her, and then she moved some man in to pay her bills. Not only did she take this man for every dime he had, she used him to start a little business of her own. Her house became a house of prostitution and gambling. Again I was right in the middle of it all. I developed a passion for gambling, and I had my pick of the girls.

Janey was very pretty and had a way with men. She could win any man she set out to get, and once she won him, she was boss. She gave the orders, and he would hand over the paychecks to her.

I wanted to ask Janey what happened to her relationship to Jesus. I wanted to say, "You supposed to be a Christian, how come you runnin' a bad house?" But how could I jump on her with accusations when I was just as guilty as she? It was the blind leading the blind—blind Janey leading blind me.

The months went by. I forgot all about Jesus. I was Janey's right-hand man. I hustled business for her, sold her liquor, ran a gambling table, roughed up anyone who wouldn't pay up, and kept a close eye over the whole operation. We pulled in more money than either one of us had ever seen. It wasn't long before Janey bought a newer and bigger house. Her prices went up and so did the class of girls she had working for her. They were college girls, and they wore fur coats. They were white-skinned and black-skinned, although most of our customers were white. White men rarely asked for white girls.

I fell in love with one of the girls. I dropped the widow's niece when I moved in with Janey, and Monica came into my life. It was a stormy relationship.

"Let's get married," Monica would plead.

"Girl, you crazy."

We would fight and she would accuse me of not loving her. We would rage and rant and break things, and many times someone else would have to come and break up the fight. Janey was afraid we'd bring the police down on us.

One Sunday night when I was dealing cards at one of the tables, Monica told me she had a headache and went upstairs to lie down. Later that night she still wasn't feeling any better, and I thought she was just faking. A couple of hours later one of the girls came down and told me she wanted to take Monica to the hospital because she was acting peculiar. I nodded to go ahead.

On Monday I went to see her in the hospital. She said she felt much better and her fever was gone. She looked pale and thin, though, and I thought she looked like she needed a good rest. When I went back to see her on Tuesday, she was dead.

I will never forget standing in that hospital room holding a bunch of flowers in my hand and staring at that empty bed. The sheets were pulled off, and the grey and white stripes of the mattress stared back at me where just yesterday a young, beautiful girl had lain waiting for her health to return.

Something broke in me as I stood there staring at that empty bed. It was as though my whole life spilled out of me onto the hospital floor. I saw the fithy trap I was in, the hopelessness, and the tragedy of it. I stood there trembling, not knowing which way to turn. Then in the silence there came a voice. It was a powerful voice, distant and yet near.

"Robert," the voice called softly, "will you not come to me now before it is too late?"

It was such a glorious sound, as though all the oceans and seas of the world were in its sound, and all love and compassion that ever existed was in those words. "Oh, Lord! Lord!" I sobbed.

I fell to my knees right there in the hospital room and begged the Lord to forgive me and take me back. After weeping and praying for a while I laid the flowers on the bed and left.

I walked the streets all night crying and begging God to have mercy on me.

Finally I went back to Janey's but locked myself in my room, refusing to eat or drink. Janey thought I was crying over Monica's death, but I wasn't. I was crying because I wanted Jesus to take me back, and I was afraid I had gotten too far away to get back to Him. It was terrible.

The following Sunday I found a church nearby. I went up to the altar and the preacher asked me what I wanted. "I want you to pray for me," I said with tears streaming down my face. He pointed to a side door and instructed me to go through it, and the elders would get me ready to be baptized.

"I don't want to be baptized, I want to be prayed for!" I argued. The preacher sent me into the side room anyway, and there I was met by three stern-faced elders who handed me a robe to put on in order to get baptized.

"I am not going in that water a dry devil and come out a wet one!" I insisted, but they wouldn't hear of it. They wanted me to join the church. "I don't want to join your church; I want somebody to pray for me! I'm a sinner and a backslider, and I want to get right with God!" They didn't seem to know what I was talking about, and so I left there, frustrated and defeated.

I went back to Janey's, but I couldn't sleep. I got out

of bed and prayed, "Show me a church where I can go, Lord!" The following Sunday I found a little storefront church. The door was open so I walked in and sat down quietly in the back. A young man was standing up near the altar praying, but there was nobody else there. He didn't know I had come in.

I sat quietly for a few moments, but then the young man's praying began to fill up the room. He was facing the front wall so he couldn't see me. He had his arms up in the air. As he prayed, I suddenly began to shake. I fell right off the chair and lay prostrate on the floor. When I looked up, there were about a half-dozen people praying over me. The young man had his hand on my forehead, and he was praying and weeping over me.

They helped me back onto the chair, and I tried to tell them what had happened and why I was there. "I know why you're here," the young man said. "You're here because you have strayed a long way from the Lord, but now you want to come back to Him." I stared at him in amazement. "How did you know?" I asked him.

He smiled at me. "The Holy Spirit told me you were coming, so I got here early to pray for you."

31

It was not easy to return to Janey's that afternoon. She was asleep and I woke her up.

"Jay," I said in a firm voice, "I'm not selling any more whiskey for you, I am not bringing any more men in for you, and I am not gambling, drinking, or carousing any more. I'm finished. Don't you ask me to do a dirty thing again."

She sat up in bed, looked at me calmly and said, "OK, Robert." Just like that.

"I went to church today and I'm going to be leading a new life from now on. The Lord has given me another chance."

Janey yawned and blinked her eyes. "OK, Robert," she said.

I moved out of the house that afternoon. I didn't even take a change of clothing. I had only about 80¢ in my pocket and no place to go, but I didn't care. I was so happy to be back with the Lord that nothing else mattered to me.

I walked down the street thanking Jesus out loud. I'd laugh and cry at the same time, and people looked at me as though I were crazy. I was crazy—crazy for Jesus.

That evening I went back to the little storefront church. The same young man who had prayed for me was there. We prayed together and talked for a long time—in fact, almost all night.

"You know, I don't even know your name," I said. He looked at me and laughed. "My name is Robert, too. Robert Jones."

Then he looked at me with an odd expression on his face. "Robert . . . Robert Sadler. I *knew* your name was familiar. And your face surely looks familiar. I *do* know ye!"

"Huh?"

"I was livin' in Seneca yonder across the road from the school where you was a student. My mama took me to the same church you went to every week."

"Lord, have mercy."

"I remember you played left tackle on the football team!"

"Do you remember that?"

"The coach, Rufus McGovern, is livin' real quiet now. In fact, he's repented of his ways."

"That's a miracle from God!"

I got a job as a caretaker in an apartment building on Harding Street a couple of days later. There was a restaurant near the little storefront church and I became friendly with the proprietor, a balding old man with silver fuzz at his ears. He had a heavy, middle-aged girl friend named Cora who sat at the counter drinking Coca-Cola in the afternoons. The day she first spotted me she had her eye on me for her niece who lived in Cincinnati.

"I want you to write to my niece," she'd tell me. At first I thought she was joking. "Where your niece is?" I'd ask.

"She's in Cincinnati and she's a fine girl. She is your type of girl."

I finally wrote to her and she answered me. We began corresponding regularly. Her name was Jacqueline Brown Graham.

One day I bought a train ticket to Cincinnati to meet Jacqueline. I walked up the steps to the nicely kept house she lived in with her parents, my heart in my throat. I couldn't figure out why I was nervous. I wasn't exactly an inexperienced boy.

Jacqueline answered the door. She was very pretty—tall and elegant-looking in a grey crepe dress with ruffles on the sleeves and the neck; she had long black hair brushed up on the top or her head in a roll. There was a gentle smile on her face.

I fell in love with Jacqueline and we were married on June 28, 1939. It was a small wedding attended by Robert Jones, Janey, Jackie's Aunt Cora, and the Baptist preacher who married us.

Jackie was a good church-goer, but I didn't realize she wasn't a real Christian. She was clean, good, and lived an honest life without smoking, drinking, or swearing, but she didn't know the Lord. I prayed for her every day, asking Jesus to save her soul and come into her heart. It took nine years for that prayer to be answered.

We moved into the upstairs apartment of a beautiful home at 99 King Street in Detroit. It was the home of a doctor and his wife. Jacqueline worked for the doctor during the day doing general housekeeping, and I worked at a hotel off Woodward near a Catholic church, shining shoes. Then Jackie and I started a little business together doing cooking and catering for the Association of Detroit Women's Clubs. Jacqueline was an excellent cook and was very good at making fancy things and delicacies.

I had a succession of jobs from caretaking to gardening, and in 1941 I went to school to learn machine operating. After I graduated, I got a job at Ford Motors. We had few financial worries in those days. I made a good living and Jackie and I were very happy.

I often took the streetcar downtown to Grand Circus Park to tell the people there about Jesus. Many gave their hearts to Him. I also held a Bible class in our home for young people every Saturday night.

From outward appearances Jackie acted like a Christian. But she wouldn't give her heart to the Lord, and she rarely accompanied me to church. She lived a more exemplary life than many people who called themselves Christians, and she didn't think she needed a personal relationship with the Lord.

She occasionally attended a Methodist church near the house. "They're quiet and reverent," she'd tell me. "Not like your church. Everyone hollering and making so much noise praising the Lord and all, it's plain *distracting*."

"Honey, the Bible don't tell us we have to be quiet when we worship the Lord."

"Well, I don't like that noise no way."

She was a good wife in every way, and we rarely argued. I didn't want to ruin the love we had for one another by arguing and fussing with her.

Though I didn't argue with Jackie, that doesn't mean that I didn't argue with God. "God, you *got* to save my wife! Lord, save her! Oh, God, save Jackie!" I begged, pleaded, moaned, groaned. I made promises and sacrificed, I fasted and did everything I could think of to impress God with the seriousness of my request. The years rolled by, and Jackie remained as cold as ever to the Gospel.

I wanted Jackie to know Jesus the way I did. If only she would love Him and trust her life to Him. I think I wanted this more than anything in the world. Sometimes I got discouraged, and I would get to feeling sorry for myself. We shared everything else in life, and yet this one vital, beautiful thing we didn't share.

Finally, I began to thank God for my wife exactly the

way she was. I thanked God and humbled myself. I knew God had hand-picked Jackie for me, and I repented for complaining that she wasn't a Christian.

The Bible study in our home began with six people. Many came to the Lord in those meetings. It grew into a group of about forty, until finally we couldn't get any more into the house. Jackie was never in favor of it. She often stayed in the bedroom or downstairs during our meetings. The young people just loved her anyhow, and went out of their way to show her kindnesses.

One afternoon at my machine at Ford, I bowed my head and said, "Lord, I'm not fasting anymore for Jackie's salvation, I'm not begging anymore, I'm not pleading anymore. Lord, you do with her whatever you want to do."

Jackie became a Christian the next week.

After Bible study at our house on Saturday night, we had gone to bed and while she was sleeping, Jackie had a dream. In her dream she saw a beautiful church. She could hear wonderful music coming from inside, which was so lovely and inviting that she ran up to it to go inside. Standing at the door, however, was a splendid-appearing man who put his hand up as she tried to enter. He asked, "Why are you coming in here?" Jackie said, "Why, I'm a member here." Then the man, who Jackie said was glorious to behold, asked if her name was written in the "book." Jackie said, "Oh yes, I'm sure of it. After all, I am a member of the church!" The man took out a great book with pages that seemed to be endless, and he looked for her name. Closing the book at last, he said, "I'm so sorry, but you may not enter. Only those whose names are written in this book belong here."

She was so frightened when she awoke she didn't know what to do first. She told me about the dream and asked me to interpret it for her. Then she burst into tears. She already knew what the dream meant. "Last week," she wept, "I would have laughed at that dream. For some reason today it's not funny. O Lord, I don't want to be left out!"

She dressed and left the house before even eating breakfast. I caught a streetcar and arrived in church just before the service began. Taking a seat, I looked up at the altar, and there was Jackie on her knees at the altar giving her heart to Jesus.

32

The Lord allowed me to help several other black people from the South come north to get better jobs. I wrote to Margie regularly asking her to come to Detroit, but she flatly refused to leave Dad. He was old and sick, and she wouldn't leave him.

Jackie and I were thrilled to be able to help our people who were still trapped in the poverty and bigotry of the South. We were able to send clothing, food, money, and help to those who wanted to come north. The employment manager at General Motors told me that he'd hire as many blacks from the South as I sent in. I was able to help over thirty men from South Carolina get good jobs in Detroit. It brought back familiar memories as they arrived in Detroit. Illiterate and knowing little more than farming, they were like lost children and were scared. Our upstairs apartment was always in use by these friends.

In August of 1945 the war was over and there were headlines in the paper saying that 22,500 blacks had lost war jobs. We trusted the Lord this far to take care of us, and we would continue to trust Him. As in the Depression, the streets were lined with more and more unemployed men and women.

Many black boys fought in the war and died for their country, but many of those who returned were refused jobs because of the color of their skin.

"My black body was good enough for that U.S. uniform," one soldier named Bill told me bitterly, "but I better not put it on a stool in a white lunch counter in Alabama! I just gave three years of my life so the white man could keep on killing me."

I had begun to feel a real burden in my heart to serve the Lord in a deeper way. I was restless, uneasy. I sometimes stayed up all night praying and writing in my journal. My job did not satisfy me any longer.

I often went to the train depot to talk about Jesus to the men who inhabited the benches. The cavernous train depot, bustling with activity, was filled with people with no place to go. They sat staring at the passers-by or sleeping in corners. They were worn out, hungry, and without homes. I sat with them and told them about a Savior who cared for them, who wanted them to know Him.

In those days after the war ended, there was little money around. One bleak morning I went to work to find that I didn't have a job anymore. I had been laid off, too. Times got pretty rough for us then, and many days saw us without bread on the table. Jackie and I went across the river to Canada to buy meat. A chicken cost us $4.50. Eggs were 25¢ apiece. We were forced to eat the way I had eaten in my days as a slave—corn bread, grits, salt pork, and molasses.

My heart was filled with joy, though, and somehow I just couldn't get despondent. I was quite sure now that God was calling me to serve Him.

If there was any sadness in my heart, it was at the way the churches were milking the people for money. Some churches were taking as many as five offerings during the service. And the pastors weren't taking care of their people. Widows who had given money to the church all their life were going hungry and had nobody looking out for them. I shed many tears over the state of the church as I saw it. It hurt me deeply to see the people so badly neglected. I prayed fervently that the Lord would let me serve Him some day.

I practiced many hours a day on the piano downstairs. I wasn't exactly popular in the neighborhood for it, but I didn't care. I wanted to play music for the Lord.

In 1947 the Lord began to speak to me about leaving Detroit. I didn't know how I was going to tell Jackie. She had long ago decorated our place with beautiful, expensive furniture, and she was proud of the fine things we owned and the fine home we had.

I was worried about my lack of education, and I wasn't sure if I was capable of serving the Lord. One afternoon when I was painting a neighbor's garage, a sudden terrible pain threw me to the ground. The pain was so awful I couldn't move. I was taken to the hospital and the doctors said it was a sprained back and they put me in traction. Then one afternoon when I was alone in the room, I felt the Lord's presence and He began to talk to me. He said, "Why don't you want to do what I have asked you to do?"

The Lord continued, "I will give you the words to speak

and the works to work. I will direct your way."

I decided there in that hospital bed to take the trust I had in education, credentials, and personal talents and put it in Jesus. If the Lord thought He could use me the way I was, it was His business.

When Jackie came to see me the next evening, I told her, "I'm healed. I'm going home tomorrow morning." She thought I was crazy. But the next morning when the doctors came around, they examined me and said, "We can't figure it out, but there's nothing wrong with you." I was taken out of traction. The inflammation and pain were completely gone and the doctors told me I was well and could go home.

A few days later we went to Lima, Ohio, to a revival meeting. Some sisters were talking after the meeting, and I overheard them mention a place called Bucyrus, Ohio. The name of that town kept going over and over in my mind. I could hardly sleep that night.

Back in Detroit, I went to the ticket office in the bus depot and bought a ticket to Bucyrus, Ohio.

I got off the bus at the square in the small town of Bucyrus. It was a cold afternoon, and the wind was blowing down the quiet, clean, main street of the town. I saw no black faces. As I walked around, I noticed many shops selling something called *bratwurst*. I went into a sandwich shop on Sandusky Street and ordered bratwurst and coffee. I discovered it was a delicious German sausage. The people in the restaurant stared at me strangely. I wondered if they had ever seen a black man before. By nightfall I was back on the bus heading for Detroit.

There was certainly nothing momentous about the trip. In fact, there was not a thing unusual about it. Maybe I had expected God to open the earth or appear in the treetops, or maybe I expected a welcoming committee of holy angels. By the end of the day I think I would have settled for a friendly hello from any old stranger. There were no signs, however, and no indications of any kind that the Lord even knew I was there. Still, I felt this was the town He wanted us to move to.

"Jackie, sit down, honey." The house was quiet, and outside in the darkness of the night there was a light snowfall spreading across the city. Jackie wrapped her bathrobe around her and sat down at the kitchen table. I poured hot coffee and smiled at her. She had the look on her face that said, "OK, where's the bad news?"

"We're leavin' Detroit," I said. "I believe we'll be movin' to Bucyrus, Ohio."

Jackie was still for a moment. "Robert Sadler, whey your mind is?"

33

In February of 1947 I left Detroit for Bucyrus, Ohio. I rented a room, had a telephone put in and took an ad in the newspaper to clean carpets and upholstery. I received so many calls I could hardly handle the work. In three months' time Jackie was able to join me.

In August of 1951 we packed the car with our belongings and moved to Clemson, South Carolina. I took Jackie to nearby Anderson for a visit. This was the last time I saw my father. He died a few months later.

I got a job as a baker in the kitchen of Clemson College, even though I didn't know anything about baking. Jackie worked in the college laundry.

Jackie and I loved children, although we had none of our own, and we began a children's Bible class. Once 30 children came weekly to these meetings. Then we were invited to have a children's radio program, so each week we brought one group of children to the radio station for our program. We had some wonderfully happy times.

Jackie wanted the Lord to use her to be a help and blessing to others and she complained to me one morning before work, "Honey, I'd sure like to lead someone to the Lord. Seem like I just never get the opportunity." That morning at the laundry she was praying with a lady friend for the radio program and the children. Then she prayed for people who were lost without God. A man was walking by the laundry door and he heard her praying. He began to cry. Minutes later, he walked into the laundry and gave his life to the Lord Jesus.

I tried to get a job as a machinist but I was always turned down, even though I was qualified and had plenty of experience. One day a white man and I were in the employment office at Swan Rubber. We got to talking and discovered we were both applying for machinist work. When I went in for the interview the personnel manager told me the jobs were filled and there were none left. The white man who went in after me got the job and was told they were still hiring.

I tried to get a job at Timken Ball Bearing when they

advertised for men, but when I applied they said there were no jobs. The same happened at Ohio Crane. The only jobs I could get were cleaning toilets or pushing a broom. Finally I made an appeal to the vice president at Swan Rubber. He went to the personnel office and insisted they hire me at the plant.

Years later a new personnel manager was hired at Swan Rubber and he was sympathetic toward blacks. He told me that he would hire any Negro I sent to him. I traveled to the neighboring towns of Crestline, Marion, Fostoria, Wyandot, Galion, Mansfield and Tiffin with the news, and the man kept his word and hired the men I sent.

Buck and Corrie Moore were living in Anderson, not far from Margie. They lived in a run-down shack just like everybody else in the neighborhood. There was an arbor of ivy over his walk leading to the broken wooden steps, and along it grew honeysuckle and roses. I ran into Buck's arms, and we rocked and embraced with the joy of seeing one another. We would never lose touch again.

Things in Anderson were not good. Many of our people couldn't get jobs. The good jobs went to the white men, and the blacks had to take the lowest and dirtiest jobs for the least pay. Many black men worked two and three jobs just to put enough food on the table. If he couldn't get a job, the white man called him a lazy nigger.

Very upsetting to me were the number of cults that black people were trapped in. Charlatans who professed to be God, or God's "prophet," were exploiting the people. One such man, Daddy Grace, had been dead for years, but his followers believed he was coming back. They worshipped his picture and forked over their money to his cult in hopes of receiving his blessing. Witchcraft, voodoo, and Satanism are very dominant among the black people of the South. Sound Bible teaching is rare.

I wanted so much to help my people. I cried out to God night and day for them. I wasn't afraid of the white man. I refused to bow and say, "Yes, Cap'n, No, Cap'n." But many of the people in Anderson were still doing it. They didn't know they were supposed to be free.

Someday, Lord, I prayed, I'll be in a place where I can help people. Black people *and* white people. I'll be able to tell them the *truth*—I'll be able to carry the gospel of love to people. Oh, someday, someday, Lord, it won't be like this.

34

"Do you love me, Robert?"

"Yes, Lord!"

"Will you help my people, Robert?"

"Yes, Lord!"

"Will you feed the poor, clothe the naked, comfort the mourning—?"

"Yes, yes, Lord!"

"Will you go without food? Without a place to sleep? Will you be content with want as well as abundance?"

"Oh, I will, Lord!"

"Will you trust me?"

"Yes, yes, I'll trust you, Lord!"

"Robert, go. Minister in my name. I am with you."

It was many hours before I stumbled out of the living room that afternoon in Clemson. I had been praying, asking God to use me in a greater way, and God had spoken to me. I knew in the deepest part of me that He had called me to minister to people. I had no education, no formal training, but I knew God was going to use me. I was willing to do anything and go anywhere for Him.

I was forty-one years old, and it was nearing Christmas time of 1952. I was laid off at the bakery and looking for work again. I strolled along the Clemson College Campus, passed Tillman Hall with its big clock tower, and I prayed to the Lord. "Here I is, out of work again, Lord. Where shall I go? Where shall I go?" I met one of the men who worked with me in the bakery, and we walked together under the broad arms of the oak and white cedar trees. He told me they were hiring in Birmingham, Alabama. I went home, packed a grip, kissed Jackie good-bye, and drove to Birmingham, singing "Thank you, Jesus" all the way.

I got a job working on the railroad on a tie gang, and when that ended I found work painting houses. One day coming home from work, I saw two scrubby little boys standing at the edge of the road. They were dirty, needed haircuts, and wore shoes without socks or laces.

The Spirit of the Lord spoke to me and told me to talk

to them. "Why don't you put some laces in those shoes?" I asked them.

"Because we don't got no money," they told me. I took them to the store and bought them some shoelaces and told them to ask their father if I could give them a haircut.

That night the pastor of the church I was attending told me to stay away from this family. "The father is an evil man," he said. "He hates preachers, and he'll stick a dirk to you just as soon as look at you."

"Well, praise the Lord," I said. "I'm going over there first thing tomorrow."

And I did. "I'm a minister of the Lord," I announced when a surly looking black man opened the door. "I'm the one who bought your boys shoelaces." He said nothing. "I told them to tell you that I would like to cut their hair." I smiled at him.

He stepped back, squinting, and said, "Come on in," I walked into a dark, cluttered room with beer cans and dirty rags piled in heaps everywhere. He closed the door behind us.

"You a minister, huh?" I nodded, still smiling.

"Hold it right there then. Before you cut my boys' hair. . . ."

My heart began to beat quickly. What was he going to do? He had the most evil look about him.

"Before you cut their hair, would you—would you—?" he fidgeted and lowered his eyes. "Would you—pray for me?"

If my mouth fell open and my eyes blinked in surprise, the man didn't seem to mind. "Of course I'll pray for you."

I didn't cut just one boy's hair, I cut the hair of everyone in the family. That family gave their hearts to Jesus that afternoon. I helped the mother clean the living room and we had a prayer meeting there that evening which lasted most of the night.

I stayed in Birmingham a couple of months, and then when work ran out, I went back home. Jackie and I had a couple of weeks together, and news came that there was work in Asheville, North Carolina. I packed my grip and went to Asheville.

The only work I could find in Asheville was shining shoes in a hotel. In a couple of weeks I found extra work doing gardening, painting houses, and then digging ditches. I knew that God was fully aware of my situation; He knew that I couldn't get skilled work even though I was qualified. He saw me shining shoes hundreds of miles away from home in order to be a man and support my wife, and surely He was with me here, too.

I knew that I would be of no use to the Lord if I allowed myself to be bitter. "I trust you, Lord; I know you're with me." I began to enjoy the hilly, beautiful town and its people.

I stayed in Asheville a couple of months, and then the Lord told me to return to Bucyrus. Happily driving along the highway, I could see the Paris mountains, beautiful and dusty in the distance, and I saw glassy lakes, streams, lush forests, and rolling hills.

The wisdom of the Lord in placing us in northern Ohio was geographically perfect and a blessing to us and to my ministry. We even had a job offer that would allow me the freedom to travel and minister.

The job for us in Bucyrus was on a large farm outside of town. We were provided with a little house to live in and a small salary for cleaning the house, keeping the yard, and being general handyman. We stayed there until 1955.

I ministered in my town, in other towns near by and some far away. The Lord sent me usually to small groups —home meetings, struggling churches, hospitals, and prisons. Many times He would send me several miles away for just one or two people who were in need. I ministered to as many white folk as black folk.

Often working in the yard or painting a house I would hear the Spirit of the Lord speaking to me to go somewhere or to help someone in need. I would try to get alone as soon as possible so I could pray, be quiet, and wait on Him for direction. Many times I had to wait for a day or two. I fasted, prayed, and read the Bible, listening for Him to tell me where He wanted me to go. Then when I knew He had spoken, I would prepare to leave.

In 1954 I was asked to hold some meetings in St. Louis, Missouri. The Lord had blessed me with a portable pump organ to take along with me wherever I ministered. I took the organ with me to St. Louis and Potosi, Missouri, for meetings.

Not far from Potosi there is a small town of about 300 people, called Mineral Point. A handful of people were attending a tiny, run-down church with no pastor, and they asked me to come minister to them. They told me they didn't have any money to pay me. I said, "I don't want your money. I just want to help you."

The first night I ministered, the people seemed cold and distant. I felt there was a spiritual wall between us.

I prayed that night, "Lord, break down that wall. Whatever it takes, Lord, break it down."

I didn't know that the Lord was getting ready to do just that.

The next night I went out to my car to go to the meeting. I started the car up and then went back into the house to get my Bible. When I came out, I saw the car rolling down the hill toward a swamp below. Though it was getting dark, I ran stumbling through high weeds and brush, trying to catch up with that car.

I saw it heading for a tree. "Please, Lord, stop it on that tree!" But the car rolled right past the tree. I sure didn't want it to end up in the swamp—it would be close to impossible to salvage from there. Another tree came in view. I prayed, "Oh, Lord, stop it on that tree," but the car brushed right past the tree. I was running with all my strength, but I couldn't get hold of the door. The car plunged into the swamp, and I watched it sink slowly, nose first, until only the back half of the car poked out of the tangle of weeds and mud.

I stood there, out of breath, scratched, my clothes torn, my car gone—and suddenly I began to laugh. A song came to my mind and I began to sing.

> I'll say Amen to Jesus,
> Amen all the time,
> It's Amen when in sorrow,
> It's Amen rain or shine. . . .

I stayed by the swamp for about fifteen minutes praising the Lord, laughing, and singing.

An old couple up on a house on the hill saw the whole thing and they saw me laughing and praising the Lord. They were amazed. Word quickly got around that the preacher's car had gotten wrecked but he was still praising Jesus. That night there were twice as many people in church, and the atmosphere was entirely different. "Brother Sadler's car is wrecked, and we never saw a happier preacher," they said. God had broken the wall!

I stayed there three months holding meetings nearly every night. I worked during the day cleaning up the church building—fixing, building, and painting it—and at night I held meetings. God broke the walls down, and love and trust replaced fear and bitterness. I became pastor of the church and traveled back and forth from Mineral Point to Bucyrus for the next five years.

I was preparing to leave for home after that first long stay in Mineral Point when Jackie called and read a letter that had come for me. It was from a fourteen-year-old girl in Sinking Spring, Pennsylvania.

"Brother Sadler, please come," it read. *"Come here because my father is an alcoholic and he need Jesus bad. Please come and pray for my father."*

The letter touched me, but I didn't have enough money to get to Pennsylvania. The Lord had been teaching me to trust Him, however, and so I prayed. I felt the Lord's approval to go to Sinking Spring to see this girl's father. The insurance company had paid enough money for me to get another car, this time a '52 Ford, and so I left Mineral Point with no money in my pocket, a tank full of gas, and a thousand miles ahead of me.

I couldn't take the turnpike without any money, because of the tolls so through the mountains I went. As I drove, suddenly the Holy Spirit spoke to me and said, "Stop here." I thought I had heard wrong and kept driving. Finally I knew that I had to obey the Holy Spirit. I turned around and went back to the spot He had told me to stop. When I got to the place, He spoke to me again and told me to take out my organ and set it up on the side of the road. I shrugged and set it up, even though I wanted to question Him. He spoke again and told me to play. I asked, "What shall I play, Lord?" He told me to play "Softly and Tenderly Jesus Is Calling."

So there at the side of a mountain, with wilderness on all sides of me, the sun high in the clear blue sky, I began to play. Cars went by, and I saw faces staring at me as though I was a crazy nut. I didn't care. I was just lifted up in the Holy Spirit and having a wonderful time. I sang all the verses to "Softly and Tenderly." I could hear my voice echoing in the mountains. Hearing footsteps, I turned around and saw a man with a young boy of about nine years. They were staring at me with wonder.

"We came closer so we could hear you," the man called. "We've been listening since you started singing." I hadn't finished the hymn yet, so I continued singing as the man and boy stood listening.

> Come home, come home,
> Ye who are weary, come home;
> Earnestly, tenderly, Jesus is calling,
> Calling, O sinner, come home!

When I turned around, the man's face was flushed and tears were streaming down his cheeks. Then the man, through tears, told me, "I was in World War II—overseas. I was in the front lines and I got shot. Bad. They rushed me to the hospital, and then they put me in the death room. I began to pray. I had Christian parents, and I knew they were home praying for me—" His voice broke.

"I made a vow there on my dying bed. 'Heal me, Lord,' I prayed. 'Let me get home to America again, and I promise I'll serve you all the days of my life.' " He wiped his face with the back of his hand. "The Lord healed me and brought me home—but—I didn't keep my promise. I've been living in these mountains—hiding out—trying to get away from God ever since.

"God sent you here. He sent you here!" he cried, "Please bring me back to God."

I stayed there with the man and his son for several hours. When I left, he had given his heart to the Lord, and he was restored and free from the bondage in which he had been trapped.

I got into my car, rejoicing and praising God. Before long I noticed that the fuel gauge was on empty. I knew if He wanted me to get anywhere, He would have to take care of that. I drove through a town in southern Illinois and noticed a church at the side of the road and a lot of people going into it. The sight of those people streaming into the church was so good that I felt I just had to join them. I pulled over and went inside. The pastor saw me and came over to talk to me. Discovering I was a minister, he asked me to speak to them that night. I spoke and sang, too, and the people took up a love offering for me. To my amazement, I counted over $100. I praised the Lord all the way to Sinking Spring, Pennsylvania.

The little girl wasn't surprised to see me. She threw her arms around my neck and kissed me. "I knew you'd come, Brother Bob, I knew you'd come!" I spent two days with her father, but he refused to see his need for Jesus. The girl's mother invited some friends, and we held meetings in their home in the evenings. I played my organ and sang. At the meetings four and five people came to the Lord each night. All except the father. He sat slumped half asleep against the wall.

I left Sinking Spring wondering exactly why God sent me there when the man I had gone to see wasn't helped at all. I stopped the car and settled it with the Lord. I gave the situation completely to Him. "I don't want Sadler's way, Lord, I want *your* way."

In 1955, about the time Dr. King led the bus boycott in Montgomery, Alabama, Jackie got a good job as a housekeeper for a family named Pickings in Bucyrus. Mr. Pickings owned a company that made copper kettles. Shortly after Jackie began working for them, Mr. Pickings asked me to work for him too. We moved into the big house next door to his where his brother Wilfred was living. Our job was to care for both houses, the grounds, and Wilfred.

Wilfred was not right in his mind. He had been an opera singer, and some said he had studied too hard and it hurt his mind. He acted like he was fighting demons.

Mr. Pickings hadn't been able to keep anybody in that house because of Wilfred. He scared everybody away. We were the only ones who lasted. In time, we came to love Wilfred. He was an elderly man, big, tall, and fierce when he was angry.

Wilfred didn't frighten us. He obeyed us as a child would his parents. I could tell him, "Wilfred, eat your carrots!" and he would obediently eat his carrots. When he was making too much noise, I would sternly tell him, "That's enough of that, Wilfred!" and he would be quiet.

Wilfred obeyed Jackie as well, and his mind seemed to improve during our time together. I felt at peace to travel, leaving Jackie in charge; and the Lord blessed her with wisdom and strength to take over.

In 1956 an incident occurred which was to have a lasting effect on my ministry. Jackie and I went to a meeting in Marion, Ohio, and there was a man from Seattle speaking and ministering the word of the Lord in prophecy. The spirit of discernment was upon him that night in tremendous power. The Lord was so near and sweet. I was sitting at the piano when suddenly the man pointed to me and said, "Come up here, brother. There is something you have need of, and the Lord wants to give it to you tonight."

Feeling a little weak, I went to the front of the church. "Open your hands," the man told me. I did as he said. He laid his hands on mine, and suddenly I opened my mouth and began to speak in a new language. It was wonderful—not that I felt any tingle or great surge of power in my vocal chords. I just opened my mouth and spoke.

I learned that what I had just experienced had been promised by Jesus to all believers in Acts 1, where He said, "Wait for the promise of the Father . . . for John baptized with water, but before many days you shall be baptized with the Holy Spirit." I had read that scripture many times before, but never *really* knew what it meant before. If the disciples needed this special power, I guess I sure did.

I began experiencing the gifts of the Holy Spirit. The Lord spoke to me in dreams and visions. I longed for Jackie to find the same wonderful closeness with the Lord. It was as though I had gone from the hem of His robe right into His arms.

It was four long years later that Jackie received the baptism in the Holy Spirit. "Why did I wait so long?" she lamented in my arms.

35

In the autumn of 1956 the Lord spoke to me in a vision. I had just bought a new portable organ—I hadn't even taken it out of the box yet. The Lord told me to go to Marion, Ohio. In the vision I saw a beer garden in front of me, and I was playing the organ. A Christian couple we knew named Toni and Mike were with me. After I saw the vision, I immediately went to the telephone and called Mike. "Can you and your wife go to Marion now?" They were at our door in less than an hour.

We arrived in Marion, Ohio, and found the beer garden that I had seen in my vision. We parked the car and I took my new organ out of the box and set it up on the sidewalk in front of the beer garden. We began to sing right there, and it wasn't long before the people began to gather around us.

We were playing, singing, and telling the people about the Lord and His love for them when a young woman burst out of the beer garden and stomped over to where we were. "You're making a lot of racket!" she shouted at me. "What are you, a religious nut?" I smiled at her and reached for her hand. Shaking it, I said, "How do you do? I'm Robert Sadler, and these are my friends Toni and Mike." She stared at me and said nothing. "Do you have a favorite hymn?" I asked her. Her face crumpled. "Ohhh. . . ."

I began playing "The Old Rugged Cross."

"How did *you* know I like that song?"

She gave her heart to Jesus that day on the street in front of a dozen or so of her friends. "I've wanted to get saved for years and years," she cried, "I just didn't know *how*."

Others gave their hearts to the Lord that day. I preached quiet, simple messages about the love of God. We passed out some literature, and then when it was time to go, everyone had left except the young woman. "I'm an alcoholic," she confessed. "What shall I do?"

Toni and Mike took her home with them to live. She was delivered from alcoholism and eventually got a good job. It was the first job she had been able to hold onto for several years. Today she is married, has a family, and teaches Sunday school. Jesus gave her a new life that afternoon in front of the beer garden.

People gave us boxes of used clothing and canned food, used toys, shoes, and small household items to take to needy families on my trips.

I packed up the car in November of 1956 with all the boxes that had gathered, kissed Jackie good-bye, and left for South Carolina.

"Lord," I prayed, "you show me where to go. You know where the needs are, Lord. You show me."

I got into Clinton, South Carolina, around supper time. I stopped at a restaurant and was looking out of the window when I saw a group of workers coming in across the field from picking cotton. My heart raced at the sight of them. It reminded me of my childhood on the Beal Plantation. I put my fork down, wiped off my mouth, and hurried outside to meet them.

The eyes of one of the women met mine, and her face froze. She looked oddly familiar. Suddenly the woman screamed and threw her hands in the air.

"Robert!" she screamed. "Robert Sadler!"

I stared at her. Then in a rush I recognized her. "Tennessee!" I hollered, my hands in the air. "Lord Amighty! It's Tennessee!"

We threw ourselves into each other's arms, laughing and crying. O Lord, Lord! Could you be so good to give me this blessing? Oh, Jesus, forgive me for not expecting it of you! I couldn't look at her enough, drink in her face. It was Tennessee all right.

We talked and shouted and cried at the same time. Finally, I was able to ask, "John Henry! Is he—?"

"He's in the store. That's our restaurant," she said, wiping her eyes. "We own that little store there."

"But I was just in there eating my supper!"

"It's John Henry who's cooking it, brother!"

She introduced me to her children. They had sons already married and with children of their own.

I stayed with Tennessee and John Henry for a couple of days and even picked cotton with them.

"Robert," Tennessee told me, "the Lord have carried us this far, the Lord gonna carry us through."

"Tennessee," I teased, "you was one mean girl, yessuh, you was a *mean* one."

Tennessee laughed. "I *had* to be, Robert. But Jesus took the meanness outa me. There ain't no hatred in my heart anymore. I don't hate Sam Beal, I don't hate any of 'em. I feel sorry for 'em. I am happy and free in my heart—free and clear, praise God!"

They lived in a small wooden house behind the store, which John Henry had built himself. Though older and heavier, both were still filled with fire and drive. They had suffered more than many blacks, and their love had survived the worst. What thrilled me the most was that they loved Jesus.

"You'd think old man Beal would drive me to the devil, but he drive me straight to Jesus, Robert. I jes knowed it had to be Jesus watching over us and helping us escape that place."

John Henry told me his mother, Ceily, had passed on to be with the Lord just the year before. At the mention of her name, I could see her face so clearly before me that I could have reached out and touched it. I remembered that day in her cabin in the slave quarter when I asked Jesus into my heart. "John Henry," I said, "your mama done took me through many a storm. . . ."

"She never forgot yoll, Robert. She often spoke of ye and prayed for yoll, too."

"I never forgot her, either," I said. "She done brought me to Jesus."

John Henry told me that many of Beal's slaves lived in the vicinity, and we went to visit some of them. Many I didn't know by name, but they knew me. I was the house slave.

"John Henry, where did Harriet settle at after she got off the plantation?"

"Harriet? She done live in Anderson till she passed about ten years ago. Her chillren still livin' there. And Mary Webb, she be livin' in Anderson."

The reunion was like heaven. I could have stayed with John Henry and Tennessee in their happy home indefinitely, but the Lord told me it was time to be going to Anderson. I left some boxes of clothing for the children and was on my way.

I got to Anderson tired and wanting to sleep, so I went to Margie's. The next morning the Lord woke me and told me to drive to Railroad Street. I drove there, got out of the car, and began walking, not knowing where the Lord wanted me to go. Suddenly a woman across the road pointed at me and squealed excitedly. "Preacher! Preacher!"

I stopped and a short, heavy, black lady ran toward me. Breathlessly, she told me that in a dream the night before, I had prayed for her. After I had prayed, she was healed, according to the dream.

"Do you need a healing, sister?" I asked.

She told me that she had been suffering with a sore on her head, and it was getting worse.

"Please come with me," she asked. "I'm on my way to prayer meeting." We got into my car and drove to a wooden shanty several blocks away where a group of women had gathered for prayer. I prayed over the sister with the sore on her head. She took off her hat and wig and showed me the sore, big and festering.

Three days later I saw the woman, and she told me that it was healing and closing over. I saw her again in seven days, and it was completely healed. She came to Margie's and handed me a twenty-dollar bill. "This is for you, preacher. God sent you here so I could be healed. I been savin' this, and I want you to have it."

A few weeks later, the Lord had me drive to Lowndesville, South Carolina, to hold some meetings. We met in the home of a woman named Myra, whose father was unable to walk and in a wheelchair. The Holy Spirit spoke to me and told me to tell the man to get out of his chair. I could feel the anointing of the Lord in the room. The man sat staring at me, not moving. I got up and walked over to him. "In the name of the Lord Jesus, get up and walk." He rose from the wheelchair and walked across the room. Then he turned around and walked back again.

Everybody in the room wept and praised the Lord. When the old man rested, he got up and tried it again. He didn't need any help, didn't need a stick to hold him up, either.

The next day he was still walking up and down in the yard and on the road. His daughter said she couldn't get him to sit down. "He's so glad to be walking, I can't keep him down!"

The old man's sons and daughters gave their hearts to Jesus when they saw what had happened to their father. Then his grandchildren gave their hearts to the Lord, too. I saw over a dozen people come to Jesus because of the miracle God did in that man.

36

When I arrived home Jackie told me Wilfred had taken a turn for the worse.

That night the Lord awoke me from my sleep and told me Wilfred was going to die. I jumped out of bed and pleaded with the Lord. "Lord, don't take him yet! Please don't take him yet." I knew Wilfred's soul wasn't ready. I began to fast and pray for him.

After six days of fasting and prayer for Wilfred, I realized he would have to be put in the hospital. "Give me a sign, Lord, that he has opened his heart to you and that he's going to heaven. Please, Lord," I prayed.

On the day he was to go to the hospital, the doctor came prepared to drug him in order to get him out of the house. Wilfred hated hospitals and thought all doctors were after him and trying to kill him. I refused to let them drug him. "Don't you put a needle to him," I insisted. "He's going to go to the hospital nicely, and he's going to behave himself." I dressed Wilfred and prayed for a miracle. To everyone's amazement Wilfred went to the hospital without a single protest. Usually, if he had to leave his house, he would scream and kick and act crazy, breaking things and terrifying everybody. This time he was like a lamb. I knew the Lord had touched him.

When Wilfred died two weeks later, I had peace in my heart that when I get to heaven, Wilfred would be there, too.

The Pickings family asked us to remain on in the house.

We missed Wilfred, though. We had gotten very attached to him, and it was lonely and quiet without him.

We started a little church right in the house. We called our ministry *Faith Mission,* and we had meetings on Sunday and prayer meetings every morning of the week.

One morning Jackie and I felt especially impressed to pray for people who were lost. The burden was so heavy upon us we continued long after the hour was over. We were praying for someone in particular, someone we didn't know. Around noon I went outside to trim a little peach tree I had planted in the backyard. Out of the corner of my eye, I saw a bum stagger by on the sidewalk.

The Lord spoke to me and said, "I'm going to save that man." "Praise you, Lord," I said. A few minutes later Jackie called me from the porch. "Robert! There's a man here and he's asking for prayer!" The bum I had seen on the sidewalk was sitting on the couch.

"I don't know why I'm in this place," he said.

"I know why you're here," Jackie said. "You're here because we been praying for you."

"Huh?"

"All morning long we been praying for you without knowing your name or who you are, and the Lord sent you to us."

The man's name was Don. We prayed over him, and he asked Jesus into his heart. He had never felt the power of God before. I took him home and he cleaned up and came back with me that night for a fellowship meeting.

That winter I felt the Lord leading me to a large convention in Minnesota. Christians were coming from all over the country to it. Jackie couldn't come with me because she was working and couldn't get time off. I packed my grip, kissed her good-bye, and left.

I noticed a rattle in the engine of the car, but I didn't pay much attention to it. The meetings in St. Paul were wonderful, and I experienced beautiful fellowship, excellent teaching, and a great moving of God. When I was leaving, I heard a man saying, "I hitchhiked to this convention. I don't know how I'll get home." I turned and said, "I'll be glad to drive you home."

"Are you sure? I live 300 miles from here!"

"That doesn't matter. I'll drive you home."

The man's name was Joe, and he was delighted with my offer. We climbed into my car, along with a blind brother who also wanted to ride with me, and started on our way. As we drove along in the heavy snow, the car began to pop and backfire. I had to stop every few miles to pour gas into the gas tank because it was leaking. We laughed and praised the Lord.

Outside the snow was coming down very heavy, and the winds were blowing. It was turning into a blizzard, and the temperatures had gone to 45 degrees below zero. After we had gone about 150 miles, the clutch gave out. I knew the transmission was gone, but the car kept moving so I didn't stop. We drove until we saw a gas station, and I headed for it and pulled in. The man in the station said, "Your transmission is gone, I'm afraid."

Not knowing what else to say, I said simply, "Well, fill it up with oil." He filled it up; I started the car up, and away we went.

The snow was really deep, and the roads were very bad. I was a little concerned about getting stuck.

We made it to Bemidji, Minnesota, but I made a wrong turn. I tried backing up to turn around, but the car wouldn't move. I tried again and again. It was useless. We were hopelessly stuck in the snow.

I looked at the face of the blind brother. He was calm and happy and trusting God. It was getting dark out, the heat in the car was poor, the storm was raging, and the sub-zero temperature was already numbing our bodies. What were we to do? Softly, we began to pray.

The three of us were staring at the storm when we felt the car moving. I sat behind the wheel with my hands on my lap, my feet on the floor. The car was turning around!

The car made a complete turn-around, then rolled up onto the road again and faced the direction we had come. It was so incredible we began to shout and weep in amazement. God had worked a miracle!

When I started the car up, it ran perfectly, and I drove on to Joe's house in Bemidji, Minnesota.

I left Bemidji with the snow flying and the temperature 40 degrees below zero. The car sputtered and popped, but I was trusting the Lord to get me back to Bucyrus. I stopped at the same gas station where we had stopped in on our way to Bemidji, and I told the attendant the miracles the Lord had worked. He drained the oil out of the car, and the pieces of gears began to fall out. "Oh, don't throw those away," I told him. "I want to keep them as souvenirs."

I drove that car all the way back to Bucyrus. Then I was home for just a couple of days when my sister Margie called to tell me that Corrie Moore was real sick and in the hospital, and I'd better come down to Anderson. The car wasn't fixed yet, but Jackie and I drove all the way to Anderson, South Carolina, without any trouble.

Corrie was in the hospital when we arrived. "How is she?" we asked Buck. With a flicker of agony, he said,

"She just had both legs taken off."

When Corrie gained consciousness and she saw me, she said with a smile, "Robert . . . sing for me."

"I done come a long way—to this, Robert," she said.

"Jesus know, Corrie, Jesus know."

Margie asked me one evening later that week, "Robert, can you do something for my pastor? He just have to get to Pompano, Florida, for a funeral and has no way to get there. Will you drive him?"

"Margie, my car's transmission is out."

"Please, Robert?"

"But, sister, the car need repair. The transmission doesn't work."

"Won't you please do it, Robert? Please?"

Finally I agreed. I had already driven the car almost 2,000 miles with the transmission gone. How much more grace was the Lord going to extend to me?

The car made it another 1400 miles with that transmission. Margie's pastor marveled. "I reckon there's a whole lot I don't know about the Lord. But, brother, now I aim to get right and find out!"

Back in Anderson, Jackie and I prayed about getting home to Bucyrus. We didn't have any money to have the car fixed. The Lord blessed us again and allowed the car to go another 800 miles back to Bucyrus. I still have the pieces of those gears as a remembrance of the miracle the Lord did.

In 1960 I was in Leesville, Virginia, in the mountains. It was a warm Sunday morning, and the air was thick with the sweet smell of the forest surrounding the highway. I was looking for a church to attend. I stopped at a gas station to get some gas, and as I waited for the attendant, I saw about twelve men standing around there. I didn't pay much attention because I was so intent on getting to church. I went on a ways, and the Lord spoke to me.

"Where are you going, Robert?"

"Why, I'm going to *church*, Lord."

"Did I tell you to go to church?"

"Well, I—"

"Did you see those men back there?"

"Men?"

"Those men back there at the gas station aren't going to church. Nobody will be preaching to them this morning, Robert."

"Lord, forgive me," I cried. I turned around and went back to the gas station.

"I'm a minister," I told the owner. "Do you mind if I minister here this morning?"

"Why, go right ahead."

Right there in the gas station we had a church service. I brought in my organ, and we sang and I preached. My congregation was those twelve men. Every one of them gave their lives to Jesus that morning. It was one of the most glorious experiences of my life.

I stayed there for three days and nights, holding meetings every night. Word got around the mountains about the meetings, and the gas station was packed every night. Men and women stood outside to hear because there was no room inside. The owner didn't even try to wait on customers. The presence of the Lord was so powerful, there was nobody who went away from those meetings untouched by Him.

I laid hands on a rebellious young man who had been running away from God all his life. He began to quiver and shake when I touched him. Then he fell to the floor sobbing and asking God to forgive him of his sins and save him. Another man, who had been an alcoholic for almost thirty years, came forward crying and asking for prayer. I laid hands on him and began to pray for him. He fell on his knees and asked Jesus to come into his heart and save him. God also delivered him from alcoholism that day.

The Lord surely touched Leesville, a place I almost missed completely. How important it is to hear the voice of the Lord. I can't thank Him enough for turning me around that day.

I've had a lot of experience with car trouble—especially in the mountains, when my old cars would break down. One time in particular, I was coming from Roanoke, Virginia, where I had held some meetings, and I was driving up a big mountain early in the morning. I got a few miles up the mountain and the car stopped dead. I got out of the car and said, "Lord, I'm not flagging anybody down. Thank you, Jesus. You know I'm here halfway up this mountain, and you know the car has stopped dead. Now I'm on a mission for you, so I'm counting on you to help me."

With that, I pushed the car to the side of the road and pulled up the hood of the car. Then I took out my organ and began to play.

The hours went by. I thought some cars that passed would drive right off the mountain, they were so busy looking at me. I couldn't blame them.

By noon I was hot and thirsty, and there was no sign of help. I just kept praising the Lord, though, repeating over and over again to myself, "In everything give thanks."

My faith grew by the hour, but my body grew more hot and weary. Shortly after 2:00 a car pulled up in front of my car and a man got out. He wanted to help me.

He insisted I get in his car and go with him to get something to eat. I didn't want to eat, but I drank a large glass of water and some soda. The man told me I'd have to have a mechanic go up and fix my car.

"Oh, no, I couldn't do that. I don't have money to pay a mechanic."

"Well, if you're going to get the car fixed, you'll need a mechanic."

The man took me back to my car and then was gone, and I never saw him again. I didn't even find out his name. In about a half an hour two mechanics pulled up in a service truck. They didn't even say hello to me; they just began to work on the car. I thought to myself, "Lord, I can't afford to pay *one* mechanic—and you send two!" They towed the car over the mountain to the station to get parts. Then another mechanic came and helped them. They put in a new fuel pump. When I saw those three men working on the car, I grew even more nervous. "Now you've sent another one, Lord!"

Finally, twelve hours after the car broke down, it was in working condition again. Gulping and trying to act casual, I asked the men how much I owed them. They thought for a moment, and then one of them said, "Give us two dollars."

The Lord is my stronghold in time of need . . .

It was in June of 1963, and I had just turned fifty-two years old. I was holding some meetings in Vicksburg, Michigan. I overheard a woman telling another woman that her son was coming from Viet Nam with his fiancee, and she wanted to paint her upstairs but just couldn't do it.

"I'll paint your upstairs," I told her. She couldn't believe it. But the next morning I showed up bright and early at her front door with my painting clothes and paint brushes, ready for work. I painted her three bedrooms and hallway in two days and had a wonderful time of it, singing and praising the Lord as I worked.

The woman's husband wasn't a Christian. When he came home from work, he couldn't believe his eyes. "You mean to tell me that *you* is the preacher man?"

He was amazed. He told me that other preachers had stayed in his house and hadn't even made their beds after themselves. "And here you is *painting* the place!"

That night he came to the meeting with his wife. The next night he came back again. The third night he gave his heart to the Lord. He had been a hardened and embittered man, and the Lord wanted to wash it out of him. His voice was gentle and soft as he told everybody in the congregation, "I know that the good Lord is *real. I know it now.*"

About a month later in the heat of the summer, the Lord put it on my heart to go to Detroit. I was near New Toledo when the Holy Spirit told me, "Don't go the expressway. Go through the business section of the city." I wondered why the Lord wanted me to go through all that traffic, but I obeyed Him. In a few minutes I saw a man hitchhiking. The Lord said, "Pick him up."

I opened the door and invited him in. He got into the car, and I felt a cold chill go through me. Then I heard the Holy Spirit tell me, "This man has murder in his heart." I gave him a quick glance and said gently, "You have murder in your heart."

"Yeah? So what?" He didn't even blink. "I'll kill him! And nobody's gonna stop me! I'll kill him!" He pulled a gun out of his shirt and pointed it at me.

"You hear me? I'll kill him!"

His gun didn't scare me. I just kept on driving. "Thank you, Jesus," I said quietly.

"*What?*"

"I was just thanking Jesus that you got into my car," I told him.

"You was—*what?*"

"Thanking Jesus. Do you know who He is?"

"Knock it off."

"Well, He knows who *you* are, and that's what counts."

I got it out of him that his wife had taken a lover, and that's what he was so mad about. He was on his way to kill them both.

"Do you mind if I pray for you first?" I asked quietly.

The man was stunned. I began to pray softly, and before I knew it the man was crying. "What are you doing to me?" he gulped.

"I'm not doing anything, son. Jesus is doing it," I explained. God worked a miracle in him, and he gave his heart to Jesus there in the car. We prayed for his wife and for the lover, too. It wasn't an easy thing for him to do, but he did it. When we finished praying, he embraced me and thanked me, exclaiming, "Hate is an awful thing."

He was a changed man by the time we said good-bye. He felt relief and peace. He confessed he hadn't been a very good husband and that he wanted to make a new start.

When I left him a couple of hours later, I turned the car around and went back home to Bucyrus. I knew God had completed what He had wanted to do on this trip.

One quiet evening in late autumn of 1963, Jackie and I were sitting in our living room in Bucyrus reading the newspaper together. It was quiet except for the purring of car engines as they passed by the house, and the ticking of the old Seth Thomas eight-day clock on the mantle.

"Look at this!" Jackie pointed. Holding out the section of the paper in her hands, she showed me a small article about a small Baptist church that had been dynamited by the Ku Klux Klan in Mississippi.

We prayed for the people there, and then I saw a knowing look in Jackie's eye, one that meant "I know what you're thinking."

"Yes, honey, I know what you're thinking. Those people will be needing help in building a new church," I said. "I better get my things together."

The next day I left for the little town in Mississippi, taking with me boxes of used clothing, canned food, and my tools and work clothes. I helped build, paint, varnish, clean, haul, and do whatever was needed.

I worked hard, but the people were closed off to me. I realized they were scared. The NAACP leader, Medgar Evers, had just been murdered in the doorway of his home in Jackson, Mississippi. No one had been killed in the blast of this church, not like the Sixteenth Baptist Church in Birmingham where four girls were killed attending Sunday school. The people were afraid of strangers and didn't know what would happen next.

I discovered another little church not far from the one I was helping to rebuild, and I felt led to go and visit the people. What a difference! They welcomed me with arms and bubbled over with the joy of the Lord. They weren't worried about the Kluxes or about what the w.. .e man could do to them.

One old man had joined the March on Washington with Dr. King and he told me, "I believe in standing up, yes I do, I believe in being a man. I believe I has a right to be a man. But if I fill my body and my mind with hate, then I ain't a man no more. I knows good and I knows bad, and one thing I knows for certain—*God* is good. I knows it. And I know He loves *me* and my black skin. Ole devil try to beat the faith outa the Christians, and it jes make us tougher.

"I done see'd hate, Robert, and I knows what killin' is. Ain't nobody who can tell me what I don't already know about hate. The young folks say it's just begun, but I say I's see'd enough. Hate don't make nothin' better nohow. It makes a man sick and despiseful."

I stayed there for a couple of weeks in Jack's shanty with him. I was with him when we heard the news that President Kennedy had been shot and killed. "The only answer for America is Jesus," Jack insisted. "Young folk think religion is jes for the old folks; they think we's foolish. They never tasted of how He can change a man's whole life—how He can cover up the hurts with love."

The church held an ordination service for me. Jack said to me, "Just remember, brother, at ordination we see how small we are—not how big."

In the sermon the preacher said, "When a man remember he not a god, then he can see God." He was direct and plain. "Black folks standin' around preaching at one another. First one preach and then the next one preach. Nobody gets nothin' from nobody. That's why God calls and sends certain ones—certain ones to lead His people right, certain ones who *knows* Him. Is you one of them, Robert Sadler?

"They's too much talk about hell and damnation and not enough about *love* and *salvation*. If they cain't see the love of the Lord in us, then we's got no right to be preachin' about Him. *Anybody can preach!* Why, we've heard men preachin' mighty fine sermons raisin' the rooftop with their fine voices, and they ain't preachin' about no God we know of. They's jes *talkin'*. I'd rather hear the truth through the mouth of a mule than hear a lie through a fine orator, brothers.

"Show them *Jesus*. Show them 'bout His love, 'bout

how He care. 'Bout how He died for the black man and *every* man. Show them 'bout how He makes strength out of weakness and 'bout how He makes beauty out of filth. Show 'em how He turns it all around inside a man and makes a *new* man where there was nothin' but evil before. Oh, great God! Show 'em 'bout Jesus!" Then he began to sing, and the congregation responded right along with him.

> *He took my feet from the miry clay,*
> "Yes, He did, Yes, He did;"
> *And placed them on the Rock to stay,*
> "Yes, He did, Yes, He did";
> *I can tell the world about this,*
> "You shure can, Revrund!"
> *I can tell the nations I'm blest:*
> "Amen, Lord!"
> *Tell them that Jesus made me whole,*
> "Well!"
> *And He brought joy to my soul.*
> *Oh, my Lord, did just what He said,*
> "Yes, He did, Yes, He did";
> *He healed the sick and raised the dead,*
> "Yes, He did, Yes, He did!"

It would be hard not to dance or clap in the enthusiastic and spontaneous joy that filled the little church.

People have come from all over the country to stay in our home in Bucyrus. Our doors have always been open to any traveler. There is enough room for at least twenty people comfortably, and often there have been more than that staying with us. Ministers began coming from all over to accompany me on my travels.

It would be close to impossible to put in a book the many miracles that God has done for me during my ministry. I have traveled to dozens of cities and towns, hundreds of churches and fellowships, and the Lord has done so many wonderful things that there wouldn't be space to tell it all. In fact, it is not easy to choose which things to tell and which to leave out, but I'll do my best to tell what I can.

I took a white minister from Aurora, Illinois, with me on one of my trips to Anderson, South Carolina. As we drove along, the Holy Spirit told me to take the next exit on the highway. I did as the Lord said, and the man with me got all excited, "Hey! You took the wrong turn! This isn't the right way!"

"The Lord told me to turn off the highway here."

"Brother, you must be mistaken. This isn't the way to Anderson!"

His protests didn't bother me much because I was used to hearing the voice of the Lord, and when I knew the Lord was speaking to me, I tried to obey immediately. I just drove along quietly, listening for the Lord to give me further instructions.

"Brother Bob! I'm telling you this is the wrong way! We won't make it on the gas—"

I looked at him out of the corner of my eye, smiled, and said, "There's no cause for you to get all flustrated. The Lord knows what He's doing."

We came to the end of the road then. It was a dead end. Before us was swamp and thick, dark woods. Then the Lord said to me, "Get out of the car, and take those clothes in the back with you."

I did as the Lord said and began unloading the boxes of used clothing. The minister with me was so disturbed I thought he was going to have a fit!

I saw a run-down shack of a house about 200 feet from the road and made my way through the weeds and brush to it. An old man, dirty and sickly, was sitting on a chair. I greeted him and said, "Would you be needing any clothing?" His eyes grew wide. He was so thin and sick-looking, I wondered how long it had been since he had eaten anything. I soon realized that he was not alone in the house. A woman came out of another room with about six small children, all thin, dirty, and sickly looking.

My minister friend was still down the road by the car fussing to himself. When I didn't return, he came looking for me and found me sitting in the dim, filthy shanty with this poor and sickly family, telling them about Jesus.

"We staying here for a while," I announced. "These people have a need."

We stayed with those backwoods people for a couple of weeks. They needed to be nursed and nourished back to health. Besides that, their shack was almost falling down. We cleaned up the tiny shack and then made a clearing to get a car through to it. We fixed the roof, bathed the children, gave haircuts, clipped toenails, cooked, sewed, plastered, painted, and did some rebuilding. Each day as we worked, their health grew better. They were thrilled to receive the boxes of clothing and household goods. The children owned no toys, and we were able to give them three boxes of toys. It was wonderful.

After one of the first days with them, my friend went walking in the woods. When he came back, his face was swollen and red, and I knew he had been crying. He hugged me and broke down in sobs.

"Oh, forgive me, brother," he cried. "Forgive me. I have never been so touched and so blessed in all my life." We were able to lead the entire family to Jesus. They were also a sight better appearing by the time it was time for us to leave. The Lord spoke to me and told me to give them my car. The man was so thankful; now he could get work in town, he said.

My friend and I took a bus back to Bucyrus. He didn't complain once.

We were at a meeting in a church outside of Minneapolis, and a young man came up to me and said, "The Lord told me to offer you my camper." He told me I could have it for very little. After speaking at some churches in the area, I had $100, which I now offered to the young man. "I'll sell it to you for $100," he said. So I left Minnesota driving a fancy, home-made pickup camper. It was like driving a little house around with me. I thanked God with all my heart.

37

For a long time I had a deep burden in my heart for American Indians. I had been on a reservation a couple of times, and I never forgot the faces and the hungry hearts. When a black brother by the name of Jesse from Minneapolis invited me to go to Canada to an Indian reservation there, I jumped at the chance. We planned to hold tent meetings and teaching sessions, and I could hardly wait.

We stopped in Detroit on the way to Canada and I visited my sister Janey. She was hard and bitter and had little to say to me.

In Detroit someone broke into my camper. When I discovered it, there wasn't a thing left in it. My organ, clothing, money, Bible, and even my dirty laundry—was stolen.

I didn't dare complain to the Lord, so I began to praise Him for it. "If you allowed it to be stolen, then that's your business. So I thank you for it, Lord."

The pastor of the church where I spoke that evening asked me to stay and minister for a couple of days. I didn't have enough clothes to wear, but Jesse and I talked it over and we decided to stay anyhow. During the meeting a woman prophesied over me, saying that the Lord was going to replace my loss and double my portion. She didn't even know of the theft.

That night an offering was taken for me. Then the next afternoon a brother handed me a check and said, "The Lord wants you to have this." We ministered in other towns on our way to Manitoba, and by the time we reached the border I had enough money to buy a much better organ than I had before, and some clothing.

Finally Brother Jesse and I made it to Winnipeg, driving through Wisconsin, Minnesota, and North Dakota. We had to leave the camper in Riverton, Manitoba, and take a boat across Lake Winnipeg to Bloodvein. By the time we got our things in the boat, the water was nearly at the top edge of the boat. I got in and thought for sure we'd sink. I fixed my eyes on the other side of the lake and prayed. Jesse saw me staring at the other side. "Brother Bob," he laughed, "we aren't going *across* the lake, we're going about 15 miles *up* the lake...." My heart jumped into my throat.

The waves were high and water was splashing into the boat all over us and our equipment. Nobody seemed worried except me. Were we going to land on the shore or the bottom of the lake? I prayed, reminding the Lord that I couldn't swim.

The water inside the boat was getting higher and higher. I thought of a verse in the 91st Psalm, "*For he shall give his angels charge over thee, to keep thee in all thy ways.*"

"Lord, send some of those angels over here to this here lake," I prayed. Then I thought of another verse, "*He shall call upon me, and I will answer him: I will be with him in trouble; I will deliver him.*"

Jesse was singing at the other end of the boat.

Wonderful, wonderful
Jesus is to me;
Counsellor, Prince of Peace,
Mighty God is He,
Saving me, keeping me . . .

My, he looked peaceful. I decided I needed some of that peace, too. I began to trust the Lord and sing along with Jesse, even though we were getting more wet by the minute. Then, seemingly out of nowhere, another boat pulled up alongside us. Our equipment was loaded into their boat. By this time the water inside our boat was already up to our ankles. The boat rocked and jerked as our heavy equipment was removed. Jesse waved and shouted something to the men, and we continued on our way. The water stopped splashing into the boat, and we bailed out what we could with coffee cans. Jesse and I started laughing. The Lord had come to our aid out in the middle of Lake Winnipeg.

We finally arrived safely at the Sioux Bloodvein reservation. The land was all rock. The people looked at us with expressions as cold as the rock. I could feel the hostility in the air.

There were only a handful of Christians and a little chapel. We met in the chapel the first night.

The following day I began to take sick during the morning meeting, and so I excused myself and went outside.

I fell down on the hard rock earth and couldn't mo
I felt as though my body was in a vise. I knew it was
an attack of the enemy, but I didn't know what his purpose was. I would soon find out.

In about an hour the meeting was over, and a couple
of the Indian Christians found me lying on the ground. They
called Jesse and he came running. Jesse is a very large
man and very strong. He picked me up in his arms and
carried me back to the chapel. He laid me down and felt
my pulse. There was none. He listened to my heart and
there was no beat. I had also stopped breathing. He called
for the believers to come, and they gathered around me
and prayed. The Lord told Jesse to command the life back
in me in His name. He did and before long my pulse returned and I began to breathe. I didn't know I had been
raised from the dead.

The evening came and the believers gathered around
me again and prayed over me. Then I slept until the next
morning.

I awoke feeling worse than when I fell asleep. The
pain in my body was terrible. I rose up out of the bed,
using every bit of strength I had. "Devil, you liar. In
Jesus' name, I will get off this bed and speak to these
people who need God."

By the time I got to the chapel, I thought I might die.
I don't believe I've ever been so sick. When the Indians
saw me there, they praised God like never before.

"This is a spiritual battle," I explained. "And Jesus
has already won."

They continued to pray over me, and I could feel the
hand of sickness and death leaving me. The Holy Spirit
moved wonderfully on that reservation. Young people, old
people, children, came to the meetings. Pretty soon there
wasn't enough room in the chapel for everybody, so we
began to use the tent. Then we began overflowing even
that.

Each day there were healings and deliverances among
the Indian people. Demons that had held families for years
and years were cast out, and the families were set free
in Jesus. A little baby who was deformed pitifully was
brought forward one evening. We prayed over her, and right
before our eyes we saw her little arms and legs straighten
out, and she was made whole.

God worked on the reservation like we never dared to
imagine He would. We fasted and prayed and God broke

many of the chains that had held the people in darkness.

There were those, though, who in spite of seeing a man raised from the dead and many other miracles, still didn't believe.

Up until now I had not told anyone much about my being a slave. Even Jackie knew very little about it. It was not until 1964, when I was fifty-three years old, that I could finally bring myself to talk about it openly. I was in a meeting in Memphis, Tennessee, and the congregation was singing *Wonderful Words of Life.*

I felt my heart begin to pound rapidly, and I could once again see the parlor in the Big House. I could hear Juanita playing the piano and singing. Then Virginia, Ethel and Thomas joined in.

> Sweetly echo the gospel call, Wonderful words of Life;
> Offer pardon and peace to all, Wonderful words of life.

Mary Webb was in the kitchen preparing cool lemonade and little cakes for the family. Upstairs Harriet was rocking baby Anna to sleep. It was hot, and my toes curled under the soles of my bare feet. That music was mighty pretty. Mighty pretty.

> Jesus only Savior, Sanctify forever;
> Beautiful words, wonderful words,
> Wonderful words of li-i-ife,
> Beautiful words, wonderful words,
> Wonderful words of life.

Almost forty years had passed since I ran away from the Beal Plantation. Yet it all flooded back in my memory that day in Memphis. I felt tears come to my eyes. Something inside me broke. When the congregation finished singing, I rose to me feet.

"I want to tell you about the first time I ever heard that song. . . . " I was able to talk about my childhood and about being a slave. I talked and talked. It all came out, easier than I thought it would.

Back in Bucyrus, I felt God wanted me to write a book on my life, and I began to seriously pray about it.

"Oh girl," I said, taking Jackie in my arms, "I knows I am not a fancy preacher man. I'm a simple man. If I can minister encouragement, faith, and love to the people, then I'll be grateful."

I grinned at her and she grinned back. "You is the

most wonderful man in the whole world, that's what you
is."

My speech problem never completely left me, and I
still mispronounced words, but I decided since it was the
Lord who chose me to serve Him, it was His problem and
not mine.

"I'm not ca'ble of preaching no fancy sermon, Jackie.
I just gives what God puts in my heart."

"And Robert, honey, that's a powerful lot. You bet."

In 1965 I took a trip to Anderson. The Lord blessed
me with some extra money, so I was able to buy Margie
a stove. She was so pleased you would have thought I
bought her General Electric itself. I visited Corrie in the
rest home and took Buck with me.

I went to Clinton to see Tennessee and John Henry.
They were so poor I asked John Henry to come north, and
I would try to get him a job in Bucyrus or Detroit. He
smiled at me with a wise old smile.

"Move up north? *Move up north?*"

"Yes, John Henry, you can make a living up north—"

"Now lissen hyar, Robert, I ain't studyin' to move up
north nohow. This hyar South is mah *home.*"

"Yes, but you don't make a decent wage—"

"The South is mah *home,*" he repeated. "Mah grand-
daddy was a slave, Robert, and his daddy served in the
Civil War for this hyar South. My daddy served in the war
in Europe for this hyar country, yes he did. He ate grits
and gravy, and they sent his battalion out first to die.
He come back, and he come back to the South!

"Robert, we was *slaves*. We and our people built and
made this hyar South what it be. We made the South rich.
Ah done give my life to this hyar land. I got me a shack
and a store and some land. Ahm an old man now, but ahm
askin' you, you want me to move up north and live in a
strange city with a lot of other poor niggers who don't know
nothin' but farming? Robert, this hyar land you standin'
on now is *mine*. Ah done built the South. Me and our people.
This hyar South is as much ours as it is the white man's.
Ain't nothin' gonna git me to move and leave what's mine
nohow."

With that, he stuck a plug of tobacco in his cheek, crossed
his arms across his chest, and gave me a shove with his
knee. It meant, "Don't mention it again," and I didn't.

38

In the spring of 1968 I took a white brother named John to Arkansas with me. I was enjoying the prospering of the Lord and had just bought a new suit of clothes and some new shoes. I was feeling so happy as we drove along, and John and I were praising the Lord together. In the distance I saw a man standing at the edge of the highway. He wasn't hitchhiking, but I felt impressed to stop. John spoke up. "What are you stopping for?"

"I see a need," I said.

I got out of the car and walked over to the man. He was dressed in shabby, dirty clothing, and his shoes were torn and without laces. I smiled. He was exactly my size.

"I don't need no ride," he told me.

"I know what you need," I said. "Come with me." I took him into the camper and dressed him up in my new clothes and shoes. First, though, I heated some water on the Coleman stove and gave him a bath, a shampoo, and shave. When I finished with him he looked like a different man. John was sitting up in front and very annoyed. "What are you doing with that man?" he asked me in a surly tone. "He's just a bum. He'll probably sell those clothes." Sometimes people just won't listen to the Holy Spirit. I didn't even bother to answer him.

When I had the man all cleaned up, the Lord spoke to me and said, "Give him one of those twenty dollar bills in your pocket." When John saw me do that, he said loud enough for the man to hear, "He'll just spend that on whiskey!" I took the man to West Helena, Arkansas, with us to attend the meeting that night and he gave his heart to the Lord during the singing. With tears running down his clean-shaven face, he confessed, "I was on my way to kill myself. I just didn't have a thing in the world to live for. Now I can see that I have everything to live for. I'm going to live for Jesus!" That man is still going on with the Lord down there in Arkansas. He led his wife and four children to Jesus, too.

We were on the road when we heard of Dr. King's assassination. I stopped driving and pulled over to the side of the road. It seemed I heard wailing and weeping from every corner of the South. John clicked his teeth. "He was a Communist, wasn't he?" For a long moment I resented that man—not for his whiteness, but for his fool insensitivity. "John, you shure don't know *nothing,* do you?"

After our meetings in Arkansas, I drove to Anderson. Margie had taken sick, and I wanted to visit her. It was one of the last times I would see her. I drove along the narrow, hilly streets looking at the familiar little wooden houses, shingle or tar-paper covered, set right on the road. Roses grew over almost every one of them. Inside somewhere in each house would be photographs of J. F. Kennedy and Dr. King, either hanging on a wall or standing on a table or dresser top.

Margie's son, Alan, was there from Detroit. I called Jackie and told her how sick Margie was, and she took a bus right down. We stayed with her for a week.

"You has did so much for me," she told me in a weak voice. "All the boxes and gifts you send."

"Now, sister, don't you remember the boxes you sent me while I was at school?"

"Robert, you is a wonderful brother. And Jackie is a wonderful sister. You gots a wonderful wife, Robert."

It pained me to see Margie suffer. She looked like Mama lying there, thin and worn. Her face was beautiful and radiant though. "I'm strivin' to make it at the straight gate, Robert," she smiled.

When I kissed her good-bye, we clung to one another. It was our last embrace.

We drove to Detroit in the summer to see Janey. Margie's son, Alan, had told us that she had cancer. Janey was living in a fancy house on the west side of town with a new husband who waited on her hand and foot.

I knew she was dying. For a brief time she mellowed. "Robert, you has been kind to send all those boxes and packages."

"You was kind to me, Jay, remember?"

"None of the other brothers ever bothered with me."

"They's just afraid of that evil temper of yours."

"I is a Christian, Robert Sadler!" she said indignantly. "I'll have you know that I is saved and on my way to glory. Now get out of here before I run upside your head!"

She shook her fist at me, and I knew she meant business. "And don't come back!" she shouted. At the door I turned, waved, blew her a kiss, and looked at her dear, angry face for the last time. Tears fell down my cheeks and chin. She had missed out on the peace and joy that she could have had living a Christian life. Maybe she had never forgotten that night in Anderson forty years ago when she gave her heart to Jesus. I prayed she'd set her heart right before it was too late. I never saw her or spoke to her again. She died a month later.

In 1970 one of the brightest lights of my life went out. Margie died. We went to Anderson for the funeral, and it seemed as though I was a boy again and Margie was not only Margie, but Mama, Ella, Pearl, and Janey, too. All my kin was gone now except for my brothers, Johnny and Leroy, and I hardly knew them.

As I stood at Margie's casket, I was overcome with a strange sense of loneliness. Many people had loved Margie and would miss her, but for me I knew there would be a hole in my heart all the rest of my life for my sister Margie.

I drove through town along Market Street and turned at a narrow, cluttered skid row street called Church Street. It is the black skid row of Anderson. The Lord spoke to me and said, "Pull over here." I thought it strange, but I obeyed and pulled over alongside a taxi stand. "Now take out your organ," the Lord said. I did as He said, and began to play right there on the sidewalk.

It wasn't long before a small crowd of men had gathered. One tall, dark-skinned man was very upset at my playing. "You a preacher?" he snapped.

"Why, yes, I am."

"I hate preachers!"

"Now, why would you hate preachers?"

"A preacher called me a rat!"

I raised my eyebrows. "And did you believe him? It's plain to see that you are not a rat. A rat has four legs and you have only two."

He stood staring at me, his mouth hanging open, and I played another song. After the song I said to him, "Will you get saved today?" He began to cry. He told me how he had been saved once, but he had fallen far from the Lord. He asked Jesus back into his heart that day.

I had a wonderful time talking with the men on Church Street. The next day I went back again. Then the Lord spoke to me and said, "Rent a building on this street,

Robert, so these men can have a place to come." I began looking for an available building and I found one. It was run-down and filthy. It would take a lot of work to clean it up and make a mission out of it. So I set to work, painting, fixing, and cleaning, and as I worked the men came by to watch, and some of them would help me.

Finally one day the sign painter came and painted COMPASSION HOUSE on the window, the name I had chosen for the mission. "Lord, always give me compassion," I prayed. "I'm going to need lots of it."

E. V. Adger, who owned and operated the taxi stand down the block, came over to see what was going on. "These men needs more religion and less whiskey; you is in the right place, brother." I discovered E.V. had been a slave on the Druid Plantation when I was a boy on the Beal Plantation.

In those early weeks of the mission, I saw the Lord touch the down-and-out men of Church Street with His hand of love, and men came to Jesus nearly every day. I played my organ, preached, and spent hours and hours talking with the men. Their response was wonderful.

39

Jackie had taken sick, and although we prayed over her and she was anointed with oil, we felt the Lord wanted her to see a doctor. We knew a Christian doctor in Upper Sandusky named Dr. Rhodes. He always prayed with his patients when he treated them. He told Jackie she was a diabetic and her kidneys were bad.

A special diet helped her, but in 1973, Jackie's health began to decline again. The Lord spoke to me in a dream and told me I'd be preaching at her funeral. Soon after, she went into the hospital with gangrene in her leg. It was spreading fast, and they had to amputate. She remained on the critical list for several days. I practically moved into the hospital to be near her. I fasted and prayed for days, and many of the Christians who knew and loved her joined me.

Finally, the dark cloud lifted and she began to recover. When she came home she was like a new girl. The droopiness was gone, and she was filled with enthusiasm and happiness. I bought her new furniture and made a beautiful bedroom for her in the music room. We celebrated her return to health by taking out the silver she had packed away for use only when company came, and her good dishes, too. "I want you to enjoy these! We are using them every day!" I bought her flowers and when they wilted, I bought her more. I was so happy that the Lord had spared her and given her back to me.

She learned how to walk with a walker, and one day she said to me, "Honey, would you take me with on your next mission trip?" I could have jumped with joy. "*Would I!*"

We had several months of traveling and ministering together. Everywhere we went the people showered Jackie with love and affection.

"Why didn't I do this earlier?" she cried one night in my arms.

Driving through Anderson with Jackie at my side, we were silent looking at the land where cotton once was king. Now the cotton fields were used for cattle pastures. Giant, modern synthetic factories took the place of the old mills, and electronic and chemical firms stood where once there was wilderness. Pre-fabricated housing developments took the place of the unpainted shacks which were once strewn across the land. Anderson was now one of South Carolina's five largest cities, called the "Electric City," and known as the fiberglass center of the world. There were no more mules, no more overseers, no more slave quarters, and no more slave masters.

My mission on Church Street expanded. I rented another building next door, so there was a place for men to sleep, as well as a kitchen. By now the number of men who had come through our doors numbered in the hundreds, and we lost count of those who had gotten saved and straightened out their lives.

We often visited Buck and Corrie Moore. Buck was in his eighties and still walked every day to the rest home to see Corrie. In December of 1973, Corrie passed on to be with the Lord. She had suffered for twelve years after her legs were amputated, and even Buck said, "Thank God. She's on the other side now. She's free."

Back home in Bucyrus, Jackie's health began to slip, and she had to go back into the hospital. She was almost ready to be fitted for an articifical limb, but her kidneys gave out. I remembered the word the Lord had spoken to me about preaching at her funeral. I wept and prayed before the Lord, begging Him to restore her. She grew worse, however, and when the doctor allowed her to come home, I knew it was to spend her last days.

When Jackie went into the hospital in March, 1974, she lay in her bed praising the Lord and worshipping Him in the spirit. I sat with her night and day, and the last words I heard her say were, "Thank you, Jesus."

On March 11, 1974, my Jackie died.

People came from all over the country for the funeral. I couldn't shed one tear. Jackie was with Jesus. How could I *dare* shed a tear? A young girl from Cincinnati asked me, "Brother Bob, how can you be happy at a time like this?"

I answered her, "Child, it's not *happy* I feel. It's *peace*. I always loved Jesus more than anything in this life, and I still love Him more."

I thanked the Lord for giving me Jackie for thirty-five years.

The funeral director was concerned about my having a plot next to hers. It didn't matter to me. "I'll never visit her grave—never," I said. "I'm not visiting no grave, because my wife isn't in no grave. She is in *heaven*. And I won't be in no grave, either, so it don't matter where we buried."

Eventually my friends had to leave to get back to their families, and I was alone. There was a hollow ache in me, but I knew the Lord would carry me through and not allow me to sink in self-pity. I sat one early Sunday morning in the mission, unable to sleep as the years of my life flew around in my mind like sand shaking in a bottle. I heard my little sister, Ella, laughing again. I saw Master Beal high above me drawing the lash back, ready to lay it on my back. I heard Pearl's voice singing, I saw the school in Seneca, and I saw Jackie smiling at me from across a steam-filled kitchen. All songs and hymns I knew became one melody, and all cries became one cry: Jesus.

I was watching the sun come up when a young man staggered in, drunk and mean. "Well, good morning, Evans," I said. He grunted. "I see you're out of the hospital."

"Preacher, if yoll let me flop here, I'll never tech another drink as long as I live. I promise."

When the people began to file in the door, I went to the organ. I heard Evans stumbling around behind the curtain and I went in to help him. "Preacher," he snarled, "how comes you don't give up on me? You been knowin' me a long time and I ain't got saved yet. How comes you still bothern' with me?"

"Didn't you know, Evans? Jesus loves you and I love you."

It was time to begin the service. I opened the curtain, walked over to the organ, and began to play.